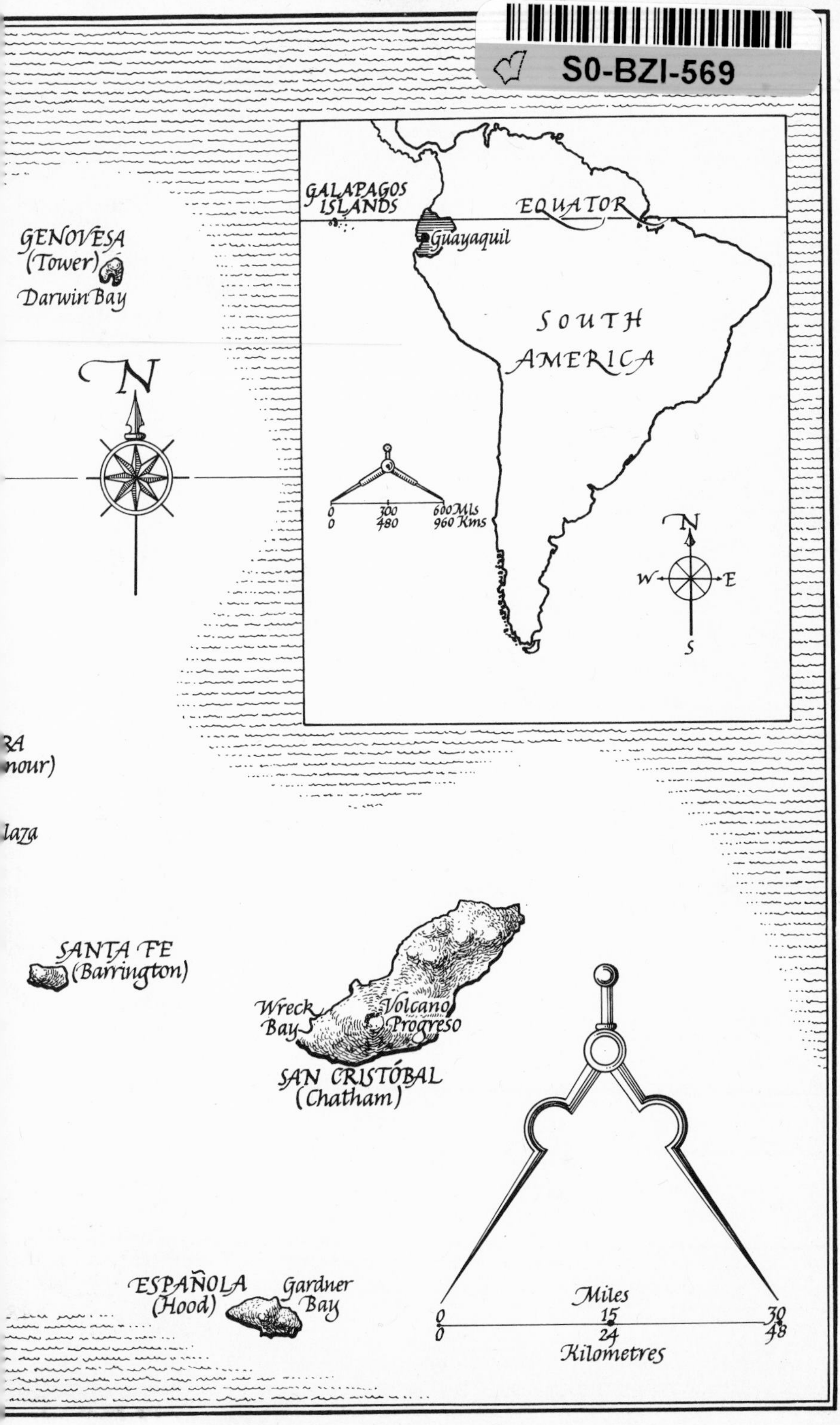

GALAPAGOS ISLANDS
EQUATOR
Guayaquil
SOUTH AMERICA
0 300 600 Mls
0 480 960 Kms
N
W E
S

GENOVESA
(Tower)
Darwin Bay
N
RA
nour)
laza
SANTA FE
(Barrington)
Wreck Bay
Volcano
Progreso
SAN CRISTÓBAL
(Chatham)
ESPAÑOLA
(Hood)
Gardner Bay
Miles
0 15 30
0 24 48
Kilometres

The Galapagos Affair

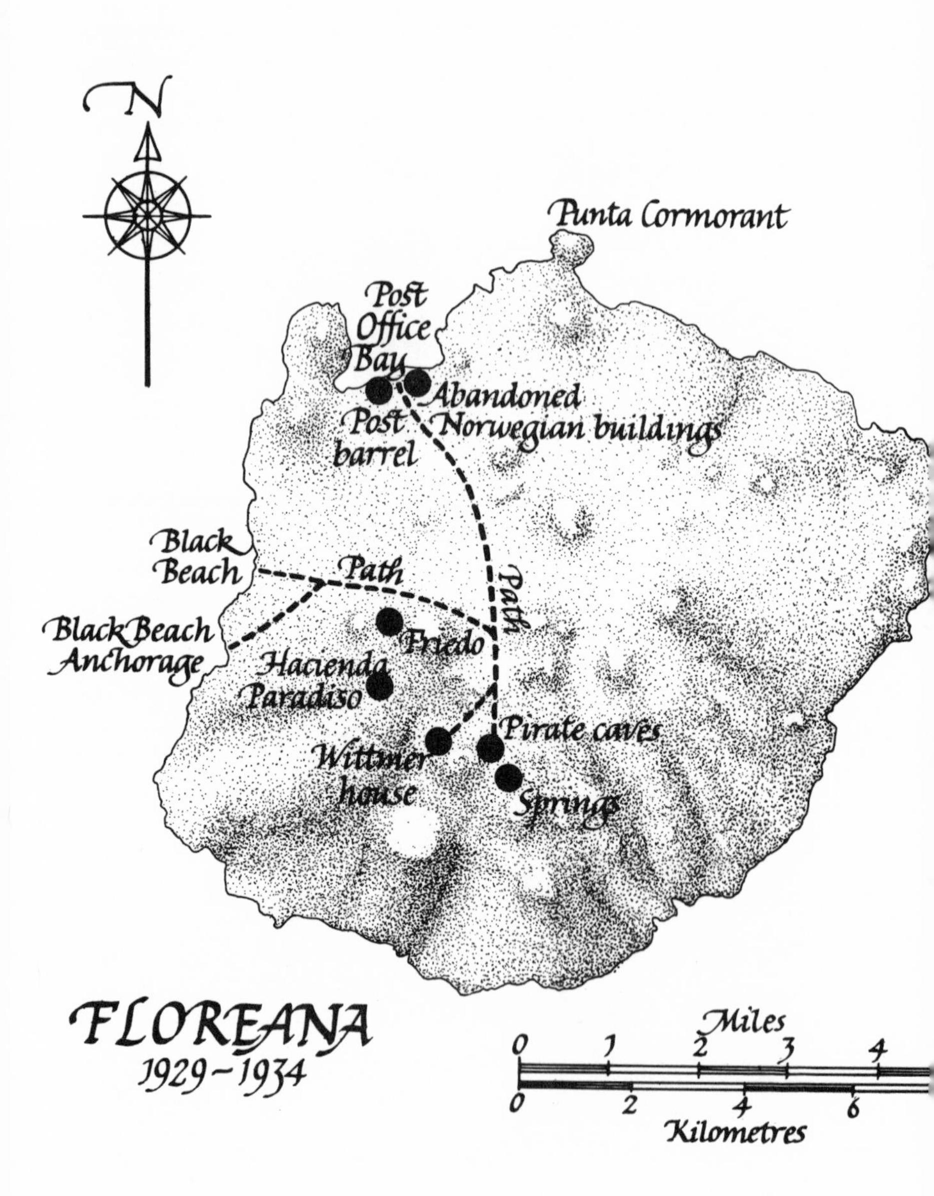

FLOREANA
1929–1934

The Galapagos Affair

John Treherne

Random House New York

First American Edition

Published in the United States by Random House, Inc., New York. Originally
published in Great Britain by Jonathan Cape, Ltd., in 1983.

Library of Congress Cataloging in Publication Data
Treherne, J. E.
The Galapagos affair.
Bibliography: p.
1. Murder–Galapagos Islands–Santa María. I. Title.
HV6535.G242S27 1983 364.1'523'098665 83-42865
ISBN 0-394-53327-5

Manufactured in the United States of America
9 8 7 6 5 4 3 2

TO REBECCA, FOR HER INTEREST AND ADVICE

It tempts no wise man to pull off and see what's the matter, but bids him steer small and keep off shore – that is Charles' Island; brace up, Mr. Mate, and keep the light astern.

Herman Melville, *The Encantadas*

CONTENTS

ILLUSTRATIONS

Figures

PREFACE

This is a story of some curious events, half a century ago on a remote Pacific island, which, at the time, excited intense interest in the world press.

In this book I have attempted to reconstruct, as accurately as possible, the bizarre series of occurrences that led to a mystery which has never been satisfactorily explained. My task has been facilitated by the surprising amount of information I have been able to unearth about these events, notably in the books, articles and letters that were written by some of the principal participants. I have also benefited from the availability of numerous documents, photographs, diaries, chapters in travel books, magazine and newspaper articles, a film and the personal testimonies of a succession of visitors to the island during the period covered by this book, as well as from a wealth of contemporary newspaper articles. Some of the information that I have used is conflicting, due to profound differences in the accounts of some of the people involved. I have, therefore, been forced to use my own judgment as to the veracity of such information, so as not to disturb the flow of the story. However, at some critical points I have emphasized the discrepancies in the accounts of some of the participants because these provide insights into their characters and actions and, thus, assist in the elaboration of a hypothesis to explain the mystery of Floreana island.

Most of the principal participants in this story were German and many of the quotations that I have used are translations of their writings. Some are, however, from letters in which the writers used English. The style of this writing is, fortunately, distinct enough to enable the reader to recognize this without further explanation.

Cambridge
October 1982

J. T.

ACKNOWLEDGMENTS

The writing of this book has been assisted and made pleasurable by the kindness and help of a number of people. I have especially benefited from the generosity of Mrs Marian Hancock Barry of Santa Maria, California, in putting at my disposal a wealth of documents and photographs that were collected by the late Captain G. Allan Hancock during his visits to the Galapagos Islands in the early 1930s; and, especially, in allowing me to see the film that was made on Floreana at that time. I am also extremely grateful to the Hancock Foundation of the University of Southern California, at Los Angeles, to Mrs Hancock Barry and to John Garth for granting permission to reproduce the photographs that I have included in this book.

I have derived much pleasure, and a great deal of valuable information, from my acquaintance and subsequent friendship with Dr John S. Garth of Long Beach, Los Angeles. Captain Fred C. Ziesenhenne of Maui, Hawaii, has also been exceptionally generous in his help to me. They were both young men when they witnessed some of the events described in this book. Their unstinting generosity in lending me their diaries, photographs and scrapbooks, and in talking to me about their adventures in the Galapagos, fifty years ago, has materially contributed to the writing of this book. I am also indebted to another participant in the events on Floreana, Rolf Blomberg of Quito, for his gentlemanly response to a potential competitor in writing on Galapagos affairs; and to a former Galapagos inhabitant, Roger Perry, for several helpful conversations.

I have, in addition, received invaluable help from a number of friends and colleagues. Above all, I am indebted to Paul Chipchase for patiently reading and commenting on the draft chapters as they were produced and to Simon Maddrell for reading the final version. I am most grateful to John Wilson and Janthea Yearley for sustaining my enthusiasm during the early stages of my literary labours and to Desmond Morris for his assistance in bringing them to fruition. I have benefited from the advice of the Master of Downing College, Cambridge, Sir John Butterfield, and the Professor of Morbid Anatomy and Histology, Professor Austin Gresham, who have educated me on relevant medical matters. Sir Martin Roth also provided some much-needed psychological insight. I am particularly grateful to Melody Siegler for her preliminary sleuthing in Los Angeles, to Peter Wallën for searching the bookshops of Stockholm for me, and to Paul Koch for his activities at Wollbach in the Black Forest. Gertraud Herbert, and her pupil Stuart Reese, of St Catharine's College, assisted and intrigued me by telling me about hitherto unsuspected Teutonic versions of *Robinson Crusoe*. I am indebted to Jonathan Harrington and Robin Wallis, of Downing College, and to Britt Ashford and Joachim Greuel for their kindnesses in translating a curious assortment of documents for me. I am grateful to various members of the staff of the Cambridge University Library (especially the bearded man at the desk in the Reading Room) for their help in a project of less than usual academic respectability; to John Westmancoat of the Newspaper Library at Colindale for his guidance; to the staffs of the Kensington & Chelsea Library and Wiener Library; and to Carmen Verlade for locating and photocopying various German newspaper articles in the Universitäts und Stadtbibliothek in Cologne.

I am also grateful to Dr Bernhard Heitmann (of the Museum für Kunst und Gewerbe, Hamburg) and to Dr Hanns-Ulrich Haedeke (of the Deutsches Klingenmuseum, Solingen) for advising me about German stainless-steel tableware *c.* 1929.

Finally, I thank Margaret Clements for her patient and efficient typing of the manuscript of this book.

The following photographs are reproduced by courtesy of the G. Allan Hancock Expeditions: 2, 3, 5, 6, 8, 9, 10, 11, 12, 13, 16, 18, 20, 22, 23, 24, 25, 26, 27, 28, 29, 30, 31, 32 and 33; Dr John S. Garth granted permission to use 4, 7, 17, 19 and 21; 14 is reproduced by courtesy of Landesbildstelle Rheinland and the Deutsches Klingenmuseum, Solingen, and 15 by courtesy of Photo Kollar and the Musée Bouilhet-Christofle, St Denis. Fig. 4 is reproduced by permission of *The Times* Newspapers Ltd. Figs 5 and 6 are reprinted by permission of the New York Times Company, © 1935/1934. The Atlantic Monthly Company granted permission to reproduce an extract from an article in *Atlantic Monthly*. The map of Floreana is based on an original drawing by John Rodford. The endpaper map was drawn by Denys Baker.

1
THE SEARCH FOR PARADISE

The two fair-haired strangers had travelled five thousand miles to the harbour at Guayaquil. They were not easily discouraged, by the noise or the equatorial heat. Narrow wooden barges crowded at the dockside unloading cargoes of bananas. Black-haired half-castes went barefoot, swarming over the little vessels, shouting and jostling. Dark-eyed women in straw hats were selling cakes from handcarts and the smoky smell of roasting meat hung in the humid air.

An ancient two-masted schooner lay alongside the quay. She had a patched and mended hull; an ugly makeshift bridge had been built below the foremast; and an engine had been added which weighed her down heavily at the stern. The decks of the *Manuel y Cobos* were still filthy from the cargo of fifty cows just discharged. The two strangers, shoving their way through the shouting crowd towards the schooner, were bent on making a six-hundred-mile voyage in her - the last leg of their long journey.

The man was small, neat and fierce-looking, with a shock of flaxen hair, a high sloping intellectual forehead and penetrating blue eyes. The woman, who walked with a limp, had a deliberately untidy and bohemian air, and showed more openly than her companion the excitement they both felt. She had short bobbed hair and a friendly face. Both were conspicuously hatless in a crowd where even the stevedores wore straw hats and the tiny Indians black felt bowlers.

Friedrich Ritter and Dore Strauch were Germans. They had left Berlin in July 1929 and their four weeks' voyage had brought them on a sweltering day in August to the Pacific coast of Ecuador. They wanted a passage to the Galapagos Islands, and the *Manuel y Cobos* made irregular trips carrying cargo and passengers from Guayaquil to Chatham Island, at the southern tip of the archipelago. The skipper was Captain Bruuns, a blunt, good-natured Norwegian. Dore Strauch and Dr Ritter were soon to discover that he had a curious reputation.

It was said along the coast that he had been a spy in the pay of German Naval Intelligence during the First World War. The most colourful version of the story claimed that Bruuns had been responsible for the torpedoing of H.M.S. *Hampshire*, and for the death of her most distinguished passenger, Field-Marshal Lord Kitchener, though the official account of this incident (that the ship was destroyed by a mine) does not bear out the legend. Whatever the truth about Bruuns's past, he had arrived mysteriously in Guayaquil some years earlier in a small boat, the *Isabela*, in which he had crossed the Atlantic with a crew of three. After negotiating the Panama Canal and sailing down the coast of South America to Guayaquil, Bruuns claimed that his identification papers had been lost overboard in a typhoon. The Ecuadorian authorities very obligingly gave him some new ones, and he was able to set up as Captain of the *Manuel y Cobos*.

As they stood on the untidy deck of the old schooner, Friedrich Ritter and Dore Strauch told Bruuns that they intended to settle permanently on one of the Galapagos Islands, and that they had a great deal of equipment to take with them. Captain Bruuns pricked up his ears at this. He had a number of pet schemes for making money out of the islands, and the two fair-haired strangers were potential business partners. At that time he had a project for butchering the cattle that roamed wild on some of the islands, and selling the dried meat and hides on the Ecuadorian mainland. He said that he had had great success with it so far. Dore Strauch later said she had 'seldom met a man so full of projects'. Captain Bruuns was disappointed when he learnt the purpose of their journey, for Dore Strauch and Friedrich Ritter had very different reasons for settling in the Galapagos.

Towards the end of August, the *Manuel y Cobos* was ready to sail. First-class accommodation was limited to four tiny cabins, one of which received the exhaust fumes from the engine. There were a hundred cows on board and sixty human passengers, most of whom slept and ate where they could. Friedrich Ritter had booked first-class accommodation and, according to him, 'we did not have to climb over cattle, but only a few tree trunks, kerosene barrels and two Indian women with children.' The first-class deck space was, in fact, usually occupied by humbler passengers who were periodically expelled by the crew. Food was served at irregular hours to both cabin and deck passengers by an agile steward with a ladle.

Dore Strauch mentioned none of these discomforts in the account she wrote many years later of their departure from Guayaquil. She saw it as the achievement of a romantic idyll, and nothing that happened afterwards was able to damage this vision: 'As we moved out of the little harbour and watched it receding from our sight, we felt a oneness with each other which we had never felt before ... a feeling of deep happiness and gratitude to the fate which had permitted us to approach our goal at last.'

* * *

This voyage into the wilderness was not a sudden decision on Friedrich Ritter's part: it was a step he had been considering for twenty years. He was born in 1886 at Wollbach in the Black Forest. His father followed several trades – farmer, storekeeper, carpenter – and was ambitious and industrious. Friedrich as a boy was undersized and sickly, and his schooldays were unhappy. The schoolmasters were strict, beating was frequent, and at the age of eight the snuffling headachey boy was subjected to the discipline of a particularly brutal master whose harshness, Friedrich said, marked him for life. He sought comfort in the country which surrounded the village, wandering in silence among the trees and watching the forest animals. He was a lonely little boy and had few close friends. In the forest, he spent hours gazing at the trout which lived in a particularly deep, clear pool that was his special haunt. He was fond of animals and hated going with his father on hunting expeditions. He once deliberately freed a bird from his father's trap. Afterwards he felt guilty for betraying his father's trust.

The boy was good with his hands. His father taught him carpentry, and he was fascinated by his mother's sewing machine. He liked to recall, many years later, how he had once dismantled the sewing machine while his mother was out and how, after he had reassembled it, it ran better than it did before. He was also fond of reading, and in particular loved the adventure stories of J. Fenimore Cooper and *Robinson Crusoe*.

After leaving school, Friedrich entered the University of Freiburg, where he studied chemistry, physics, philosophy and, later, medicine. At the age of twenty, while still a student, he married Fräulein Mila Clark, with whom he had been living for two years. She was studying to be a singer, and Friedrich's parents vehemently opposed the marriage. Friedrich, however, took charge of his wife's career and pushed her rather successfully; she sang a number of roles, including that of Carmen, with the Royal Opera at Darmstadt.

In the early stages of the First World War, Friedrich volunteered for the Army and served in the trenches with the artillery. At the end of the war he returned to Freiburg to complete his medical studies, and then moved with his wife to Berlin, where he set up in medical practice. His relationship with Mila had by this time deteriorated badly. She wished to abandon her operatic career and devote herself to housekeeping and helping Friedrich, but Friedrich had ambitions for his wife and would not tolerate it. In this clash of temperaments, it is easy to see that Friedrich's strong and aggressive character dominated the passive Frau Ritter.

Friedrich held a position in the Hydrotherapeutic Institute at the University of Berlin. It was here that he met Dore, then

Frau Koerwin, who was undergoing treatment for multiple sclerosis at the Institute. She could not help noticing the impressive young doctor. 'He made a strong impression on me because of the deep furrows in his forehead and the extremely harsh expression of his eyes. It would be too much to say that he looked brutal, but there was a strange absence in his face of any trace of amiability. It flashed through my mind that I hoped I would never be examined or treated by him.' Some days later the young doctor came to Dore's bedside. He discussed with her the 'powers of thought' and told her that even multiple sclerosis could be subdued by appropriate mental processes. He lent her books dealing with this psychological approach to illness. He came each day, and soon Dore was quite captivated by the striking and intellectual young man. When, after two weeks, she was discharged from hospital, Friedrich suggested that he should become her physician. In fact, he became her confessor as well, for Dore told him 'everything without reserve'. In particular she told him about her marriage, which was in very bad shape.

Dore Strauch, at the age of twenty-three, had married a man of forty-five. Herr Koerwin was a schoolteacher and at that time principal of a high school. Dore's father was a grave, sedate man, settled in his ways, and her new husband resembled him. Herr Koerwin seems to have been drawn to Dore by her natural cheerfulness, and Dore, in turn, was attracted by the prospect of thawing out this grave middle-aged man. They married, despite the misgivings of the bride's parents, and Dore found herself the wife of an elderly schoolmaster.

At the time of her marriage, Dore was working in a bank and, despite the high rate of currency inflation at that time in Germany, was bringing home an adequate salary. Nevertheless, she was conventional enough to feel it strange that she should be working when she had a husband to support her, and she longed for a child. It was at this stage in their marriage that Dore developed multiple sclerosis; it left her with a permanent limp and no possibility of having children.

When she returned home from hospital, after her first attack of the disease, she became discontented. She found that she could not bear housework and, without her bank job, had no desire to be a *Hausfrau* whose horizon was 'bounded by the four walls of a few scruffy rooms'. Her artistic and romantic temperament clashed with that of her narrow-minded, unimaginative husband. She had bohemian aspirations. She was a passionate supporter of the Revolution of 1918 in Germany and read Nietzsche eagerly. She was soon disenchanted with her hidebound husband, and by the time she met Friedrich Ritter, she knew that her marriage was a failure.

The strange young philosopher-doctor was able to speak to her of Nietzsche and Lao-tse. She became his disciple at once, 'for I have always felt drawn to everyone who seemed by nature allied to greatness'. Dore cast him in a heroic Nietzschean role. She was fascinated as he admitted her into his inner world and enchanted when he told her that he recognized in her 'a fellow pilgrim on the way to final wisdom'.

Dore spent as much time as Friedrich could spare for her in his private medical practice in Kalkreuthstrasse. Between seeing patients he could take Dore up on to the roof of the house and talk to her of his philosophy and his strange dreams of journeying out into the wilderness to realize his 'great ideal of solitude'. Dore recounted, long afterwards, how they 'would lie up there in the sun letting our fancy wander, pretending that the clouds that drifted by were our remote island of refuge and the blue sky the ocean in which our earthly Eden was set'.

Friedrich had a little black book in which he made notes about these earthly paradises. He and Dore discussed them endlessly and lost themselves in island fantasy. They were very close: Dore wrote, long after, that she 'shared Dr Ritter's life in every way'. But there was awkwardness at home when Herr Koerwin heard about Dr Ritter. He forbade Dore to meet Ritter, but Dore persisted in her visits to Kalkreuthstrasse. Eventually, Herr Koerwin seems to have accepted the inevitable and made no more scenes. Dore despised her cuckolded husband for his acquiescence, for she felt, despite her newly-acquired fashionable attitudes, that 'a real man must be the

Circle
of the
World as „Empfindung" – Sentiency.
Key of the relations between reason + „All".
Philosophical System by Dr. Ritter.

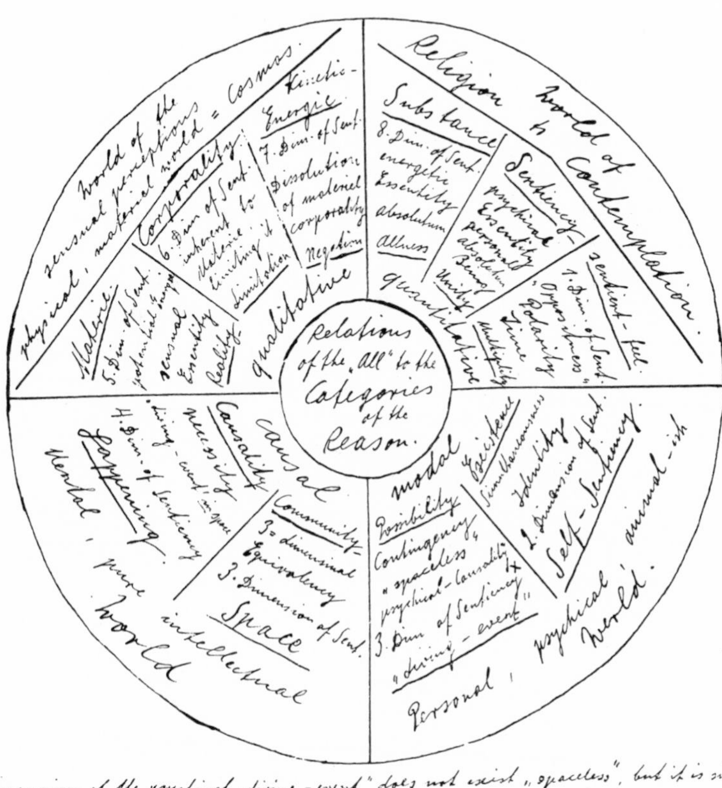

x The 3. dimension of the psychical „living-event" does not exist „spaceless", but it is situated as unequal-time-dimension within the identity-within the plane": I·I·V-7 – not out of it, like by the 3=dimensional „spacious" space.

Fig. 1 Diagram by Friedrich Ritter illustrating his philosophical system

master in his own home'. She despised Koerwin even more when she realized that his toleration of her affair with Friedrich arose from an anxiety to avoid public scandal.

Dore's health began to improve as she fell beneath the spell of her forceful lover. She had found someone to whom she could give freely her love and admiration. However, the affair was not entirely a bed of roses for Dore. Friedrich's 'great mind and spirit' made it necessary for Dore to make 'more compromises so as not to hinder our great mutual quests, than most women would in any relationship to any man'. She had to accept that 'in his human contacts he was rough and unskilful, and the fact that one was a woman - perhaps the only one he did not despise - entitled one to no special clemency or favour at his hands'.

Even Dore's descriptions cannot disguise the fact that Friedrich was a fierce and selfish bully. To Dore, however, he was her heroic philosopher lover. Through him, she believed, her life would be fulfilled: 'I prayed that my body might become the vessel of the beautiful and divine.' Dr Ritter made it clear, on the other hand, that he could not have, as he later wrote: 'a love-sick woman of romantic notions trailing after me into the wilderness'. But that is what he got.

* * *

Dore and Friedrich spent two years as lovers in Berlin before they left for their island Eden in the Galapagos. It was a particularly difficult time for Dore. In her own home she had to keep up appearances and 'play the model *Hausfrau*, appearing with my husband at social functions wearing an evening dress and high-heeled shoes'. Life was also difficult for the unfortunate Mila Ritter; her ideal of an orderly home life with Friedrich would have been difficult to achieve even without the adoring disciple Frau Koerwin.

As Friedrich's plan for departure to their island matured, Dore worried about the unhappiness their going would cause to her husband and to Frau Ritter. She hit on a plan of striking boldness and simplicity. Frau Ritter was an excellent *Hausfrau* and Dr Koerwin a typical bourgeois husband. *Ergo*, bring the two together, leaving her and her superman free to escape into the wilderness.

> It was my plan that Frau Ritter would come to my husband's home and manage his household. This is an occupation which German ladies often undertake, and does not imply the social inferiority of the 'housekeeper' in other countries. It was, of course, essential that this arrangement be kept secret, for the sensation-mongering world, even in a large city like Berlin, is always eager to ferret out unusual situations and make a public scandal of them.

Dore seems to have had no difficulty in persuading her husband to accept this arrangement. According to Dore, he even considered the possibility of joining her and Friedrich in the Galapagos and gave her two thousand marks to help them in the costs of their project. Dr Koerwin was, however, worried about the likely reaction of the neighbours and demanded that Dore should write a letter explaining why she was leaving, especially emphasizing that there had been no quarrel between them.

The next stage of Dore's plan was more difficult. This involved a visit to the ancestral Ritter home in the Black Forest, where Friedrich's wife was living with his mother at this time. Dore's arrival in the Ritter house in Wollbach must have created quite a sensation, for it was, according to her, 'Dr Ritter's wish that I should disguise myself as a man in order to escape identification.' Friedrich presumably wished to avoid any scandal in his home village. Dore was apparently delighted with the success of her disguise as a youth and recalled that 'both Friedrich and I enjoyed my performance in this role'. Not surprisingly, Dore got a cold reception from Mila when she shed her disguise. However, Friedrich and Dore did not argue in vain, for Frau Ritter was finally persuaded to fall in with their plan; she would move in with the long-suffering Herr Koerwin. Dore was overjoyed, 'as the last obstacle to our venture seemed to have been removed.' Dore even seems to have made a hit with Friedrich's mother. Dore found her to be 'quite charming'. After some initial reluctance on the part of Frau Ritter senior, Dore recalled: 'she embraced me lovingly, and we both wept a little.' The rest of the Ritter family raised great objections to the proposed arrangements, but Friedrich paid no attention.

Dore returned to Berlin, leaving Friedrich at Wollbach to pack some of his belongings. She had to face a last emotional hurdle: her own parents. After the first, expected, impulse of dismay and horror, Dore's mother showed some understanding and promised Dore that she would do all she could to console Herr Koerwin and Frau Ritter. Dore's father, on the other hand, was deeply wounded at the prospect of losing his favourite daughter to Dr Ritter, whom he had never liked (Friedrich, perversely, expressed a great liking for Dore's father).

Having arranged things so satisfactorily in this neat and unlikely pattern, Friedrich and Dore began to prepare for their departure. Despite their romantic and high-falutin' approach to emigration, Friedrich and Dore were quite practical in their choice of equipment and supplies. Dore was at pains to emphasize that they were not like 'certain nature apostles, who reject on principle every modern appliance and tool'. On the contrary, Friedrich collected an impressive quantity of tools, garden implements, boxes, metal containers, essential books and some materials for use in house construction. Dore accumulated, in a more haphazard way, kitchen utensils, bedding, sewing equipment and a supply of 'stainless metal ware' that was to be her pride and joy in the Galapagos. All this they stored in a shed in the garden of the Ritter house at Wollbach. The shed was before long filled to overflowing.

Dore was anxious that Friedrich should take an adequate supply of drugs and medical equipment. Friedrich was furious at her suggestion that he should take morphine and a syringe, maintaining that their future life in the wilderness would teach them to overcome pain 'by the power of the will'. Dore, for her part, was equally incensed at Friedrich's suggestion that he should take a rifle. This, Dore maintained, was to deny their 'principle of living at peace with the animal creation'. For once Dore got her way. In the event, however, they were to have urgent need of both these items.

Towards the end of June 1929, Friedrich Ritter gave up his medical practice in Berlin. All that remained for them was to supervise Frau Ritter's move to the Koerwin household and take their farewell. By this time Frau Ritter had arrived in Berlin. Dore spent a couple of days with her showing her around the Koerwin house and taking her to her favourite local shops. Friedrich put in an occasional appearance, carefully timed during school hours so that he would not encounter the still resentful Herr Koerwin.

Everything went well. 'The meeting between my husband and Frau Ritter had passed off with less tension than I feared,' Dore wrote. 'One afternoon at four o'clock, when he came home from school, he found her there, and when I introduced them, he behaved so calmly I could conscientiously tell myself that this experiment, too, was starting favourably. The only thing my husband objected to was to call Frau Ritter by her married name, so they arranged that he should use her maiden name instead. It was natural that the name of Ritter should only call up bitter associations in his mind.'

On the last evening before their departure, Dore held a supper party to introduce Frau Ritter to Herr Koerwin's circle of friends. Only the family knew that this was also Dore's farewell party. The guests at this curious occasion were: Dore's mother and teen-age sister, a schoolteacher friend and his wife, a cousin of the Strauchs (who was an engineer), and a female friend of Dore's, with whom she had quarrelled and was anxious to be reconciled before she departed.

Dore's mother was much cast down, as were Dore's sister and Herr Koerwin. Dore 'was not blind to this', but 'contrived to keep the conversation going brightly', for she knew that 'none of those outside the secret suspected anything unusual.' Frau Ritter sang. It must have been a deeply embarrassing evening for Frau and Fräulein Strauch, poor Frau Ritter and the cuckolded Herr Koerwin. Dore described the evening as 'one of the happiest that I had ever known'.

After the guests had departed, Dore took her farewell from her husband and Frau Ritter. Herr Koerwin made Dore promise that she would never attempt to return to him. He then escorted her from their home, arm-in-arm, and put her on a tram car. As the tram receded Dore watched her husband waving to her 'with a grave and sad expression on his face'.

The next morning Dore Strauch, as she now wished to be called, and Friedrich Ritter left the Ritter home with rucksacks strapped to their backs, looking, Dore hoped, like 'a pair of week-end trippers'. This must have been unlikely, however, for they had some exceptionally heavy suitcases to carry. Dore wanted to call a taxi 'but he would not hear of this, insisting that all our theories obliged us to put our will-power to this initial test'. And indeed this test was a fitting prelude to the far harsher ordeals that awaited her.

* * *

Friedrich and Dore sailed from Amsterdam at nine o'clock in the evening of 3rd July 1929, on the S.S. *Boskoop*.

Friedrich was disappointed that a delay in their departure prevented them from 'seeing by daylight how we got away from the continent'. However, on the following morning he was exhilarated by the scene as the Dutch steamer ploughed steadily westward along the English Channel. He stood with Dore in the bows and enjoyed the throb of the engines beneath his feet, the wind blowing through his untidy hair, the regular heaving of the ship and the occasional splash of sea water in his face: 'a wonderful sharing of the endless battle between progressing machine power and the waves makes us forget any feeling of disturbed balance.'

On 10th July Dore and Friedrich saw ahead the cloud-shrouded peaks of the Azores. Friedrich was interested to see them for he had contemplated the possibility of settling in the Azores during his long search in the Berlin libraries for their island paradise. He was relieved that they had not chosen to settle there because, despite the pleasant climate and some uninhabited islands, he had heard that 'many Jews are supposed to have settled, also many European capitalists are said to have found refuge against future revolutions'.

Past the Azores the air became warmer and the ocean a deeper blue. Dore must have enjoyed watching flying fish shooting across the ocean surface, the leaping dolphins, occasional sea-birds and, once, a party of whales.

By 19th July the *Boskoop* was sailing close to Curaçao, in the West Indies. Friedrich calculated that 'the heart of our ship – the 4 cylinder engine – has beaten 2 million times since our departure – day and night – each minute 80 times. 500 to 600 horses would be necessary to do the same work. 80 cwt would have to fall 1 meter deep each time in order to turn the screw just once. And all the other things that depend upon this strong "heart": light dynamos, ventilators, refrigerators, sweet-water distillation, pumps, winches, cranes, rudder etc.'

The *Boskoop* reached Curaçao on 20th July and then sailed on to Bilbao, through the Panama Canal and reached Guayaquil on 3rd August 1929. There Friedrich and Dore learned that the ship that would take them to the Galapagos would not return to Guayaquil until later in the month and, it was predicted, would sail on 29 August.

Friedrich decided that they should use the time to visit Quito, the capital of Ecuador, perched at 9,500 feet in the Andes. On 7th August they boarded the ferry which took them four miles across the Rio Guaya to the railway station. Dore and Friedrich travelled second class, tightly packed among diminutive Indian passengers in the sweltering heat. At first they saw dry swamps and dried-up reedy pools with occasional huts raised on stilts. Their train chugged on through scrub and forested land. At the occasional railway stations ('a few Nigger or Indian huts') dark-eyed women sold fruit and fried maize.

Higher up, the train climbed into the jungle. Friedrich was not particularly impressed: 'The primeval forest ... never shows a tropical abundance with giant trees and dense shrubbery, as it is mostly described. One can not say that the forests are rich in wood, as we understand it. Proof of this are the crooked railway sleepers and bent construction lumber ... Even where water is more plentiful the forest only grows denser, not exuberant. Climbers, orchids and other parasites seem to hinder the growth'.

Higher still the jungle thinned, yielding to grass and willow trees. Friedrich, who may have been mentally depressed by the thin mountain air, considered that the 'vegetation in general is rather monotonoüs and strange'.

At sunset they reached Riobamba and slept the night at the Hotel Guayaquil. Next morning they saw the glorious peak of Chimborazo and a succession of small snow-covered peaks, before climbing aboard a bus which was to take them on to Quito. The bus was even more crowded than the train had been. They sat on hard wooden benches packed with silent Indians and their baggage. At a meal stop Friedrich succumbed to carnivorous habits by eating the 'deliciously crisp leg' of roasted Guinea pig.

They reached Quito at seven o'clock that evening. In the morning they explored the old-fashioned, narrow streets, visited some of the numerous ornate churches and were shown gruesome shrunken human heads. The following day they left their boarding house at sunrise to climb Mount Pinchincha. They were soon tired by the lack of oxygen and the steepness of the ascent, but steadily continued to climb for six hours before they reached the summit. There they were rewarded by a fleeting glimpse of Cotopaxi amidst the surrounding clouds. During their descent they experienced alarming symptoms of mountain sickness. Poor limping Dore seems to have been totally exhausted. They were helped down part of the way by a friendly shepherd boy but did not reach the road until darkness had fallen.

They did not eat that night, because Friedrich decreed that 'one should not eat even fruit when oxygen is scarce.'

After a few more days of sightseeing they returned by bus and train to Guayaquil, to make the final preparation for their voyage to the Galapagos. There they bought last-minute supplies to add to the mountain of equipment that they had so laboriously accumulated in Herr Ritter's shed at Wollbach.

The humid heat and squalor of Guayaquil must have been unpleasant after the temperate, perpetual spring of Quito. Despite the heat, Friedrich decreed that he and Dore should go about conspicuously and uncomfortably bare-headed in the noisy, crowded streets: 'we considered our hair the best protection against the sun, better to have it bleached by the sun instead of having it become poor and gray in a damp hot atmosphere.' Friedrich clearly enjoyed this opportunity to make himself conspicuous. With characteristic conceit he recorded that 'the greatest sensation is our hatlessness'.

Dore, with her love of animals, must have been distressed by many of the sights in Guayaquil in those days: donkeys and mules with open wounds caused by the immense loads that they were forced to carry, bound chickens struggling in the dust, bull fighting, and dead and dying dogs in the gutter. Friedrich considered that the 'dog diseases' of Guayaquil were caused by 'protein poisoning'. 'The dogs, which get plenty of meat here, do not use it up through action, that is, work, nor for the generation of heat, and the unused remainder causes cramps and other forms of intoxication. These diseases might be prevented through lesser intake of proteins. I never saw these symptoms in vegetarians'.

Friedrich was also incensed by other aspects of life in Guayaquil in 1929 that did not conform with his philosophy: 'smoking, drinking, wearing black clothing and taking medicine'. However, he would soon have the opportunity to put his philosophy to the practical test in the solitude of his chosen island Eden, for he and Dore sailed down the Rio Guaya in Captain Bruuns's battered schooner on 31st August 1929.

2
FORGOTTEN ARCHIPELAGO

The choice of Galapagos was singularly appropriate for Dr Ritter and his disciple. After all, a tropical island as it is popularly imagined, abundant and soft, with golden sands and Pacific palms, would not have been an apt setting for their dark, Nietzschean romanticism. How much more challenging for the heroic philosopher-superman to choose the remote Galapagos, with its strange fauna, its misty volcanic landscape and associations with the genius of Charles Darwin. Even the prototype of Friedrich's childhood favourite, Robinson Crusoe, whose name he would link with his own when he called himself '*der Robinson auf Galapagos*', had been in the Galapagos.*

Friedrich's 'Robinson' is, however, very different from Defoe's castaway: a sensible, pragmatic fellow who makes himself comfortable on his island, persuades a black man to work for him and departs on the first passing ship. Friedrich's 'Robinson' is clearly romantic and Utopian, very much in the genre of some Defoe-inspired novels (*Robinsonaden*) that were written in mid-eighteenth-century Germany and which were very popular at the end of the nineteenth century.

The most famous of the *Robinsonaden* novels was Johann

* The marooned Alexander Selkirk was picked up from Juan Fernandez island in 1708 by two British ships, the *Duke* and the *Duchess*, under the command of Captain Woodes Rogers. After the piratical sack of Guayaquil the two ships and their prizes, together with Alexander Selkirk, sailed to the Galapagos to refit.

Gottfried Schnabel's *Die Insel Felsenburg*. In this novel four castaways welcome their escape from civilization and attempt to establish their own paradise in the wilderness. They first live in a cave previously inhabited by buccaneers, then establish themselves in a volcanic valley, in the centre of the island, where there is a waterfall that they divert for their own purposes. Very significantly, in the light of the events that Friedrich and Dore would experience on their island, there is a murder and a suicide on Schnabel's island.

However, it was William Beebe's book, *Galapagos: World's End*, that finally caused Friedrich to choose a Galapagos island for his version of paradise. This book, published in 1924, described in considerable detail the observations of the Harrison Williams Galapagos Expedition of 1923. The members of the expedition had come to the archipelago in the steam-yacht *Noma*, on which they had lived with considerable comfort. They did, in fact, spend less than one hundred hours ashore. Nevertheless, the lavish illustrations and Beebe's excellent narrative did more to bring the Galapagos to public attention than any other book since the *Voyage of the Beagle*, whose author himself spent only five weeks in the archipelago.

From Beebe's book, Friedrich and Dore derived their knowledge of the geography, the natural history and the human history of the Galapagos. There are five major islands, ten smaller ones and a scattering of hundreds of islets and rocks, spread over an area of about sixteen thousand square miles, straddling the Equator, six hundred miles out in the Pacific Ocean from the Ecuadorian coast.

The Galapagos are, in fact, the tips of a series of gigantic volcanoes that rise up for more than ten thousand feet from the ocean floor. They are washed by the cold Humboldt Current that flows three thousand miles northward from Antarctica to cool the tropical air and cause the mysterious obscuring mists that gave rise to their early name: *Las Islas Encantadas*, the Enchanted Isles. The mountains of the Enchanted Isles are, in fact, hidden by mist and clouds for the greater part of the year. These provide enough moisture to support rich tropical vegetation and sustain a few freshwater springs in the highlands of some of the islands. The lower slopes and the smaller, low-lying isles, however, are virtually waterless for much of the year. Here desert scrub and cacti are found, in conditions quite unsuitable for human habitation, as Herman Melville described: 'Cut by the Equator they know not autumn, and they know not spring; while already reduced to the lees of fire, ruin itself can work little more upon them. The showers refresh the deserts; but in those isles, rain never falls.'

Melville was wrong in supposing that the Galapagos climate is unchanging, for, as Friedrich and Dore were to discover, the islands have their own strange cycle of seasons. For the greater part of the year there is a temperate climate as the cool Humboldt Current and the south-east trade winds pass through the archipelago, producing condensation only on the higher mountain slopes, in the form of almost continual mists and drizzle. During the short Antarctic summer, however, the Humboldt Current changes its course and the islands are bathed, from about January to April, by warm water. Then the Galapagos have a tropical climate. This is a time of heat and rain, when the dry vegetation on the lower island slopes becomes suddenly green and the birds and reptiles breed. By May, when the cool south-east trade winds return, the rains cease and the vegetation on the lower slopes and low-lying islands becomes dry and brown again, as Melville saw: 'Tangled thickets of wiry bushes, without fruit and without name, springing up among deep fissures of calcined rock, and treacherously masking them; or a parched growth of distorted cactus trees.'

Friedrich and Dore had chosen for their home a smallish island, in the south-west of the archipelago. It is reasonably lush, for the Galapagos, for it possesses at least two freshwater springs and abundant tropical vegetation on the higher slopes of its extinct volcanoes. Their chosen island was thrice-named (fairly modest by Galapagos standards – one island bears eight names). First of all, in 1684, it was called Charles Island by the English buccaneer Ambrose Cowley. Its official Ecuadorian name is Isla Santa Maria, but this is rarely used by the inhabitants of the Galapagos, who prefer to call it Floreana. At Friedrich's and Dore's time the place was referred to indiscriminately as Floreana or Charles. This confusing system of nomenclature is still used in the Galapagos, and bluff British names (Indefatigable, Chatham, Albemarle, Narborough) persist alongside their beautiful Spanish equivalents (Santa Cruz, San Cristóbal, Isabela, Fernandina).

* * *

The island had a violent and sordid history; at first sight not an appropriate setting for Friedrich's philosophical idyll. But in fact it exactly conformed to the island of Schnabel's 'Robinson' castaways (which had been inhabited by buccaneers), for Floreana (Charles Island), like Santiago (James Island) and Santa Cruz (Indefatigable Island), had been a refuge for pirates and buccaneers during the late-seventeenth and early-eighteenth centuries. These islands had safe anchorages, freshwater springs, plentiful tortoises, birds and fish that could be easily captured, and, most importantly, they were far from the usual Spanish shipping routes.

After the buccaneers came the whalers. Later in the eighteenth century, and well into the nineteenth century, British and American whaling captains stopped their ships in the Galapagos to refill their water barrels and take on board fresh food supplies. Tortoise flesh was highly regarded. The giant Galapagos tortoises could be kept alive, unfed, for months in ships' holds, and the whalers would load hundreds of these reptiles when they anchored in the Galapagos. This depredation started the decline of the giant tortoises, which were said to be extinct on Floreana long before Friedrich and Dore landed there in 1929.

The downfall of the tortoises was accelerated by the domestic animals released by the early seafarers, for they ate the only vegetation that the giant reptiles could reach with their short necks. When Friedrich and Dore arrived on Floreana they were to find the island populated with thousands of cattle, wild goats and donkeys as well as feral dogs and cats. The descendants of the cattle released by the eighteenth- and nineteenth-century seafarers on Floreana formed the basis of Captain Bruuns's lucrative butchery business, which he had discussed with Friedrich and Dore on board the *Manuel y Cobos* in Guayaquil, and which he pursued despite their refusal to participate.

A memento of the eighteenth- and nineteenth-century whalers remained on Floreana and was to become very familiar to Friedrich and Dore. This was a barrel placed on a pole, on the shore of a bay at the north end of the island: its purpose gave the bay its name: Post Office Bay. It was the custom for outbound ships to leave their mail in the barrel and home-bound ships would pick it up. The post barrel was erected on Charles Island in the late-eighteenth century by Captain James Colnett, who spent eighteen months cruising in H.M.S. *Rattler*. (The information derived from the letters left in the post barrel was used by the American Captain David Porter to locate and capture British shipping passing through the Galapagos in the war of 1812.)

As well as visitors, Floreana had had settlers in the past; it was quite common for them to cherish dreams of sovereignty. One was an Irish ruffian called Patrick Watkins, and another was the 'Dog King of Charles Island' described by Herman Melville. According to Melville's rather fanciful account, the 'Dog King' was a Creole who had been granted the island as a reward for bravery in battle. He succeeded in attracting eighty subjects to the island, and kept them in subjugation with a pack of large, vicious dogs. His subjects eventually rebelled, and after a battle which left three men and thirteen dogs dead on the beach, the 'Dog King' fled.

The desolate Galapagos seem to have had a special quality that bred the desire for kingship. The ancient schooner which took Friedrich and Dore from Guayaquil had belonged to, and still bore the name of, the tyrant of Chatham Island: Manuel Cobos. In 1880 Señor Cobos kept as slaves on his plantation prisoners who had been banished to Chatham. He minted his own coins (oval in shape) and dispensed his own savage punishments: shootings, lethal floggings and maroonings on uninhabited isles without food or water. Manuel Cobos's reign came to an abrupt end like that of Melville's 'Dog King' – in his case when his wretched slaves rose and murdered him.

The prisoners enslaved on Chatham Island by Manuel Cobos had been taken from a penal colony on Floreana. Several penal colonies had, in fact, been established on the island since the first batch of prisoners was banished there in 1829 by the Ecuadorian Government. Charles Darwin saw the prisoners in this colony six years later, when he landed on the island from H.M.S. *Beagle*. Their colony was high up on the mountain slope in the damp forest zone. As Dore and Friedrich were to find, abundant food could be obtained at this altitude. In his diary entry of 23rd September 1835, Darwin wrote: 'The houses are irregularly scattered over a flat space of ground, which is cultivated with sweet potatoes and bananas ... The inhabitants, although complaining of poverty, obtain, without much trouble, the means of subsistence. In the woods there are many wild pigs and goats; but the staple article of animal food is supplied by the tortoises.' The inhabitants subsequently had more to complain of than their poverty when they became subjects of the 'Dog King of Charles'.

Besides prisoners, pirates, buccaneers, castaways and tyrants, there were settlers with straightforward commercial ambitions. In 1925, a group of twenty-two Norwegians arrived on Floreana. They had been attracted there by false stories of the riches that could be made by hunting, fishing and farming on the island. Each member of the group had contributed $900 for the fare from Norway, the right to a hundred acres of land and a share in jointly-owned assets. Within a year most of the Norwegians had left, defeated by the hardships of life on Floreana. Twelve of them remained in Ecuador, and eventually died there, presumably without the means to return to Norway.

After four years, only two of the Norwegians remained on Floreana, along with an Ecuadorian. Together they owned a sloop for fishing, and they dried and exported their catch. The three men lived on in the two-storeyed house that the Norwegian settlers had built of corrugated iron and wood near the beach at Post Office Bay. There they had a small iron pier, a hundred yards of narrow-gauge railway for transport to and from the shore, and a small blacksmith's shop.

Friedrich knew of the existence of the Norwegians and the Ecuadorian on his chosen island. He was not pleased at the threat they posed to the solitude that he and Dore were so anxious to find in the Galapagos. But he need not have worried, for yet another human failure had occurred on Floreana to remove his unwelcome potential neighbours.

The discovery of this failure was made on 28th June 1929, at about the time of Dore's extraordinary farewell party in Berlin, when a schooner sailed close in to Post Office Bay. She bore a name that was to become very familiar to Dore: the *Mary Pinchot*. Dore would see the name carved on the trunk of a tree on Floreana and, in her romantic way, would imagine that Mary Pinchot was perhaps the sweetheart of some poor shipwrecked man who had cut the name on the tree in a desperation of love. The schooner, in fact, belonged to Gifford Pinchot, the Governor of Pennsylvania, who was cruising in the Pacific.

Gifford Pinchot had come to Floreana to replenish the fresh water on his schooner and to get some fresh meat, by shooting one of the island's wild bulls. As the *Mary Pinchot* sailed past Post Office Bay, the Second Mate spotted the Norwegian buildings on the shore. These surprised the men on board, for they had supposed Floreana to be uninhabited. The *Mary Pinchot* anchored a little way down the coast, at Black Beach, while Gifford Pinchot and his party searched for water and attempted unsuccessfully to shoot a bull. The next morning they sailed back to Post Office Bay.

Gifford Pinchot was first ashore. He walked up a broad path, bordered by lava blocks, which led in a gentle curve to the house. Pinchot was surprised to find, in such a desolate place, that the building was 'friendly and home-like, painted brown, with white trimmings and white doors, and with a flight of steps leading up to a broad veranda'.

All was silent and deserted, except for a half-starved dog that came to meet Pinchot and his party. They knocked at each of the three doors that opened on to the veranda, but there was no reply. The visitors walked in to find a room containing a ship's medicine chest, and another room leading to a second veranda at the back of the house. This room contained 'two clocks, several chairs, a trophy of whale harpoons, two stands of shot-guns and rifles, and a large talking machine.' In the centre of the room was 'a table with a table-cloth, and knives, forks, and spoons; a sugar bowl well filled; a plate on which were a couple of limes beginning to dry out; a white cut-glass decanter; a bottle of pickles; an unwashed egg cup; and some plates with fragments of food still on them.' Everywhere they looked were signs of recent habitation, but no inhabitants.

Outside they found the empty blacksmith's shop with three or four big tubs containing salted fish. Near the blacksmith's shop was a huge steel tank, presumably for water storage. Chickens were rooting about in the scrub behind the house. A second lean dog appeared and then two puppies, 'tickled to death to see us, and as fat as butter'. Most surprisingly of all, the party found a croquet pitch delimited by a row of lava boulders, complete with hoops and stakes and, nearby, balls and mallets.

Returning to the building, they found papers and diaries, written in Norwegian. With the help of a Norwegian crewman they learned from these something of the life of the occupants of the building. The diaries concerned the trivial things that easily magnify themselves in the minds of isolated men: efforts to keep the house clean and attractive, memories of friends back in Norway, and detailed accounts of the games played on the strange lava croquet lawn. But where were the writers of the diaries? All that could be learned from the last diary entry was that the inhabitants had returned from a fishing trip three weeks before. There was no solution to the mystery and the *Mary Pinchot* sailed away leaving the puppies and the dogs guarding the empty house on the shore.

After cruising around the archipelago the *Mary Pinchot* eventually sailed to Chatham Island. There they found the *Manuel y Cobos*, moored at the end of the long wooden wharf at Wreck Bay. To their amazement, they saw on the deck of the old schooner the two fat little puppies they had last seen playing in front of the mysterious deserted house on Floreana.

It turned out that Captain Bruuns had arrived at Post Office Bay on the *Manuel y Cobos* on the same day that the *Mary Pinchot* had departed from Floreana. Captain Bruuns had realized that something was wrong, as the sloop was missing, and set off to find her and her crew. He came upon them at another settlement, at Academy Bay on Santa Cruz, where they had taken refuge after being blown off course. One of the Floreana settlers was ill and he had come with Captain Bruuns to Wreck Bay. The other two remained at Academy Bay until the kindly Gifford Pinchot towed them back to Floreana. However, they appear to have finally lost heart in their enterprise, for they were not on Floreana when Friedrich and Dore arrived there a few weeks later. The Norwegian house stood abandoned and empty – a symbol of human failure on Floreana that would not be lost on the imaginative Dore Strauch when she set foot on the island that was to witness her tragic failure in the great enterprise she and Friedrich had planned with such confidence in Berlin. Years later she wrote: 'It was impossible to suppress a qualm of fear at the thought of all the disappointed hopes of our predecessors on this island.'

3
ESCAPE TO THE WILDERNESS

From the deck of an approaching ship, Floreana first appears as a cluster of seven grey-green volcanic mountains, like an untidy muddle of small inverted pudding basins. Closer in, with petrels scuttering over the waves and frigate birds overhead, the sloping foothills can be made out, with their curious covering of regularly spaced bare white trees. Below them is the low sweep of a mangrove and lava shore and then the long white beach of Post Office Bay, dazzling in equatorial sunshine.

Friedrich Ritter and Dore Strauch landed there in early September 1929. It was a brief visit, merely to put ashore some equipment, for Captain Bruuns had invited them to return on board the *Manuel y Cobos* to sail with him and see the other islands in the archipelago.

On 19th September they returned. Waiting for them was the only person on the island, a fourteen-year-old Indian boy called Hugo. He had come to Floreana to hunt and fish for Captain Bruuns and during their brief first visit had agreed to stay to help them until the ship next returned.

Dore stayed on board while the remaining supplies were unloaded. Leaning on the rail she watched Friedrich attend to a sailor from the schooner whose hand had been injured handling one of their large boxes. In the clear water there were shoals of small fish, but Dore was worried about the bigger, darker shapes that she could see moving in deeper water. What she could see of the land was no great comfort. The strange volcanic landscape was dry and grey: a twisted and fractured lava slope, with thorny trees and cacti, rose to the foothills of an extinct volcano, its head obscured by whispy clouds. On the shore were the wooden buildings deserted by the Norwegian fishermen.

The *Manuel y Cobos* left before dark. Dore watched it depart with apprehension, for it left them, with only an Indian boy for company, in a strange and desolate place. She explored the abandoned Norwegian buildings, and found a derelict poultry yard and some rusty tanks. As the nights can be cold at that season in the Galapagos, they slept on the shore in the deserted buildings.

In the morning they rearranged their supplies, making their foodstuffs and plants safe from animals. They packed their rucksacks with three days' supplies and, together with Hugo, who had with him an old-fashioned gun and several dogs, started to explore. Dore was enchanted: 'The light was different from the light of other days, the air was sweet, the landscape full of more than earthly charms. The sun-parched lifeless Galapagos bush seemed different here, from the same vegetation in Isabela and Santa Cruz.'

On that first day they discovered how difficult it is to cross a Galapagos lava field; even through their heavy shoes, the sharp edges lacerated their feet. The slopes of the largest volcanic mountain became greener and richer as they climbed. They came across lemon trees, heavily laden with fruit – the first Dore had ever seen. They also discovered the zig-zag tracks of wild cattle, pigs and donkeys, descendants of the animals left by earlier settlers on the island. Hugo shot a large boar which they dismembered and stripped of its flesh. Friedrich, the vegetarian, disapproved of this slaughter, and lectured Hugo on the subject; it was decreed that Hugo must not shoot any animal until he had consumed the meat of the one before – a counsel of perfection in a tropical climate.

Later that day they found some rough caves in the black lava, formed, Friedrich supposed, as a result of air pockets trapped in the molten lava when the volcano had been active.

Some of the caves also appeared to have been hollowed out by human hands. The biggest one had been enlarged to a floor area of some twenty feet deep by fifteen feet wide. On one side and at the back of the cave, ledges of about six feet by two feet had been hewn to form seats and bunks. There was also a fireplace with a curved opening and a chimney that ran upwards through the lava.

Like Schnabel's castaways, Friedrich and Dore decided to spend their first nights in the shelter of these caves. The cave was thought to have belonged to the Irish pirate Patrick Watkins,* who was possibly the first real inhabitant of Floreana. This man, who jumped ship in the early-nineteenth century, kept alive for some years by eating tortoise and growing a few vegetables. He was terrifying to look at, menacing in manner and verminous, with matted hair and an unkempt beard. His freckled skin was blistered by the sun and barely covered by a few dirty rags. He eventually escaped to Guayaquil after murdering his slave crew in an open boat.

This disagreeable figure haunted Dore Strauch's imagination. She thought of him crouching in the darkness of the cave, plotting to kidnap visiting sailors and declare himself King of Floreana.

Watkins's cave showed signs of recent habitation. There was an improvised bed of corrugated iron covered with a layer of grass and a tarpaulin sheet. A large rat ran from beneath the tarpaulin. The cave was, in fact, occasionally used as temporary shelter by hunters who came to Floreana to shoot the wild cattle and pigs.

Young Hugo made it quite clear that he would not stay in the cave alone, but the presence of Friedrich and Dore reassured him and he slept there that night. It was cool and damp and they lit a fire to help dry the place out.

The next morning, Friedrich and Dore awoke to find the landscape obscured by misty rain. Their intention was to

* Patrick Watkins was described by Captain David Porter in his diary published in 1822. He appears as 'Oberlus' in Herman Melville's *The Encantadas*, but transposed to Hood Island.

explore the dry, grassy plain lying to the north-east of the cave. There they attempted to capture some of the wild horses to help them with transport, but they succeeded in catching only one aged horse which they eventually cornered outside the cave. Dore was troubled by the animal's fear of recapture. She sensed that its spirit had been broken by previous captivity, and regretted the necessity of having to use it.

On the second morning they emerged from the cave into a brilliant sunlit landscape, for the early-morning mist had dispersed before sunrise. Friedrich and Dore decided to return to Post Office Bay. They headed north, led by Hugo and the horse, enjoying the exquisite morning and the astonishing tameness of the small birds that accompanied them.

When they saw the sea again, they were surprised to see the faint outline of Isabela away to the north-west instead of the curving white beach of Post Office Bay. They had, by following a donkey trail, turned too far to the west. Hugo told them that there was another spring in the direction in which they were walking. He did not, however, want them to go there and raised numerous objections as they continued along the donkey trail. Poor Hugo did not, apparently, want them to choose a site which was so far from the grassy plain where the hunting was so good.

At around noon they came to an extinct volcanic crater, at five hundred feet above sea level, to the east of the island's large, central mountain. The crater formed a natural basin full of luxuriant tropical vegetation. In the centre, they found a clear spring. This was the source of a small stream that flowed across the floor of the crater before tumbling down towards the sea through the open ends.* This opening in the crater wall provided a marvellous view of the sea and a superb site for a house.

Friedrich and Dore realized that this was the ideal place for them to build their home and establish their farm. There was

* Their discovery of a hidden volcanic valley with a waterfall is, again, an unusually precise parallel with the adventures of the castaways on Schnabel's Utopian island.

a scene of some emotion – at least on Dore's part. She wrote years later that 'tears of joy and thankfulness' flowed down her cheeks; and according to Ritter 'she danced to the music of Nature's silent melodies.' Young Hugo must have observed this with astonishment.

Hugo told them that they had again unwittingly chosen the site of one of Watkins's habitations. It had been called *Casa Piedra* and Hugo said that murder had been done there. Unabashed, Friedrich devised his own name for the house they would build: Friedo. According to Dore Strauch he announced this rather disconcertingly suburban combination of their names with the statement: 'This is our place, Dore, and we shall call it Friedo.' The pronouncement Ritter remembered making was longer, nobler and totally unbelievable: 'In the name of the Ritters I take possession of thee, O lovely valley, against all comers, and with thine own pure waters I christen thee Friedo, our Garden of Peace.'

That night they slept in the open at Friedo under an acacia tree and became aware, for the first time, of the animal life with which they were to share their new home. The whole bush was alive with braying and barking and bellowing creatures which, Dore felt, watched them as they slept.

Next morning Hugo woke them up with herb tea which they drank with the juice of freshly gathered lemons. Poor Dore was severely rebuked by Friedrich for sweetening her tea with sugar. She was deeply wounded by this reproach. Though it was a trivial incident, she saw it later as a landmark in their relationship, 'the beginning of a violent struggle, which, from that day onward, Friedrich and I were to wage.'

The following days were arduous and painful for Dore and she struggled to help Friedrich, Hugo, and the aged horse transport their belongings to Friedo. She never forgot her suffering at this time – not just from the crushing physical labour but from the conflict which had blazed up between her and Friedrich.

They had brought an enormous quantity of equipment and supplies. There were two large and heavy wooden boxes which could be adapted for use as a table, and three wooden cases that could also serve as cupboards. Breakables were packed in two zinc bath-tubs and they also had two full-sized milk churns for food storage. They had a complete carpenter's outfit, wire, rope, roofing felt, canvas and a variety of garden implements. There were ten hundredweights of seeds and plants with which to stock their proposed garden. They had mattresses, sheets, blankets, a hundred-yard bale of calico, and sewing needles stored in paraffin to prevent rusting. Friedrich had brought his medical instruments and some drugs. Dore's pride and joy was her 'Nirosta ware'. They had spent a thousand marks on this ultra-modern purchase, which apparently comprised cutlery and dishes, and Dore took a jackdaw pleasure in her shining metal pieces. Unfortunately she had brought only one set of cutlery, which created problems, especially when entertaining visitors. They also had a small library, including Dore's Greek and Latin textbooks, a volume of animal stories and her particular favourite, Nietzsche's *Thus Spake Zarathustra*. Friedrich had a number of medical books and a large supply of writing paper on which he was to commit the great philosophical works of which his devoted Dore believed him capable.

All this had to be carried across jagged lava fields, where a single stumble could result in a broken ankle or a painful laceration, and through tangled trees and cacti that tore at the face and eyes. Fortunately, they found a wooden transport saddle in the abandoned Norwegian buildings at Post Office Bay. With this they used the old horse to move the pots and pans, the plant shoots and the garden implements. Hugo, however, refused to carry anything more and frequently disappeared.

More than a century earlier Captain Porter's muscular sailors of the U.S.S. *Essex*, hardened by years at sea, found transportation on Floreana to be a formidable task. Porter's crew had found a spring 'at the distance of three miles from the beach and the water, after cleaning it out proved excellent. But it was found to be extremely laborious work getting it down to the beach, as our stoutest men were exhausted after taking down one keg each and it was found that each man could not carry any more than three kegs in twenty-four hours, owing to the distance, the badness of the roads and the excessive heat on shore.'

For more than two weeks the caravan of Friedrich, Dore and the horse continued, every other day, to move the mass of materials from Post Office Bay up to Friedo. Despite the cool and rainy nights at that season, the sun soon burned off the clouds and mists each morning and beat down with equatorial violence. This was very different from Dore's previous hiking experience with the German Youth Movement. She was frequently stretched to her physical limits and often cried and pleaded for help from Friedrich. He ignored her. He left her sobbing and exhausted on the ground beneath her heavy load, and at these moments Dore was filled with pure hatred for him. She later used some unplaned wooden planks as crutches to help her struggle over the lava.

Dore was upset when she realized that their aged horse was also nearing its physical limits. Weeping, she released it from captivity when Friedrich's back was turned. To her dismay, Hugo recaptured it and brought it back to Post Office Bay later in the day. Despite her own fatigue, Dore bitterly protested to Friedrich about using the sad creature. He insisted, however, that it was essential that they should go on using it. As it turned out, this was its last journey. At Friedo they turned it loose and its corpse was found by Hugo later that day. Next day when they passed by, it had been picked clean.

By early October, things began to improve. They had now shifted much of their material to Friedo. The shoots and seeds which they had planted in the rich, freshly-cleared soil began to sprout with amazing vigour. At night they slept in hammocks slung between the branches of the acacia tree. Hugo had constructed a bed of saplings resting on a frame and uprights to keep him off the ground.

On 1st October three Norwegians from Santa Cruz sailed into Floreana to hunt cattle. They borrowed Hugo and, before they left, gave Friedrich and Dore a strong horse which they had captured to transport carcasses to their boat. With this new horse Friedrich was able to move the heavier things, including the roofing felt. The Norwegians promised to bring over building materials when they next came to Floreana.

The vegetables in their garden had grown so prodigiously in the ground which had been cleared that, after only three weeks' planting, they were able to eat their first radishes. They were as large as European turnips. Tomatoes and cucumbers were also growing at a rate which amazed Dore, who had taken charge of the garden. They had discovered several kinds of tropical fruit growing in an abandoned orchard near the caves in which they had spent their second night on the island. This provided them with oranges, lemons, aguacates, guavas and papayas which supplemented the rice and maize they had brought with them.

Despite this improvement in the food supply, Dore was still physically exhausted, lonely and desperately unhappy at Friedrich's neglect of her: 'The little tendernesses, all the spontaneous expressions of love, so trifling when enumerated, and yet so indispensable, had disappeared entirely from his behaviour towards me. He had become impersonal, almost cold. He seemed impatient of even the slightest demonstrativeness on my part and so I, too, suppressed my warm affectionate impulses, though not easily.' She contemplated leaving the island. There were sufficient funds for her to do so for they had buried money on the island and left some funds with the German Consul at Guayaquil. It was a combination of obstinacy and adherence to their original idea that she afterwards believed kept her on the island – to face further hardships and, ultimately, terrible tragedy.

Their regular journeys across the rough lava slopes had torn their European shoes to shreds. The lava also split the rough wooden clogs which Friedrich had made for her. To the lacerations of her feet were added the painful swellings of *nigaus* (swellings, usually on the toes, caused by sand fleas, or jiggers,

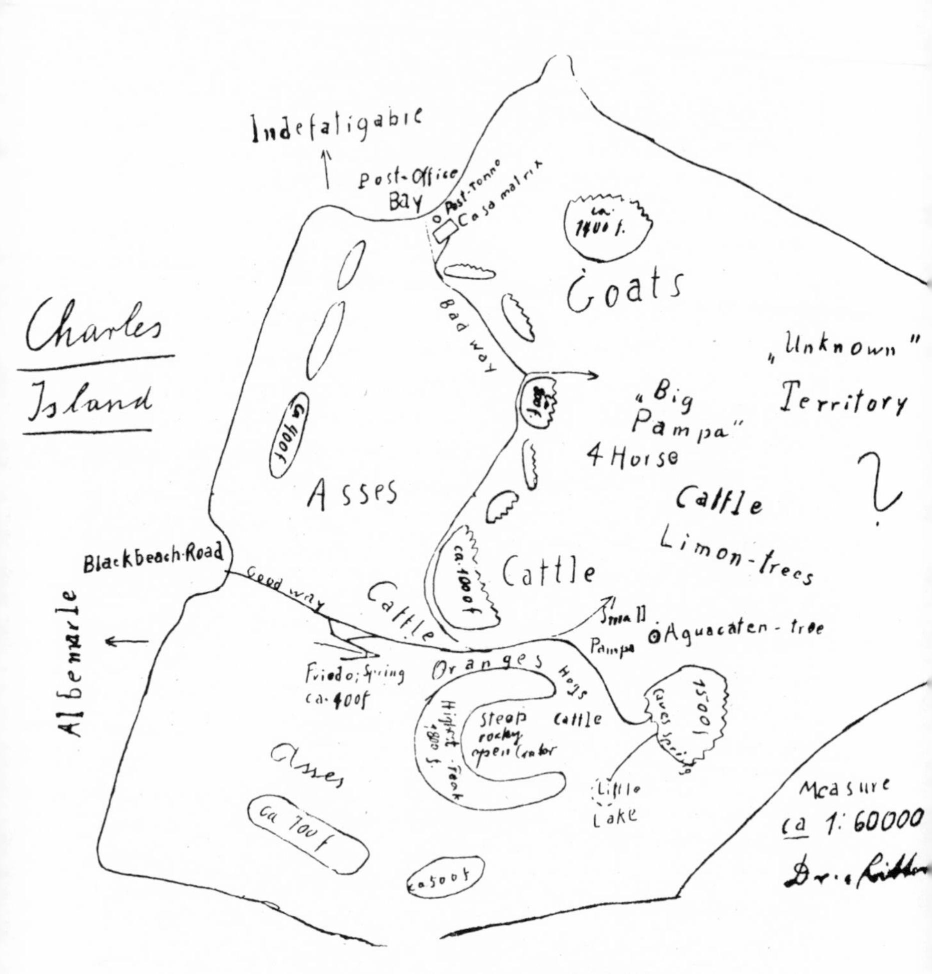

Fig. 2 Sketch map of Floreana drawn by Friedrich Ritter

the adults of which burrow deep into the skin). Friedrich removed these from Dore's swollen and painful feet and did his best to reduce the pain. He also persuaded her to adopt his own protective strategy – for Dore to erect a 'strong-defence-psychology' around her feet so that through 'sheer intensity of consciousness' she would deflect the parasites. Dore believed this to have been a successful remedy against the *nigaus*.

Dore's next injury was not susceptible to Friedrich's 'defence-psychology'. Whilst clearing up after an outdoor meal cooked by Hugo she knelt on a pile of white ash at the edge of their primitive hearth. Beneath the deceptive whiteness were red-hot coals which burned her knee nearly to the bone. This accident left an appalling wound that added further torture to the long journey to and from Post Office Bay.

An outbreak of painful and unsightly body sores added further miseries, to both her and Friedrich. These, she believed, resulted from Friedrich's unexpected decision to abandon their vegetarian diet. This repulsive change in diet she felt to be the worst of her misfortunes at this time. Friedrich justified it by arguing that, as a servant of Captain Bruuns, Hugo was inevitably involved in animal slaughter. They were, therefore, morally obliged to make the fullest use of Hugo's animal victims.

Friedrich refused Dore's passionate request to order Hugo to stop cattle-hunting on Floreana. This, Dore suspected, was because Friedrich feared that Captain Bruuns might have power to evict them from the island. Friedrich did not, apparently, want to antagonize the captain by interfering with his cattle-slaughtering business.

Friedrich later became more dramatically involved in Hugo's hunting. Hugo was charged by a wounded bull and badly gored through the armpit. The bull returned and charged them again. Friedrich, with great coolness, took Hugo's gun, reloaded, and shot the bull.

After Friedrich had tended Hugo's wounds, Dore asked him to wash the mud from her burned leg, which she could not bend sufficiently to reach. Friedrich refused. Dore was furious at his callousness. She bent her leg sharply in her rage, and tore the bandage so that blood gushed from the wound. Only then did Friedrich tend her leg. Dore regarded this incident as another milestone in their deteriorating relationship.

Hugo, shaken by his injuries, departed with Captain Bruuns on his next call. Dore missed the boy and was surprised to discover that Friedrich too had grown fond of him. In her dislike of what she must have regarded as her cold, indifferent lover she apparently found it difficult to credit him with even the capacity for friendship with the boy who had shared their life and hardships of the past weeks.

* * *

Meanwhile, the construction of the house at Friedo continued. It was a difficult task. Friedrich had decided that acacia was the most appropriate timber, despite its curving growth. He adapted his design to the sinuous acacia by building a circular wall with a covering of roofing felt. This structure withstood its baptism by the Galapagos rain. Later, however, the sun dried the wood, which buckled and cracked until Friedrich thought the structure 'looked like the skeleton of some prehistoric monster.' By good fortune, the arrival of the Norwegian ship, with its promised load of building materials, brought thirty-six sheets of corrugated iron. These were unloaded at Black Beach, which was much closer to Friedo than Post Office Bay; Friedrich used them to cover the roof. Fortunately the weight of the corrugated iron held the wall boards in place. Dore was enchanted when, after the rainy season, the acacia-wood walls came to life and sprouted leaves.

Friedrich continued to clear ground to enlarge their vegetable garden. The clearing of trees and shrubs and especially the removal of lava boulders and moving of soil was hard, back-breaking work. Friedrich laboured from dawn to dusk, using axe, shovel and bucket. After four months his labours were lightened by a gift from Eugene McDonald, the owner of a cruising yacht the *Mizpah*, who gave Friedrich more tools, including a wheelbarrow, a rifle and dynamite. The first officer came ashore especially to demonstrate the detonation of dynamite, despite Friedrich's insistence that he was a student of chemistry with wartime experience of explosives. The dynamite enabled him to blast out tree stumps, and the wheelbarrow to shift soil – more than fifty thousand barrow-loads, according to Dore.

Friedrich eventually laid out two pathways in the garden of Friedo: one leading to the west, to Black Beach, and the other over the mountain, to Post Office Bay. Around their spring they

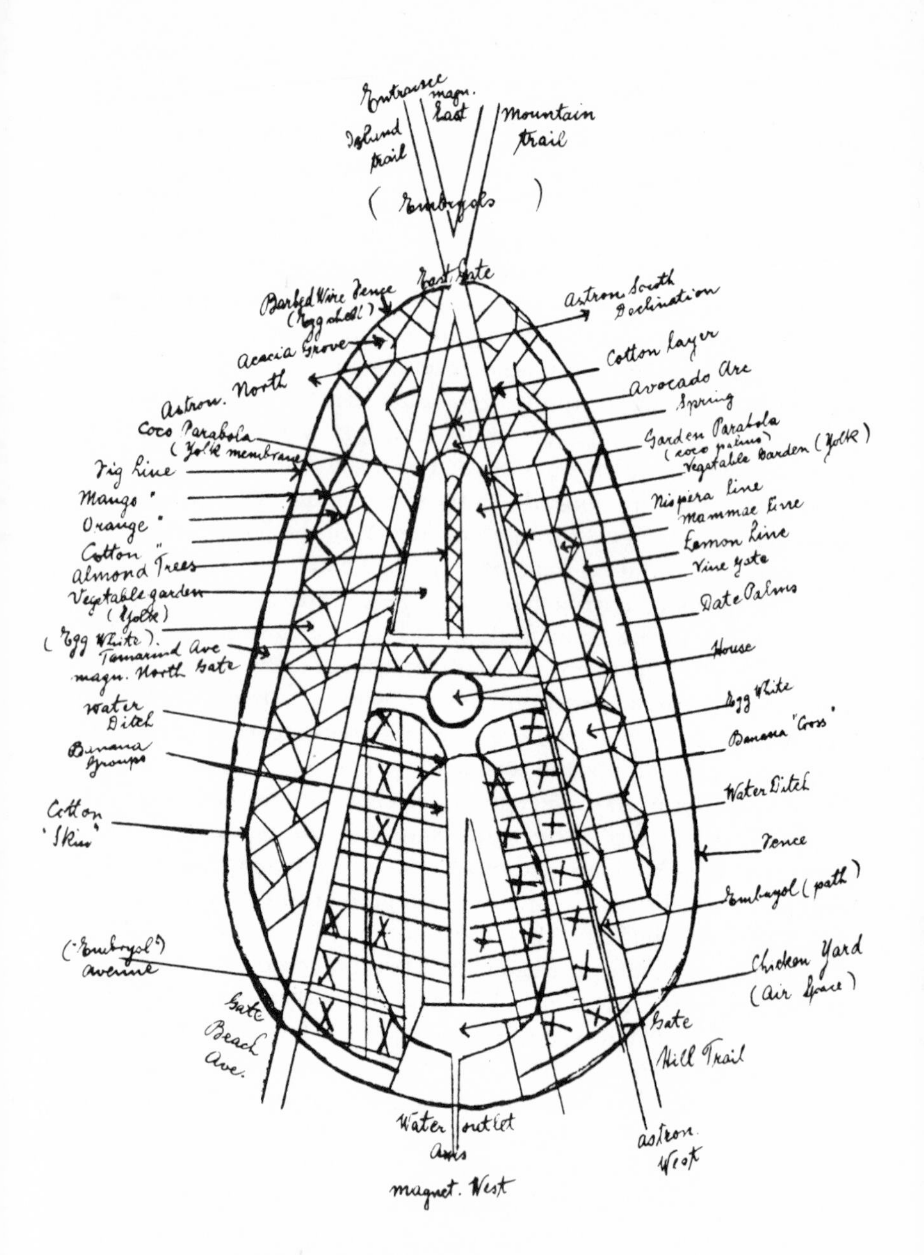

Fig. 3 The 'Friedo Egg' or 'Garden Symphony'. A sketch, by Friedrich Ritter, of the garden at Friedo designed according to his philosophical system.

planted palms. The water from the spring flowed in two small streams around the vegetable plot. Here they grew beans, tomatoes, peas, cabbages, radishes, cauliflowers, onions, celery and spinach. Their first planting was a great success. Friedrich described how the tomato plants grew to more than six feet in height with fruit whose average size was as large 'as a baby's head'. In another part of the garden they cultivated bananas, papayas, oranges, coconuts, guavas, lemons, pineapples and yams. They also planted sugar-cane and Friedrich constructed a primitive wooden device, from a tree stump, which involved Dore swinging to and fro at one end of a wooden lever, to squeeze the sap from the cane. Their chickens they established in an enclosure in a recess in the crater wall, well protected from animals.

The garden at Friedo never again achieved the fecundity of the first season. This may have resulted from exhaustion of the soil, but certainly the animals were partly to blame. The seedlings and shoots of the second season in particular were attacked by an astonishing variety of insect pests. The ants were worst of all. Their undiscriminating appetites caused terrible damage to most kinds of vegetable and fruit in the Friedo garden, as well as the stored food. They smothered the plants with their bodies, built nests in the potato patch, chewed holes in boxes, stole sugar (despite all precautions) and even invaded their beds.

Friedrich was enraged by the predation of the Friedo ants. He saw the 'socialism' of the ants as 'nothing but a systematic robbery from all other life'. He raged against them in his philosophical writings at the time. He regarded their social organization as a parallel to human socialism, which was so repellent to a disciple of Nietzsche. 'In the battle against them one drops every respect for this by the moderns so highly praised "solidarity" and recognizes the whole misery of an endeavour where "one hand always wants to wash the other".'

Of the large mammals the wild pigs distressed Friedrich and Dore most. Despite his early lectures to the Indian boy on the subject of animal slaughter, Friedrich found himself engaged in a protracted private war with one most troublesome boar. This enemy he credited with satanic qualities. He first attempted to shoot it with his inadequate rifle; then he tempted it with poisoned bananas. When this failed, he dug a pitfall trap which he covered with leafy branches and baited with yucca. The boar took the bait, but escaped leaving even more devastation. Friedrich then constructed an elaborate guillotine, which incorporated 'a strangulation device with the axe'. This also failed. Next, getting very cross indeed, he constructed an elaborate trap made of logs, to crush the animal. When his enemy escaped again he resorted to dynamite. This ultimate weapon still failed to kill the beast, and it is hard to imagine what Friedrich would have done next, but apparently the boar had had such a shock from the explosion that it finally left the Friedo garden alone.

Things had become a little easier for Dore and Friedrich by February of 1930. Their hard-won garden was yielding them food and their house had withstood the heavy Galapagos rainstorms. The conflict between them seems to have abated somewhat and after the departure of Hugo their diet became, again, vegetarian. In that hot damp season Friedrich said that they worked in 'complete nakedness'. They rose with the dawn: bird song was a relief after the nocturnal clamour of the donkeys, pigs, wild cats and dogs. Friedrich gathered fruit for their breakfast. They would then work at their allotted tasks; Friedrich in building and cutting wood and clearing more ground and Dore in tending the chickens and cultivating the vegetable garden. They took their second, and only other, meal at midday. They rested in the overpowering heat from two until about three or four o'clock. Friedrich would read or write and Dore engage in needlework or writing. As the day cooled they would return to their outdoor work until after the quick equatorial sunset.

They ceased their labours at about seven o'clock. Friedrich would work at his book on philosophy or read aloud to Dore while she darned or made rugs and mats by twisting together dried banana leaves. Between eight and nine o'clock Dore usually fell asleep. Before he slept, Friedrich would go outside to catch some of the cockroaches and moths that attacked their precious plants and fruit trees, to feed to their chickens in the morning.

Their two daily meals were simple and possessed a certain ritual quality. At breakfast they ate freshly gathered melons, cucumbers, tomatoes or whatever else was in season. For their midday meal they alternated two days of sweet food with one of salt. The sweet food would consist, according to Friedrich, 'of two beaten eggs, raw, with bananas or other fruit and cane-sugar sap, either fresh or as a syrup'. Their salt food was composed of 'several raw or cooked greens and root vegetables, with peanut butter or oil'. They ate no grain. Friedrich was glad that they were 'entirely rid of flour dabbling', for he believed that the 'chronic "flour-diseases" with which mankind is afflicted could rapidly be eliminated if people would simply omit bread from their diet.'

Friedrich seems to have had strong views on dietary matters. For years in Berlin he had, according to Dore, practised a system of eating that required 'intensive mastication of each mouthful' and, as a consequence, had worn his teeth to stubs. Before leaving for the Galapagos he had these extracted, partly for the 'scientific desire to find out whether gums might be so far toughened as to substitute for teeth in chewing.' Nevertheless, Friedrich had equipped himself with stainless-steel dentures for special occasions.

Friedrich's dentures subsequently became the object of malicious interest to some visitors to the island. A Danish visitor claimed, for example, that Dore also was toothless and that they were forced to share the now famous stainless-steel dentures, presumably like the 'Nirosta' cutlery, by using them alternately. Dore was sensitive on this point. Years later, she went out of her way to produce her rigmarole about Friedrich's scientific mastication to explain his toothless condition.

Dore's improved relationship with Friedrich continued

during February, March and April. She afterwards looked back at these months as their happiest on Floreana: 'It was the time of our hardest work but of our brightest hopes. A sense of permanence had allied itself to peacefulness, a kind of strange assurance had filled us, that we had been in some way put to a test of fitness and had been accepted.'

In early May, however, Dore received another painful shock. The mail arrived on the *Manuel y Cobos* together with newspapers from Germany. These told of Friedrich's flight to the Galapagos with her. Dore was appalled by the cheap sensationalism of the articles and ashamed at the effects which the scandal would have on her husband and family in Germany. With the newspapers were forty-six letters – mostly from Germany and all from strangers. The privacy of Friedo was breached. Soon others would come to Floreana and put an end to their solitude.

* * *

The first news of intruders came, unexpectedly, from the captain of the *Manuel y Cobos*. On one of his visits, Captain Bruuns announced that he had decided to live on Floreana and to refurbish the disused fishing station at Post Office Bay. Dore suspected that he had heard the rumours, which had apparently spread through the islands, that she and Friedrich had received generous presents from wealthy Americans in the few yachts that had called at Floreana. Dore strongly disapproved of Captain Bruuns, not only for his cattle-slaughtering enterprises but also because she suspected that he had stolen some of their belongings stored in the Norwegian buildings at Post Office Bay. She was particularly outraged by the loss of a small rowing-boat, a recent gift from another passing yacht.*

The first of the would-be settlers who had been stimulated by newspaper stories of their island idyll were five young Germans. They arrived separately, but joined forces and, like Dore and Friedrich before them, moved into Watkins's caves.

* The yacht was, in fact, the *Mary Pinchot*, whose name, carved on a tree, had so intrigued Dore on her arrival on Floreana.

Differences subsequently arose between the members of the group, one of whom constructed and moved into his own hut at a distance from the caves.

Dore recounted how she and Friedrich helped the young Germans, entertaining them all, despite their quarrels, giving them help and advice and sharing their plants with them. The new arrivals apparently behaved 'with much tact and kept well out of sight, except when we invited them to call.'

Hard on the heels of the young Germans came a 'nature-worshipping' lady from Berlin, accompanied by her consumptive husband, a cook and a menagerie consisting of several monkeys, a parrot, a dog and a rabbit. She wore a silk gown, silk stockings and her fingers were bejewelled with diamond rings. The lady was cold-shouldered by the cave dwellers, but was received at Friedo. There she poured out her life story, examined everything in detail and, according to Dore, expressed unbounded admiration for their little estate – especially for the spring and, presumably, the 'Nirosta ware'. She was so charmed by all that she saw that she decided there and then to move into Friedo. This arrangement had the additional advantage that Dr Friedrich could have kept his eye on her consumptive husband whose health, she confidently expected, would greatly benefit from a prolonged stay on Floreana. It was also, apparently, her intention to enrich the island fauna with her menagerie.

It took several hours for Dore and Friedrich to persuade this extraordinary visitor that she could not live at Friedo. She eventually departed, for Post Office Bay, where she was the guest of Captain Bruuns in his newly refurbished establishment on the shore, and left the island within the week. Unfortunately, the monkeys were abandoned by their departing owner, and all quickly perished.

There are some curious and revealing differences between Dore's and Friedrich's accounts of their relationship with the early would-be settlers on Floreana. As described by Dore, their attitude to the increasing number of visitors was invariably most considerate: 'It sounds discourteous to designate our visitors as intruders, yet pleasant as most of them were as human beings, we did at times resent their coming. Of course it might have been said that had we seriously wished it, we would have easily refused to talk to anyone or entertain a single stranger in our Friedo seclusion. Sometimes, indeed, we were almost tempted to do this, but when we thought of the sheer physical effort that it cost to clamber up the rough hill-side to get to us, we felt that to turn our backs on these no doubt well-meaning callers would be too churlish. So we never did.'

Compare this with Friedrich's account of their treatment of such visitors: 'They came expecting to be treated like invited guests, and the only way we can deal with them is to make it clear in the beginning that we want to be alone and consider them intruders. We refuse to have anything to do with them.'

There is also an odd discrepancy between their accounts of the death of one of the abandoned monkeys. Friedrich said that it attacked them and was shot by him; Dore said that it attacked and was shot by someone else in a hut on the island.

These differences are, of course, trivial. But they shed an interesting light on Dore's and Friedrich's personalities and attitudes. Dore's accounts exhibit an underlying desire to be conventionally kind and considerate to strangers – even though they had disturbed their precious privacy. Similarly, her transposing of the monkey slaying to another (non-existent?) settler's hut must have arisen from her gentle desire not to associate her Friedrich with animal slaughter.

Friedrich, on the other hand, seems to have deliberately struck a pose in boasting of his rude and churlish behaviour to the visitors. However, such a pose would be quite consistent with monkey slaying, which can therefore be truthfully described, for the tough-guy disciple of Nietzsche had, according to Dore, once said: 'There is only discipline. We must conquer by will . . . with brutality, too, if it must be.'

* * *

By this time the fishing enterprise had transformed the scene at Post Office Bay. The derelict buildings had been restored and ten Indians worked there at long benches, gutting, cleaning and salting fish. The fish offal that was thrown into the sea had dramatically changed the marine life at Post Office Bay, for the sea there was crowded with shoals of sharks. Dore was terrified of them: 'One almost heard the impact of their great bodies as they collided, crowding ravenously around this new and inexhaustible feeding place.' She was also repelled by the pervasive stench of fish. This, together with her antipathy to Captain Bruuns, led her to shun Post Office Bay, which she had, in any case, always felt to be a sinister place. She only occasionally went down there with Friedrich, who, despite his frequently announced desire for total solitude, seems to have been a more frequent caller there than was Dore.

On one of these visits to Post Office Bay Dore was surprised to meet Captain Bruuns's new partner in the fishing enterprise: a Dane, called Knud Arends. Dore was surprised that Bruuns had acquired such a presentable partner. Arends was, apparently, a dark-haired young man of 'more than usual good looks'.

Dore, who seems to have been quite susceptible to handsome men, was later also surprised and charmed by one of Captain Bruuns's visitors. He too was a Norwegian. Dore described him as a highly intellectual and aristocratic-looking man of about sixty years, who had formerly had a high position in the Norwegian consular service, chiefly in Africa. He was Artur Wörm-Muller, who also charmed a visiting Englishman, Roydon Bristow, during his visit to Floreana in the fifty-two-foot Cornish ketch, the *Gold-digger*. Wörm-Muller had been involved in the disastrous Norwegian enterprise on Floreana. He seems to have returned to the island to fill in time before his wife returned from Guayaquil after a trip to Chicago.

Captain Bruuns's partnership with the handsome Arends and his friendship with the distinguished-looking Norwegian visitor altered Dore's view of him. In her kind way she was glad that the Captain should have formed a firm friendship with a middle-aged English doctor who had shown up at Post Office Bay. He arrived on a small yacht with a single half-caste crewman. Dore discovered that he had been a medical officer in a lunatic asylum. However, he seemed to have some personal psychiatric problems, for he was 'alternately dully and violently miserable' and 'smoked continuously drawing one cigarette after another, in an endless chain out of a large tin, which bulged out of his misshapen pocket of his coat.' Like many of the odd assortment of people that have been drawn to Floreana, he had fled from unhappiness in the civilized world – in his case, an incompatible wife. According to Dore, he and Bruuns became inseparable and spent each night together, in the fishy atmosphere of Post Office Bay, drinking *guaropo*, a powerful distillate of sugar-cane.

This odd friendship came to an end when Captain Bruuns was drowned whilst on a voyage to Isabela to purchase food and salt.

From high up at Friedo, Dore had watched Captain Bruuns put to sea in his thirty-five-foot cabin cruiser, the *Norge*. She was enraged to see her little rowing-boat towed behind. With Captain Bruuns were eight of his Indians, the Governor of the Galapagos, who was staying with Bruuns, and the English doctor, who, according to Dore, was leaving the island for good.

The party arrived at Isabela, took on board the supplies and started back to Floreana. But there was not enough petrol on board to bring the *Norge* back against the powerful current and the boat was swept into St Pedro's Bay, on the south-west tip of Isabela, fifty miles from the settlement of Villamil.

The stranded party decided on two courses of action. One group, including the Governor, was to walk across the terrible volcanic terrain to Villamil, while Captain Bruuns and two Indians attempted to sail back to Floreana in Dore's and Friedrich's little rowing-boat, in which Bruuns had improvised a sail, to fetch a second motor-boat from Post Office Bay. The doctor and two Indians remained on board the stranded *Norge*.

Captain Bruuns failed to make any progress against the same current which had impeded his motor-boat and, eventually, made for the settlement at Villamil. There he was joined by the exhausted members of the overland party. Shortly afterwards the *Manuel y Cobos* arrived on a scheduled call at Isabela. The whole party returned to St Pedro's Bay on the old schooner with fuel for the *Norge*, towing the rowing-boat. The skipper of the *Manuel y Cobos* suggested that the fuel should be taken to the *Norge* in the rowing-boat and that his ship would then accompany the motor-boat back to Floreana. But Captain Bruuns would have none of this. He wagered the skipper of the *Manuel y Cobos* that he could get the fuel to the *Norge* in the rowing-boat and would be back at Floreana before the schooner. The skipper accepted the wager and sailed, with the Governor on board, for Floreana. But Captain Bruuns and the Indians with him were soon in serious trouble in the heavy swell and the rowing-boat became waterlogged. The crewmen swam for the shore. Captain Bruuns stubbornly remained in the boat, attempting to bale it out. But the rowing-boat quickly sank and Bruuns took to the water. He was unable to get to the beach and was flung against some jagged rocks.

The English doctor, who had watched from the *Norge*, attempted to revive his friend, but Captain Bruuns was dead. They buried him beneath a lava cairn close to where he was swept ashore.

The party were still stranded, for the fuel had been lost when the rowing-boat capsized. They then decided to attempt to row the *Norge* to Villamil using the six oars that they had on board. They kept close to the shore, to avoid the tremendous sea, and eventually got near to Villamil before running aground. They walked the last few miles over the lacerating lava to the settlement.

Arends was in Guayaquil when Captain Bruuns left for Isabela. After returning to Post Office Bay, and finding that his partner had not returned, he set off in the other motor-boat to look for him. While searching for Captain Bruuns, Arends's boat also capsized in St Pedro's Bay. He was cast up on the shore close to a lava cairn, which to his grief he discovered was the grave of his friend and partner.

Arends was eventually found with the *Norge* at an anchorage close to Villamil, by Roydon Bristow and the crew of the *Gold-digger*. The *Norge* was beached in a small creek, with a leaking hull and a damaged engine. With the aid of a fifty-gallon drum, to provide buoyancy, and a bilge pump, the *Norge* was towed slowly back to Floreana by the *Gold-digger*. Wörm-Muller was overjoyed to see Arends once again, and the old Norwegian, the young Dane and his English rescuers celebrated that night in the Norwegian buildings on the shore at Post Office Bay.

Arends did not stay on Floreana, but moved to Academy Bay on Santa Cruz to stay with a Danish couple and Post Office Bay became once again the scene of quiet decay which Dore and Friedrich had encountered on first landing on Floreana. The five young Germans had also left the island. However, this did not mean that Dore and Friedrich were left entirely to themselves. Visiting yachts still called and their owners and guests climbed up to Friedo. Much worse, journalists now invaded their privacy and, even worse, Dore and Friedrich learned that her husband and parents and his wife and family had been pestered by them.

Dore and Friedrich agreed to write magazine articles about themselves and their life on Floreana. They did this, they claimed, to correct the sensational press distortions and to present a true account of the 'Adam and Eve of Floreana'. Dore was particularly annoyed with newspaper stories that they promenaded about the island stark naked, except for high boots to protect them from thorny undergrowth. She discussed the technicalities of insular nudity in relation to the Galapagos vegetation and concluded, rather coyly: 'If we did sometimes play Eve and Adam in our little Eden, it was only when we knew ourselves to be completely alone.'

Dore derived much consolation and pleasure from a stray donkey, one of six that the five young Germans left and, apparently, had cruelly ill-treated. This animal she tamed and called Burro. She could not, however, bear to see him captive and eventually released him. She was thrilled when Burro came back to Friedo. However, even her fondness for the donkey was to be used to cause her future pain, for poor Burro would be a victim of the conflicts that would later arise on Floreana.

4

THE LAVA EDEN

In their second year, Friedrich and Dore commenced work on a new house at Friedo, as they both longed for a more comfortable home than the simple shelter which they had built during their first weeks on Floreana. Friedrich approached the problem with philosophical detachment: first, 'What is the ideal solution?' The ideal solution, as Friedrich saw it, would be to build as near the centre of the garden as possible without unduly covering their precious soil. The ground plan should be circular, for the best aesthetic and philosophical reasons. A dome would be the most beautiful roof. In the end Friedrich settled for a compromise: an octagonal ground plan with a pyramid for a roof. The house was to be set on pillars, sunk in lava shafts as corner stones, and the space between these would be filled with smaller rocks to make walls. The bedroom should occupy the eastern side, to admit the rising sun, and a workroom the western wing. On the shady northern side would be a kitchen, storerooms, staircase and a lavatory.

A certain amount of mystery surrounds the building of this house. Having outlined his still rather grandiose compromise, Friedrich wrote about the 'refractory nature' of his materials. He complained that he was not equipped with the tools of a stone-mason and was frustrated by the 'incalculable internal tensions' within the lava rocks which caused splinters to be 'continually breaking off at unexpected moments to threaten eyes and shin bones'. He told of the difficulties of lifting rocks when the walls were breast high and described how they piled up earth to make an incline to drag them into position. According to Friedrich, in an article published in late 1931, they had been nearly a year labouring on this stone-built house and in a few months the roof would be added.

Dore, on the other hand, wrote quite firmly that building commenced on 23rd September 1931, that their old house 'dwindled rapidly into a mere shack next to its broad imposing neighbour' and that the new one was finished in three months. She described a wall-less building, with a slightly tilting corrugated-iron roof, in which the awnings of sail-cloth could be easily let down at the sides. The roof frame and props were formed of acacia and hardwood. The floor was stamped clay covered with bamboo rods. This is indeed the rather ramshackle building shown in the faded photographs taken by visitors to Friedo. Friedrich's impressive stone building seems to have been a mythical edifice, presumably abandoned at an early stage in the face of intractable building materials, concocted purely to impress the readers of the *Atlantic Monthly*.*

However, both he and Dore agreed about the most marvellous of his inventions – a piped water supply. This, to Dore, was the 'chief glory' of their new home and took pride of place with her 'Nirosta ware' when visitors were shown around their little estate. Friedrich used an old pipe salvaged from the buildings at Post Office Bay to convey the water from their spring to a natural rock in the corner of Dore's kitchen. A tap was constructed from an old cartridge case, 'controlled by a slide'. To Dore, 'this piece of plumbing was the admiration of all beholders, and an incalculable boon to me.'

The marvels of Friedo were, in fact, admired by several visitors who were drawn to Floreana to see the now notorious Friedrich Ritter and his mistress. Some that walked up to Friedo

* Friedrich did, in fact, devote considerable efforts at this time to the design of some even more grandiose buildings which conformed to the principles of his philosophical system. These would have been more suitable on Schnabel's mythical island than on Floreana.

from their anchored yachts were rich and powerful men. One such was G. Allan Hancock, a multi-millionaire from Los Angeles who was to play an important role in the tragic events that were later to take place on the island. The foundation of the Hancock wealth was the possession of the historic Rancho la Brea, which subsequently became most of Hollywood and the Willshire district of Los Angeles. Land bought for $2.50 an acre was sold, years later, for $2,500 per foot of frontage. With this wealth Hancock founded banks and established numerous business corporations in oil, railways, the construction industry, farming and packaging.

Hancock also owned and captained the *Velero III* (he had a master's ticket). This was not a typical millionaire's pleasure ship, but a vessel that was dedicated to Hancock's dual interests, biological research and music. The *Velero III* was well equipped with laboratory facilities and usually had on board a number of distinguished American biologists. The ship was, in fact, used for the Hancock Pacific Expeditions which the multi-millionaire sponsored. The biologists came from a variety of universities and institutions.

Hancock, usually a rather withdrawn and taciturn man, was able to relax among the scientists and other guests on board his great yacht. He was largely responsible for navigation and especially enjoyed handling the ship's mechanical gadgets, and, in the evenings, playing his cello with the other musicians on board.

Allan Hancock stopped at Floreana with his party on Saturday 2nd January 1932. With him was a young biologist, John S. Garth, who described in his diary their visit to Friedo. The party from the *Velero III* landed at Black Beach after a thirty-minute launch trip. Garth was surprised to find that a twenty-foot-wide track had been cleared, leading to Friedo. It was a long hot climb, and they were pleased to hear the welcoming braying of a donkey 'which brought Herr Ritter running out in his nightgown. Dore followed in a soiled blue housedress. Both were glad to see us but Dore was much more demonstrative. After the greetings in German and English we all ducked under the two enormous plum trees and entered the hermitage. The abundance of fruit and its excellent quality were remarkable. Besides the plums, which were so thick on the ground that we crushed them with every step, were two kinds of bananas, papayas, limes, water melons, sugar-cane, coconuts, besides corn, tobacco, yams, tomatoes and other vegetable staples.' The party admired Friedrich's device for squeezing sap from sugar-cane and inspected Dore's two cats which were 'useful because sparrows were needed to stuff feather pillows'. After being conducted around Friedo, Allan Hancock invited Friedrich and Dore to come aboard the *Velero III* the next day.

Very considerately Allan Hancock moved the yacht around to the Black Beach anchorage early the next morning and at ten o'clock Friedrich and Dore came aboard. A crewman, Sam Clover, described their visit:

> Through their glasses those on board could see the donkey descending the trail and arrive at the beach. Dore bathed her feet in the ocean, donned rolled socks and white tennis slippers and in a blue, sleeveless dress, with a white slip under it, made a most presentable appearance. The doctor was clean-shaven and neat in well-washed, though stained clothes. Dore appeared like a typical artist of the standard type; not unusual, but with much vivacity, which is her great charm. The captain arranged a musical program for his visitors.

Hancock was, in fact, an adequate cellist and Dore described how 'he played on an instrument whose tone was one of such extraordinary beauty as I have never heard before.' Dore and Friedrich were filmed with a ciné camera as they listened to the recital by Allan Hancock with Arthur Jensen, violin, and John Garth, piano. Dore sat in the corner of the saloon, with Friedrich standing by her, to one side of the trio. Her face was alive with excitement and enjoyment. Friedrich frequently glanced down at her in a proprietorial manner, as though he had been responsible for the whole occasion. John Garth describes how

Dore was 'moved to tears'; characteristically, Friedrich 'spoke of the psychological unity of music'.

Allan Hancock was especially generous to Dore and Friedrich. When Hancock asked Friedrich what provisions they lacked he replied that they needed only oil for their lamps. Dore, when pressed, said that they needed soap and, much to Friedrich's disapproval, flour. They also accepted gifts of rice, chocolate, cooking oil and, again much to Friedrich's disapproval, coffee. John Garth estimated that they had enough food for a year. Allan Hancock also gave Friedrich a handsome Winchester repeating rifle with several boxes of cartridges, several steel traps, a shovel and two mattocks. Dore was especially grateful for the gift of a cooking stove.

As they went over the side, the *Velero III* gave three blasts from her whistle to honour the Adam and Eve of Floreana.

* * *

Such occasional visits must have relieved the strained relations between Dore and Friedrich. However, during the long weeks of solitude they seem to have tussled about many things. Dore believed that Friedrich was jealous of her affection for Burro, and that he resented her attentions to a cat which she had tamed, and to its newly-born family. There were fierce battles about Dore's attempt to establish a flower garden at Friedo. Dore longed for some familiar childhood flowers, especially roses, carnations and dahlias. Friedrich forbade her to order seeds from Guayaquil. She managed, however, to get some carnation seeds from an American visitor and defiantly planted them, dreaming of their familiar blooms in her own little flower garden.

When Dore fell ill she begged Friedrich, between her bouts of fever, to water her carnation bed. She emerged from her sick bed to find that Friedrich had destroyed her precious plants. She planted her seeds a second time only to find them destroyed again. The appearance of seedlings at her third attempt led to a severe lecture from Friedrich on her frivolity.

Years later Dore attempted to rationalize such events, by

believing that Friedrich was trying to free her 'from the domination of fleeting wishes and irrational desires'. He apparently told her that *his* theory of energy conservation did not allow for time to be spent on unimportant things.

Despite her wildly romantic action in running away with her lover to a remote Pacific island, Dore was, nevertheless, basically rather conventional in her attitudes. She was certainly not the typical *Hausfrau*, as she repeatedly stresses and illustrates with examples of her culinary incompetence. But Friedrich probably regarded her as rather bourgeois. She seems to have possessed a great capacity for love and she willingly assumed a subordinate role in their relationship – to the extent of at first, and posthumously, crediting Friedrich with god-like qualities: 'I think that no one ever loved a man more wholly than I this man. He was for me perhaps more than a man, and nearer to a god.' One suspects that she would gladly have endured every hardship and humiliation – except neglect by her lover.

Friedrich seems from the beginning to have had a remarkably detached attitude to his devoted companion. He once maintained that on leaving Germany he 'wanted to go alone without being linked with another fate. However, my companion declared that I could not prevent her making the same trip.' He also told a visitor to Friedo in early 1932 that it was hard for a woman to live without comfort and to be content with a life without diversion, in total solitude. He believed that civilized woman still had 'a natural longing for a soft, secure nest for her young ... her only serious ambition – however she may try to avoid it.' Dore also subscribed to this view. She told the visiting English sailor, Roydon Bristow: 'If the woman disobeys, her man is justified in beating her. Woman's most important duty in life is the reproduction of the species.'*
But Dore had no young. The only object for her love was Friedrich and, as substitutes, her animal pets.

* Dore was obsessed with her idea of the subjugation of women to their male masters. She wrote a lengthy letter to Captain Hancock exclusively devoted to the subject, expressing views that would seem outrageous today.

Dore wrote that her many disagreements with Friedrich were concerned with everyday things, but that 'on the spiritual and intellectual plane, our lives were as nearly perfect in harmony as could well be imagined . . .' This was written long after the events and leaves the impression of an attempt to give their relationship a vestige of dignity. After all, if there had been hatred and argument between them then the whole outward purpose of her life was lost and the years on Floreana would have appeared merely as a series of sordid incidents.

It is also difficult to accept Dore's vision of their perfect intellectual harmony because she seemed hardly concerned with intellectual matters. Her little library, for example, consisted merely of two school textbooks (to brush up her Latin and Greek), a book on animal life and Nietzsche's *Thus Spake Zarathustra*. It is inconceivable that she would have chosen the latter by herself, a book which extols violence and holds that women are incapable of friendship but are at best mere cows. This pseudo-prophetical work must have been chosen merely as a symbol of her love for Friedrich.

Friedrich gave no indication, in his writings, of any serious disagreements such as Dore described, just as he never revealed his lapses from vegetarianism (which were subsequently confirmed by other witnesses) or the truth of the building of their new house.

Friedrich's treatment of Dore, as described by her, is quite consistent with the behaviour expected of an obsessional follower of Nietzsche. After all, contempt for women is a primary tenet of that philosopher's ethic, whose 'noble' man is devoid of sympathy and is ruthless and cruel in the pursuit of the 'higher culture'. And yet Friedrich seemed anxious to project a public image of a congenial relationship with Dore. She expressed surprise, for example, that he would boast of her achievements to visitors to Friedo, but never uttered a single word of praise while they were alone.

Some idea of the image which Friedrich sought can be gained from a newspaper account which he quotes with approval in a magazine article. It was published in *El Telegrafo*, of

Guayaquil, and consisted of an interview with an Ecuadorian naval officer who had visited Friedo. Friedrich translated it thus:

'We have been told, lieutenant, that a cultivated German doctor has been living a primitive life on one of the Galapagos Islands in an amazingly eccentric manner. Is this true?'

'Absolutely. A German couple are living as man and wife on Floreana in a very primitive fashion, distinguished from that of our early ancestors by the fact that both of them are highly educated and have moved in cultured European circles. They are living on a vegetable diet, shunning the use of meats, and they appear to thrive on it. Their thoughts are free from the prejudices of the civilized world. As for myself, I was surprised at such novelty and self-possession.'

'And how do this Adam and Eve procure their food?'

'From a small garden, hardly sufficient to guarantee their daily bread. Vegetables and fruits of every description form their meals and are prepared in natural dishes. While they eat they carry on a spirited conversation in German as though they were at a banquet. They are always cheerful and in harmony. They have completely forgotten the bitter struggle between man and man which characterizes life in society.'

'Did you notice any weariness or mental depression?'

'Quite the opposite. Rejoicing manifested itself in all their gestures, contentment at the sight of their surrounding wilderness. Neither the woman nor Dr. Ritter was the least bit excited by my visit. They are happy in their natural life, void of prejudice, affectation, and sordidness. Faith which cannot be shaken animates them. They seem to possess a supernatural ability to stand the silence – that mighty silence which is disturbed only by living creatures such as birds, reptiles, and other wild things.'

'What else did you notice worthy of comment?'

'Curiosity and a desire to see and speak with this German couple led me into the temporary dwelling where they have been living for several months. Decidedly original in its construction, it is built of branches to give it security and covered with corrugated iron plates. The interior is not at all inviting, being plain and sturdy for necessities of life. Dr. Ritter speaks Spanish indifferently. He told me that he intends to study nature at close range, and that he wishes to close his life in the midst of the primitive forest.'

This then was the impression that Friedrich wished to create of their life on Floreana. One even suspects that he might have had a hand in writing the original article for the visiting naval officer.

Compare this account with that of the Danish writer, Hakon Mielche, who visited Friedo some years later:

> Ritter was a philosopher. He was fairly small, his legs had been screwed on wrong, so that his toes pointed inwards. His nose was long and pointed, he had watery, protruding eyes and the hair of a prophet. His disciple, Miss Dora, smiled a toothless welcome.
>
> Miss Dora wore beach pyjamas and had large, naked, black feet. Her neck had not been washed for at least a month, and had been given a marbled effect by the passage of drops of sweat.
>
> ... Ritter sat in a wooden chair and philosophized with Dora kneeling at his turned-in feet ... his philosophy was a comprehensive cocktail of the strangest ingredients, a curious mixture of foreign words, faded theories and well-chewed phrases. His ambition was one day to map the human brain but so far he had not finished measuring it.
>
> When I asked to be allowed to photograph him, he agreed readily and got up on to his bed. He worked at a board which hung suspended over the bed, and above his head swung a storm lantern 'made in Thuringia'. This he lit – it was midday and blazing sunshine – then he ran his hands through his hair, put a finger to his forehead and asked me straight out if I didn't think he looked like Faust.

5
INTRUDERS

The fishing boat was far away, a tiny silhouette against the bright sea. Dore and Friedrich first saw it in the early-morning light from high up on their veranda at Friedo.

The boat was making slow progress. The wind was contrary and she had to contend with the Humboldt Current.

Dore and Friedrich had eaten their midday meal, of egg-nog and bananas, before the boat dropped anchor at a small bay close to Black Beach. They saw a dinghy move back and forth, three times, between boat and shore. Within the hour they watched the boat sail away into a shifting sea mist.

Five hundred feet below were the three people who had been put off on the black lava shore: a bald, amiable, middle-aged man, a younger, rather attractive woman and a twelve-year-old boy, together with two Alsatian dogs. These were the Wittmers: Heinz, his pregnant wife Margret and Harry, his son by a former marriage. They were tired, for their voyage to Floreana had been exhausting and uncomfortable.

The Wittmers had spent three weeks on Chatham Island (San Cristóbal) before the Ecuadorian Governor there arranged for a small fishing boat to take them to Floreana. They left on 22nd August 1932. The boat was crowded, with a crew of three, the Wittmers, their dogs and luggage. They were soon cold, drenched with flying spray and Margret was seasick. The night was as black as pitch.

They were close to Floreana by dawn of the following day.

They saw Post Office Bay and the abandoned Norwegian buildings on the shore, grey and uninviting in the cold early light, and two hours later Black Beach. Then the wind dropped and the island was completely obscured by thick clouds. The strong Antarctic current carried them away from Black Beach and they spent a second miserable night, cold and wet, on the deck of the twenty-five-foot fishing boat. Next day was spent in hopeless attempts to get to Black Beach and for a third night they huddled on the open deck. They were now short of water, cold, hungry and definitely worried. Fortunately, the current carried them north to Isabela where they obtained water and food, including a giant tortoise, and salt-dried fish. That evening they enjoyed hot strong coffee, roast bananas and sweet potatoes before they settled down to another uncomfortable night at sea, now troubled by the smell of dried fish.

At dawn, Margret, Heinz and Harry saw the outline of Floreana through clearing mist. The boat lay offshore that night and on the following morning worked its way laboriously into the bay near Black Beach, watched by Dore and Friedrich from their veranda up at Friedo.

Charles Darwin, landing on the Galapagos a century earlier, had seen a 'broken field of black basaltic lava, thrown into the most rugged waves and crossed by great fissures ... everywhere covered by stunted, sunburnt-brushwood, which shows little signs of life'. Herman Melville had doubted whether 'any spot of earth can, in desolateness, furnish a parallel.' To Margret, five months' pregnant and tired out from six days' voyage, it must have looked especially grim. As she sat among the lava on the shore Margret felt she 'was no longer on this earth but had landed on some distant and deserted planet'.

She and her husband had been drawn to Floreana by romantic magazine articles describing Friedrich and Dore's supposed idyll on the island. Like Dore and Friedrich before them, they had been enthralled by William Beebe's book *Galapagos: World's End*. Life had been hard for them in Germany. Heinz had been a lieutenant in the Army Reserve before the First

World War and had served in the trenches. After the war he faced insecurity and unemployment, while inflation destroyed his savings. He became a secretary to Conrad Adenauer, then *Oberburgermeister* of Cologne, but like many of his generation, Heinz was mentally scarred by his years in the trenches and depressed by economic insecurity. He worried about his son, Harry, whose health was poor and whose eyes were bad; they could not afford to send him to a sanatorium for two years, as they had been advised.

Heinz first broached the idea of starting a new life in the Galapagos at Christmas 1931 when, according to Margret, they were standing, newly-wed, looking in the window of a men's outfitters, contemplating the purchase of a new suit. To Margret's surprise Heinz suggested that it might be more useful to buy a rifle – to take with them to the Galapagos. This was the first that Margret had heard of Heinz's secret, but from that moment their plans grew to go to Floreana, at least for two or three years, to escape from the difficulties of life in Germany and to give Harry the healthy outdoor life that he needed.

They made arrangements to sell their apartment in Cologne and used their savings to purchase equipment and supplies. To prevent their friends and family from attempting to dissuade them, they kept their plans secret. On the morning of their departure they left messages for the families and Heinz sent a letter of resignation to Dr Adenauer. They sailed from Amsterdam in July, arrived on Chatham Island from Guayaquil in early August 1932 and, after three weeks, departed on their exhausting voyage to Floreana.

Like Dore, Margret was fascinated by her first sight of the animals on the shore at Floreana. Warmed by the sun which had penetrated the mist, she saw thousands of small fish jumping in the shallow water of the Bay and much bigger ones further from the shore. In front of her were two marine iguanas, the dragon-like creatures that Darwin called 'imps of darkness'; overhead frigate birds dipped and soared, and pelicans flew towards the mangroves, landing like clumsy flying boats. All about her were finches and mocking-birds, unbelievably trusting. She heard their two Alsatians joyfully chasing a wild donkey through thorny scrub.

Fifty yards behind her, Heinz had erected their largest tent. A tarpaulin covered the sacks, boxes and crates containing their stores. They had brought plenty of food: 'two hundredweights each of rice and beans, a hundredweight of flour, twenty-five pounds each of coffee and Quaker oats, five pounds of cocoa; plus three bottles of brandy, washing soap, matches, oil, tinned milk, and potatoes and onions for planting'. During their stay on Chatham they had also bought seeds and plants: 'sugar-cane, yucca [a sort of tapioca], banana shoots, coffee beans, atois and camotes [two kinds of sweet potato], pineapple, pumpkins, mangoes, papayas and avocados, also a cock and two hens'. They had tools, pots and pans, a rifle, a large crate of books, a bale of yellow cloth and a typewriter.

Margret used the crate of books for a table and covered it with a tablecloth. They used boxes for chairs. Margret made a huge rice pudding, which tasted marvellous. Then they swam in the cold sea and emerged feeling refreshed and clean. Heinz was anxious to meet Friedrich Ritter and Dore Strauch so they started the half-hour climb up to Friedo.

Dore looked forward to meeting the Wittmers. She had been told that they were coming by the crew of a ship, the *Esperanza*, that had called at Floreana three weeks before. She particularly welcomed the prospect of a friend on Floreana and, no doubt, anticipated the occasional womanly chat about her 'difficulties' with Friedrich.

Despite his famous rudeness to visitors, Friedrich walked down the Black Beach path to guide the visitors to Friedo. Dore was surprised and disappointed when only Heinz arrived. What is more, she was unimpressed with his appearance. Poor Heinz was definitely not in the same class as Knud Arends or the late Captain Bruuns's distinguished Norwegian friend. 'He was a person of middle age, bald and bespectacled,' she wrote. 'His rather gaunt legs stuck out of a pair of shorts very brief indeed, his bare feet were protected from the thorny undergrowth by nothing more appropriate than a pair of felt bedroom slippers.

The charm of his appearance was not enhanced by several days' growth of stubble on his face, and the finishing touch consisted of a large and clumsy canvas bag which he had bound to his shoulders like a haversack.'

Dore was definitely not amused. She found it hard to believe that the wife of a man in carpet slippers would be worthy of her friendship and she and Friedrich evidently gave poor Heinz a cool reception. 'Friedrich and I behaved as hospitably as we could to this curiously attired person, but it could not be helped if we showed him somewhat clearly that his get-up had not won our sympathy. He was not stupid and soon took his leave.'

Quite soon Heinz reappeared at Friedo, this time with Margret and Harry in tow. He was quite transformed: he had shaved, Dore noted, and 'had changed his absurd costume, and came back dressed like a sane human being'. It seems that Heinz had adopted his first strange outfit to fit in with what he imagined to be appropriate for the bohemian Ritters. After all, the newspapers had contained extraordinary reports of their nudism and stainless-steel dentures. Poor Heinz had badly misfired in his first attempt to make a good impression on Friedrich and Dore. Fortunately, Dore at first was pleasantly impressed by Margret Wittmer. 'She looked much younger than she actually was, and had especially attractive eyes.' Dore wondered how in a pregnant condition she would cope with life on Floreana.

For her part, Margret was not particularly impressed with Friedo. It 'turned out to be a sort of bungalow, four stakes with a corrugated iron roof over them. As we found out later, there was a cage of wire mesh inside, enclosing another four stakes. The cage was about ten feet in diameter, and had two beds in it.'

Margret was relieved, remembering the nudist stories, to find Friedrich clothed in shirt and trousers. She noticed that his eyes shifted uneasily and had the gleam of a fanatic. He was, she suspected, a boor. Dore was short and untidy with a pronounced limp. When she shook hands with her, Dore 'made a face as if she had burnt her fingers'. The two women then engaged in some feminine sparring concerning the appropriateness of Margret's costume for life on Floreana. Dore also could not forbear showing off by quoting Nietzsche and Lao-tse to the tired and overawed Margret. However, Dore was concerned for her and was surprised 'that there was something very pleasant in the feeling'. This feeling is, however, hardly surprising in a sensitive woman, capable of deep affections, who had spent three years in virtually total isolation with a man who showed no signs of love for her and who seemed altogether more concerned with his public image than with his private responsibilities.

Dore was concerned not only about Margret's pregnancy, but also about their having brought Heinz's twelve-year-old son to the island. She behaved more like an outraged small-town gossip than a woman who had abandoned her husband and family to live on a remote Pacific island as the mistress of a Nietzschean superman. 'I thought it a most extraordinary thing for a father to have done, to bring a boy to a desert island. This circumstance seemed to me by far the strangest in the whole affair, and as time went on I understood it even less.'

Dore was outraged when she learned that Heinz had chosen Floreana not only for its supposed idyllic qualities, but also for the presence of Dr Ritter the physician. She very much resented the presumption of the Wittmers in regarding Friedrich as their local medical practitioner, who would presumably be expected to keep an eye on Harry's health and also attend at Margret's imminent confinement.

Despite his strongly expressed hatred for modern civilization, on which he had irrevocably turned his back, Friedrich questioned Heinz very closely about recent events in Germany. He asked whether he knew Berlin and Margret detected an underlying homesickness in him. She sensed that he did not intend to remain at Friedo for ever. Perhaps Friedrich did indeed secretly contemplate a return from the wilderness. He was by that time something of a celebrity and might well have relished the prospect of lecturing the civilized world on its sins and providing his own peculiar panacea for its improvement.

Friedrich took obvious pleasure in showing the Wittmers around the garden during their first visit to Friedo. Margret was surprised to find only a half-acre plot, but was impressed by its expert cultivation and their crops of bananas, date palms, tamarinds, ciruela plums, mangoes, papayas and figs. Friedrich seems to have lectured them on the virtues of the vegetarian way of life, and expressed the confident opinion that it was possible to live exclusively on figs. The hen-house in the crater wall and its twenty occupants were also admired by the newcomers, who must have been becoming uneasily aware of the hard labours which faced them on Floreana.

Later in the afternoon the Wittmers prepared to leave. They were feeling distinctly out of place and embarrassed by the feeling that they were 'not entirely welcome' at Friedo. However, Friedrich told them of the pirate's caves, which would make a temporary home for them. He offered to guide Heinz to them on the following day.

When they reached the beach, they found Harry had fallen asleep and were unable to awaken him. Margret prepared stew for her supper with Heinz. Fresh water was precious, so she diluted it with a third of sea water to make a stew from beans, a large onion and otoi tubers. She wished that she had some pork to go with the beans.

After supper Margret and Heinz sat in the flickering firelight in front of their tent and discussed the visit to their extraordinary neighbours. 'Mulling it over, we begin to feel that we can hardly blame Dr. Ritter for his coolness. He can hardly be expected to fall on our necks – three perfect strangers. Nevertheless, something seemed to be lacking. Knowing, as they did, of our long sea voyage they might have stressed the intellectual side of life a little less and the human side more. We would be the last to refuse to bow down to knowledge and wisdom. So for the present we determine not to force ourselves on the Ritters.'

Heinz and Margret were glad to get to bed that night. They

slept very comfortably. The tent had a rubber groundsheet and they slept on air-beds, although the soft sand would by itself have been comfortable enough for their tired bodies.

* * *

On the following morning they were awoken by the braying of donkeys. It was a damp, foggy morning, but they bathed in the sea. Margret prepared a breakfast of rice, with fruit and coffee.

After breakfast Heinz and Harry left to meet Friedrich and climb up to the pirate caves. Heinz had a pack on his back and the plants that they had brought with them: sugar-cane, banana and pineapple. Harry had their cock and two hens, their legs bound together, suspended from his neck.

Left to herself, Margret wandered along the donkey trails, accompanied by a particularly inquisitive donkey, collecting wood for her fire. She tore her blouse on the thorny bushes. From higher up she could see not only the little bay at which they had landed, but also Black Beach. The small bay had been cleared of lava rocks by previous settlers. Like Dore, three years before, on her first day on Floreana, Margret felt apprehensive at this symbol of previous occupation and, presumably, failure on the island.

Carrying her firewood back to the camp Margret could see the lava and sandy shore exposed by the low tide. The wet lava is always brilliant with the red and blue bodies of scuttering Sally Lightfoot crabs together with inquisitive sea lions.

She made her preparations for the meal that she had planned for Heinz and Harry. She knew that they would be hungry after their journey to and from the caves. She even improvised some biscuits for them using a potato-like fruit, carmotten, which she had been given during their enforced call at Isabela. These she sliced and fried in hot fat until they were crisp and brown.

Heinz was excited when he returned with Harry from their visit to the caves. He told Margret how, with Dr Ritter, they had loaded their belongings on to Dore's donkey and marched for two hours until they had reached the caves. They had found a marvellous spring close to the three caves that Friedrich had told them about. He thought that they could live there while they built a more permanent house. At least it would be more comfortable than a draughty tent. It was, in any case, essential for them to move closer to a spring for they had very little fresh water left in their water bag. They should start the move the next day.

After hurried cups of warmed-up coffee early next morning, Heinz, Margret and Harry started their climb up to the old pirate caves. They took only essential things: food and utensils with which to cook and eat it, bedclothes and some tools.

Heinz reckoned that it would take them about two hours to climb up to the caves. They followed a donkey trail across broken lava and then climbed over dusty ashes, scratched by cactus spines. After thorny brushwood the trees became greener: acacia, *palo santo* and mayuyu trees. Then at six hundred feet they were in misty dampness, with black soil underfoot and green leaves with ripe lemons and oranges overhead. Here the braying of donkeys was replaced by the sounds of herds of wild cattle.

After three hours, they rested and watched the lowering clouds. Soon it began to rain. They realized that they were lost when they came upon one of the lengths of white thread that prudent Margret had been hanging on branches, every hundred yards or so. It took them another three hours to find the caves that Heinz had so easily reached on the previous day.

Like Dore, Margret found Watkins's caves uninviting. She sat down on one of the hewn benches and looked around her at the rough fireplace and sooty walls. Other users, most recently the young German would-be settlers, had left their relicts – including a rough home-made table and two warped stools. In front of the cave were trees loaded with papaya fruit and ripe lemons.

Heinz and Harry showed Margret the spring that they had discovered on the previous day. Margret was enchanted: 'We were in a fairy ring of green trees. It was wonderfully cool and pleasantly dark in the shade of their thick foliage, after the glare of the sun which had beat down on us for the last part of the march.' Frances Conway, a later settler on the island, also described that spring. 'The Wittmer spring would have been beautiful in anybody's land. A generous stream gushed out of a rugged ledge ... and flowed into a lava pool, partly natural and partly artificial. Ferns and long streamers of moss made the rocky niche into a fairy grotto.'

The spring water was icy cold. They cooled their hands and faces and then drank from their cupped hands the best water that they had ever tasted.

Margret, like a good *Hausfrau*, immediately started to sweep out the caves with a besom. Heinz went out to shoot a boar for supper and Harry collected dry wood and picked papayas, lemons and oranges from the trees at the entrance to the cave. When Heinz came back he found that Margret had transformed the cave. It was now as clean as it could be and water was boiling in a saucepan.

Heinz brought in the heart of the boar that he had shot and then departed with Harry to haul back the rest of the animal. When they returned they found the cave bathed in warm candlelight, the rough table covered with a spotless white tablecloth and their supper cooking on the fire.

That evening seems to have been a happy one for the Wittmers. Margret describes their shared sense of satisfaction as they sat in the warmth of the fire. They had, after all, reached their chosen island safely, if extremely uncomfortably, had already transformed Patrick Watkins's dirty cave into something like a home and eaten a good meal with plenty of fresh meat. However, much hard work lay before them, because the Wittmers had still to haul up their food and equipment from the bay near Black Beach.

Heinz suggested that it would lighten their labours considerably if they could use Dore's donkey to help carry their goods. He walked over to Friedo the next morning to ask if they could borrow the animal. According to Margret, 'he was met by Dore, who told him they were always needing the donkey, it would be inconvenient to lend it'. They were, apparently, hurt by Dore's unfriendly attitude, which confirmed Margret's feeling that they would not 'find this couple easy neighbours'.

Dore's account of these events is entirely different. 'We gave them everything we thought would help them to start their lives most favourably on the island, both good advice and many plants. They seemed to appreciate our good intentions towards them, and Herr Wittmer set to work with extreme energy, wanting to do everything at once. The severest strain put upon my hospitality was when I had to lend them our Burro for their transport. I could not forget that the predecessors of these people had been the authors of all his woes until we found him, and I had often vowed a vow that he should never under any circumstances fall into any other hands than ours, as long as he lived. It was, therefore, with sad reluctance that I lent him, and the way he raced home that night after his hated journey to the caves of evil memory told an eloquent tale.'

It appears, from Margret's account, that Burro was being led by young Harry when it had 'a stubborn fit – suddenly refusing to go further and trying to escape into the thorns'. Harry was forced to let the donkey go and the Wittmers worried that the pack-harness would get caught in a tree or bush. They told Friedrich immediately of the donkey's escape and, according to Margret, blamed themselves bitterly for the incident. It seems as though they scarcely deserved Dore's insinuation of ill-treatment of Burro.

Margret describes an incident at this time which was to her distinctly odd. Friedrich appeared, in amiable mood, and suggested that Heinz might like to exchange the head and one of the hams of the boar which he had shot for some vegetables from the garden at Friedo. Despite his very recent lecture on the benefits of vegetarianism, Friedrich seems to have suffered one of his periodic carnivorous lapses.

With or without Dore's donkey, which even by her account was lent for only one day, the transport of the food and equipment from the shore must have been a daunting task for a middle-aged man, a pregnant woman and a sickly boy. In almost continual rain they carried their belongings over the slippery lava and, higher up, the black soil would have been soggy and difficult to walk through. It took them about a week to move everything up to the caves. On one occasion Heinz had caught Dore making a thorough inspection of their belongings remaining on the shore. Margret was furious when she heard of this, for she seems to have had a strong sense of property. Heinz advised keeping out of Dore's way to avoid conflict between the two women. This they seem to have done for Dore commented that they 'did not trouble us as I had feared they might'. Margret, in fact, rarely set foot in Friedo for another eighteen months.

Long after the events described in this book, Dore wrote that she felt strong forebodings about the Wittmers as though 'through these people directly, or indirectly, some harm would come to us and Friedo'.

Heinz began clearing the ground near the caves, to expose the rich underlying humus, even before they had finished carrying their belongings up from the shore. He cut down bushes with axe and machete. He chopped down the trees, cut free the branches and stacked the trunks for use in the future building operations on their house. The branches were burned and the ashes used to fertilize the soil.

The ground destined for the vegetable garden had to be cleared of the roots of trees and shrubs. This, as Friedrich had found three years earlier, was an exceptionally hard task. Heinz left the roots in the ground in which bananas, coffee and sugar-cane were to be planted. He worked the rich but shallow soil with a pick, then turned and hoed it. After some weeks, and a great deal of hard labour, they had planted enough in the first piece of ground to be able to look forward to supplementing their diet of wild fruit, freshly killed meat and the groceries which they had brought with them.

From time to time Heinz would leave his clearing operations to shoot a boar or a bull. Their trails were everywhere, some used as main roads by the settlers. The donkeys were on the dusty lava slopes closer to the shore. Higher up, the damp greenery was criss-crossed with the tracks of wild pigs and cattle. Here the scent of damp earth and greenery mixed with the fragrance of orange blossom and the smell of cattle dung and regurgitated lemons.

The bulls were fearsome, as poor Hugo had discovered three years earlier when he was gored by a wounded animal. For a city dweller, Heinz Wittmer seems to have been a remarkably adept hunter. Frances Conway, an American settler on Floreana some years later, tells how Heinz dealt with a dangerously wounded bull: 'The Mauser cracked twice – it was a gun with authority ... he had fired first at the heart and the bull had fallen. But when he had stepped forward to give the *coup de grâce* – a knife thrust in the heart – the bull had struggled up again. Wittmer had fired at a distance of four feet, right into the brain.'

The thrifty Wittmers made good use of the victims of Heinz's Mauser. The meat was cut from the carcass and that which was not eaten immediately was preserved by smoking it. The kidneys were cut away from the embedding fat, which was melted down and used to make candles. Heinz would carry the hide down from the damp mountainside to the shore and stretch it out in the tropical sunshine to dry. He eventually learned to cobble most excellent cowhide boots for the family.

Heinz's slaughter of bulls and boars was necessary not only for their meat supply, but also to protect their garden. Margret was horrified when she first saw the devastation that a bull caused to their hard-won vegetable garden.

> I found that the radishes, lettuce and parsley had been trampled down, and by the tracks I could see that a bull had broken in during the night. The little plantation was fenced in with a proper hedge, laboriously built with stakes and thorn-bush. The bull had simply shoved it aside with his horns, and laid waste everything we had taken so much trouble on. We had cleared the land, cut down trees and bushes, hacked out the roots, tilled the soil, covered it with the mud which had collected under the spring, and cherished

lovingly the little green plants that came up. Now all this was in vain.

Night after night the bulls came back, tearing down the fences, trampling young plants and eating young banana leaves, camotes and maize: the same devastation that Friedrich had experienced from his 'satanic' boar. Heinz eventually won the battle by persistent slaughter of the intruders.

The Wittmers were also troubled by wild dogs during their first weeks on Floreana. Margret was frightened by a large yellow one that she found lurking in the semi-darkness of their cave. She straight away set a trap, baited with strips of dried meat. On each of the next three nights they caught a dog, trapped by a paw in the steel trap. Heinz shot them through the head. Unfortunately, the fourth victim that he shot was their own Alsatian bitch, Hertha.

On 16th September Heinz and Margret celebrated Harry's thirteenth birthday. Margret made him his favourite dish: 'bananaschaumei'. This was one of Margret's special concoctions and consisted of bananas mashed in egg yolk which was then mixed with the whipped egg whites. Margret wrote in her diary: 'One would have to see Harry's face while eating it to truly appreciate the situation.' Margret also made pancakes from otoi tubers for the occasion. The three of them spent the afternoon playing cards and clearly enjoying the break in their hard, back-breaking routine.

It was at this time that the Wittmers decided to start work on their new home. This was to be a log cabin, twenty-two by twelve feet when completed, not far from the caves. The foundations consisted of lava stones. The corner posts were to be four stout tree trunks and the walls were to be made of logs plugged with moss. They intended to make a waterproof roof with sugar-cane.

The Wittmers had, in fact, settled in quickly and effectively. Within a few weeks they had laid the foundations of what was to be a tiny fragment of Germany, far out in the Pacific. Margret attempted to preserve Teutonic orderliness and thriftiness, whether eating from packing cases on the shore or living in a primitive cave. Frances Conway, years later, described Margret as 'rosy and whiteaproned'. 'Frau Margret asks no odds and never rides in the back seat' was her assessment of this determined and attractive woman.

She provided valuable support for her older and rather odd-looking husband, support which enabled him to establish them so effectively on the island. Heinz was tough and resourceful. He was obviously a good-natured man and seems to have been content with his new life on Floreana.

Heinz and Margret were neighbourly and hospitable to subsequent visitors to the island. However, they had a strong sense of property and seem to have resented intrusion. Frances Conway, for example, considered that 'nothing infuriated the Wittmers more than pilfering and housebreaking'. She recounted, some years later, how Margret kept a loaded 0.22 rifle to hand and Heinz 'added a gun to the ever present machete' to deal with a twelve-year-old Indian boy, who had come to work for a later settler on the island and had stolen some of their meat and garden produce. 'If I see José I will shoot at his legs,' Wittmer said. 'Then I can catch him. He is half animal, and you have to hunt him like an animal.'

The Wittmers were a down-to-earth couple. They had no sympathy for the romantic high-brow approach of Friedrich and Dore. They too had turned their backs on Germany, travelled to a remote Pacific island and faced danger and hardship. But for Margret and Heinz this was a strictly practical affair to be tackled in a businesslike way and with determination that nothing should hinder them.

With amazing foresight, in view of subsequent events, the visiting Danish writer Hakon Mielche predicted that when the other settlers on Floreana had 'turned to dust ... Wittmer will still be sitting in his cosy little house smoking his pipe. The sun will rise and set, and he will forget to count the days.'

6
THE BARONESS ARRIVES

Just after dusk on 18th September 1932 the island of Fernandina erupted. Dore and Friedrich, watching from Friedo, and the Wittmers, standing at the entrance to their temporary home in Watkins's cave, saw the darkening sky to the north-west change suddenly to a fiery red. Later, the reflections of huge yellow flames were visible on the clouds behind Isabela.

Both Dore and Margret wondered whether the eruption would spread to Floreana or the sea would rise and engulf the island. Dore and Friedrich watched and waited for most of the night. She afterwards wrote that they were not frightened: she and Friedrich 'had never felt so bound to one another as at that moment, nor so safely and indivisibly of one mind'. She rather resented Heinz Wittmer's reaction to the event, for her solid and unimaginative neighbour was quite unmoved by the violent volcanic spectacle. For Dore, the sulphurous clouds and the nightly volcanic glow only encouraged the presentiments of approaching evil which she later said she had felt since the arrival of the Wittmers on Floreana.

On a bright sunny afternoon a month later Heinz Wittmer rushed into Friedo in what was for him an unusual state of excitement. It was mid-October 1932 according to Margret Wittmer, and November according to Dore Strauch. Heinz had brought the mail and also news of the arrival of another group of settlers just landed at Post Office Bay. The odd thing was that *all* of the mail had been tampered with. Every letter had plainly been opened and some of them even lacked envelopes.

Heinz told Dore and Friedrich that their mail had been brought by the apparent leader of the new arrivals, a German woman, a Baroness. She had a retinue of men and had temporarily established herself in the wooden Norwegian buildings on the shore at Post Office Bay.

The Baroness appeared at Friedo with her male companions soon after Heinz's visit. She was riding on a donkey with her male companions walking beside her. Dore saw a small, slim, platinum blonde. 'Her very wide red mouth, with the rather prominent protruding teeth, were her most conspicuous feature. Her eyes were hidden behind dark spectacles. She wore a kind of workman's overalls, with sandals on her bare feet, and a beret sat jauntily upon her head.' Her appearance and manner were contrived for maximum effect. 'If this was a mere Baroness, she certainly behaved as though she were at least a queen,' Dore thought.

One of the male retinue helped the Baroness to dismount and, without permission, placed one of Ritter's deck-chairs for her. When seated, she held her hand to Dore as though expecting it to be kissed. Dore noticed annoyance flash across her face when she merely shook the proffered hand.

Dore, in her odd way, was relieved that this strange woman was not a mere bourgeois *Hausfrau* (like the sensible Margret Wittmer), nor a 'foolish romanticist' or 'an imitation "seeker of the light"'. Here, at least, was a potential adversary of unusual and formidable qualities.

The Baroness was given the usual conducted tour of Friedo. She was, apparently, exceedingly gracious. She was intrigued by the house, admired the 'cunning contraptions' (presumably Friedrich's piped water supply) and was impressed by the flourishing vegetable garden. She told Dore and Friedrich that she had read of their idyllic life at Friedo and was presumably drawn there, as were the Wittmers, by the newspaper accounts of the Adam and Eve of Floreana.

Friedrich, according to Dore, was unimpressed by the

Baroness and was impervious to her flattering remarks on the marvels of Friedo. He seems to have enjoyed talking to her male companions, although one of them seemed to have no eyes for anyone but the Baroness.

There were four men in this retinue. The most attentive was a German called Rudolf Lorenz who looked about twenty-one, though was in fact thirty. Dore was quite bowled over by him. 'He was tall and very graceful, with a slender, well built figure. His complexion had a youthful freshness, and his very bright blue eyes had something so nice and candid in their expression that he inspired a certain sympathy and confidence, despite the touch of obsequiousness in his manner. Towards us he was pleasant and entirely unaffected.' Characteristically, she noticed that 'he seemed to come of rather simple people, and his speech betrayed only a very moderate education.'

The other three men who came up to Friedo that day were not members of the party who intended to settle on Floreana with the Baroness. They seem to have been an Austrian settler from Chatham Island, called Hagen, his friend Herr Schimpf and the captain of the ship that had brought her party to Post Office Bay.

At the time of their arrival Lorenz was greatly favoured by the Baroness and he was entirely fascinated by her. Dore describes, for example, how he kept close to the Baroness while the other three men were conducted around Friedo. He assumed a tragic attitude when the Baroness complained of the ship's food on their voyage. He worried that she had lost more than a stone in weight.

The Baroness seems to have had Lorenz constantly at her beck and call at this time. He answered her repeated commands with 'undiminished eagerness and pleasure'. According to Dore it was: 'Lorenz, take off my glasses for me' and 'Oh, Lorenz, come and show me how this thing works'.

Dore, who had a quick eye for these things, noticed that the Baroness exercised an unspoken power over Lorenz. When Lorenz politely helped Dore to feed Burro, in that first visit to Friedo, she noted his extreme caution in answering her questions about the Baroness. She also picked up the sharp and menacing look which the Baroness shot at Lorenz when they returned and noticed that 'an almost imperceptible shaking of his head seemed to reassure her'.

It was late in the afternoon before the Baroness and her retinue had finished their tour of inspection of Friedo – too late for the long walk back to Post Office Bay: it is dangerous for newcomers to walk in the dark in the Galapagos. Friedrich and Dore had no choice but to offer them hospitality for the night.

Lorenz and the three other men slept on the floor on home-made mattresses, which Dore had stuffed with banana leaves, and covered themselves with blankets. The Baroness was given a hammock, covered with a length of the muslin which Dore had brought from Europe. One suspects that Dore might have contrived to provide the Baroness with rather inadequate covering as compared with what she gave the men. The newcomers were tired after their voyage and their long walk over difficult terrain. They therefore went to bed fairly early in the evening, leaving Friedrich and Dore to spend the night writing letters which could be taken off next morning by the ship which had brought the Baroness.

Friedrich described the scene in one of the letters that he wrote that night:

> Some settlers have just arrived – an Austrian baroness, her 'husband', a companion and an Indian, with cows, donkeys, hens, 80 Zetner* of cement and other necessary equipment. – Your letters. We are only interested in visits in so far as they bring and deliver mail, everything else is a waste of time (we don't need to be disturbed or have our privacy infringed upon). For example, it is now one o'clock in the morning – a splendid night with a full moon and about 4 deg Celcius: the baroness is sleeping outside in a hammock and her company of four men are lying on the ground, both their donkeys are chewing sugar-cane.

* About 71 cwt.

Friedrich and Dore scribbled away at their letters, and all was silent. But in the small hours Dore heard the Baroness turning restlessly in her sleep, apparently troubled by a cough. Lorenz slept on. Dore and Friedrich went on writing. Soon 'the Baroness began to bark in a most alarming way. But it was no cough, only an hysterical imitation of one.' Again Friedrich and Dore went on with their writing. Friedrich wrote: 'Let us hope that the present settlers don't remain here longer than the first ones ... This baroness, this import from Paris, is coughing through cold and hysteria.'

Eventually, Lorenz was roused by the Baroness's coughing. Dore and Friedrich heard them whispering together in the darkness. Lorenz then appeared at the door of the 'cage' in which Dore and Friedrich were working, and asked if it would be possible to make the Baroness a cup of tea as she was extremely cold. This was hardly surprising in view of the covering Dore provided. Dore regretted – possibly with relish – that this was not possible: the fire had been extinguished and could not be relit in the middle of the night. According to Dore, the Baroness increased the intensity of her performance when she was told that tea would not be forthcoming. By this time the entire household was awake and Dore left her writing to fetch some sackcloth to cover the Baroness. The Baroness almost immediately went back to sleep, leaving the others disturbed and wakeful.

Dore was depressed by the events of the night; they symbolized the trouble she feared would lie ahead for them while the Baroness was on Floreana. She could not write. At dawn, she lit the fire and started to cook breakfast for their guests. This was not easy, because she had not enough pots and pans and was, by her own account, an indifferent cook. Nevertheless, the four men ate their breakfast with gusto. The Baroness, on the other hand, ate very little and pushed Dore's 'laboriously prepared dishes away from her with an expression of disgust'.

As the Baroness and her retinue prepared to leave Friedo, Dore was distressed to see the state of their donkey. Despite the sores on its back they saddled it so that the Baroness could return to Post Office Bay in regal style. Dore was also annoyed when they tied a rope around the animal's muzzle to prevent it eating on the return journey. Their departure was also the occasion for a display of bad temper by the Baroness. According to Dore, one of the men in the party had complimented Friedrich. 'To come to Floreana without seeing Dr Ritter would be like going to Rome without seeing the Pope.' This so incensed the Baroness that she left Friedo in a jealous fury.

Friedrich, despite all his published claims about turning his back on visitors, was eager to lead the Baroness's party down to the shore. Dore felt vulnerable and lonely when they had gone. 'I watched the Baroness go away as I had watched Frau Wittmer, sadly convinced that now no woman friend for me would come to Floreana. It was a long and melancholy day, and I waited with impatience for Friedrich to return. He came back very grave. He, too, felt that no good would come of this thing. The new arrivals' equipment had proved to him they expected, and were, in fact, determined, to make a long stay.'

At Post Office Bay he had seen the two other permanent members of the Baroness's retinue. Robert Philippson was also German. He appears to have been about Lorenz's age and was considerably younger than the Baroness. He was well built with dark curly hair. Margret Wittmer, when she saw him, thought him good-looking, but with a rather off-hand manner. The third man in the group was a large Ecuadorian, called Felipe Valdivieso. He too was a young man, but seemed to have had a different status from Lorenz and Philippson and Heinz Wittmer regarded him 'more as the hired man of the party'.

On the shore there was a vast stack of equipment brought by the Baroness. There were two cows and two donkeys from the mainland as well as ducks, hens, turkeys, rabbits and pigeons. Seventy hundredweights of cement had also been unloaded at Post Office Bay. Friedrich Ritter and Heinz Wittmer both thought that this Baroness did indeed intend to settle on Floreana.

Margret Wittmer, busy with her housework, first met the Baroness and her party when they emerged from surrounding trees and shrubs on to the grass outside the caves. Their approach had been heralded by the excited barking of her Alsatian, Lump, and then by the noise of breaking vegetation. It was the same party who had visited Friedo: the Baroness, Lorenz, the ship's captain and the Austrian, Hagen. Margret was delighted to see Hagen for she had met him when the Wittmers had been delayed on Chatham Island before their voyage to Floreana.

According to Margret, the Baroness dismounted and abruptly inquired: 'Where's the spring?' Startled, Margret pointed to the spring. The Baroness went over to the spring, where Lorenz took off her shoes and washed her feet – much to Margret's outrage, for this was their drinking water. The Baroness then complained of fatigue. Margret, very hospitably, offered their tent for her to rest in. The Baroness accepted the offer. Lorenz followed her inside – 'it seems that he also is in need of rest', Margret commented sardonically.

Heinz Wittmer returned while the Baroness and Lorenz were in the tent. He too was pleased to see Hagen. Hagen expressed considerable concern about the Baroness and her strange companions. 'There's something not quite right about her. I noticed some funny things on the boat. I'd be a bit careful if I were you.'

Hagen was interested to see how the Wittmers were getting on. He inspected the house that they were building near by and told them that they had thatched it wrongly. Using sugar-cane as a thatching material, they had started from the top of the roof instead of from the bottom. This depressed the Wittmers, for it meant a lot more hard work, but the advice was appreciated.

After her siesta the Baroness announced that she intended to live close to the Wittmers while she and her companions selected a suitable site and built a house. Heinz and Margret reluctantly agreed and suggested that the newcomers could camp in their orange grove close to a small spring.

The Wittmers were pleased to receive the mail which the Baroness had brought. This had not been tampered with as had the letters for Friedo. Friedrich Ritter believed that it was the Baroness who had opened their mail. Friedrich said to Heinz: 'She's even taken photos out of some of them, the dirty bitch.' Heinz suspected that the Baroness had asked him to deliver the violated letters as a subterfuge to create ill-feeling between the Wittmers and Dore and Friedrich.

The Baroness also became involved in some funny business about a bag of rice that had been brought on the boat. The captain had, apparently, brought a hundredweight of rice which the Wittmers bought from him for eleven *sucres*. The sack was left at Post Office Bay until Heinz had time to collect it. The Baroness offered to look after the rice, with her stores and equipment at Post Office Bay. This rice was a very precious commodity for the Wittmers. Not only was it a very welcome addition to their diet, but it had also been purchased from the very few *sucres* which the Wittmers possessed.

On the following Sunday Heinz and Harry Wittmer walked down to Post Office Bay to collect their rice. They were met there by the Baroness, dressed in riding breeches, shirt and riding boots, with a revolver in her belt. She carried a riding whip. She was heavily made up and received Wittmer senior and junior while lolling on a couch in the old Norwegian building on the shore. Here Heinz met Robert Philippson for the first time. He was introduced as the Baroness's 'husband'. Heinz noticed, with surprise, that although Lorenz and Philippson were German and the Baroness, apparently, Austrian, they conversed mostly in French.

After the introduction Philippson retreated, as he explained, to complete a magazine article that he had been writing. When they were alone the Baroness revealed her plans to Heinz Wittmer. She told him that it was her intention to build a luxury hotel on Floreana especially for American millionaire guests. It would be called the Hacienda Paradiso and it would be run jointly with her two partners, Lorenz and Philippson.

The prosaic Heinz must have been greatly surprised and alarmed by the news of these grandiose projects. But before he could inquire further about her plans or about the whereabouts of his rice, the Baroness launched into a venomous attack on

Friedrich. 'Dentist and doctor indeed! Dental mechanic at most, more like a male nurse.'

When the Baroness finally got round to the matter of his sack of rice, Heinz discovered that he was to be charged no less than twenty-eight *sucres* for it – by the Baroness. When Heinz protested that he had already bought the rice from the captain, the Baroness merely repeated the price of twenty-eight *sucres*.

In the face of this impudence Heinz told the Baroness that she would be no longer welcome in his orange grove. This the Baroness dismissed, according to Margret's account of the proceedings, with the threat that she had three men with her and that she could be as good as a fourth. She tapped her revolver.

In the face of this threat the Wittmers gave up their claim to the bag of rice, which must have been a blow to the thrifty Margret. Even worse, the Baroness continued to live in the Wittmers' orange grove.

On 15th November, according to Margret, about four weeks after her arrival, the Baroness caused another unpleasant incident. This concerned Kristian Estampa. He was a handsome Norwegian who lived on Santa Cruz with his pretty Norwegian wife. Although differing on some details, both Dore and Margret recount how Estampa arrived on Floreana in his Norwegian fishing boat, the *Falcon*, bringing with him a German travel writer called Franke. The first that Dore claimed to know of their arrival was when she and Friedrich were roused from their sleep, at Friedo, by the sound of voices. They lit a lantern and in the lamplight recognized two Indians who were employed by Kristian Estampa. Dore and Friedrich realized that there must be something very unusual happening, because the superstitious Indians would not normally venture out alone at night on the haunted island of Floreana. The Indians were breathless and incoherent and answered Dore and Friedrich's questions only with queries of their own as to the whereabouts of the Baroness and her men.

It turned out that Estampa had dropped anchor at Post

Office Bay and landed there on a small raft with his friend Franke. Franke wished to stay on Floreana to write, in peace and solitude, an account of his recent travels, and Estampa wished to do some hunting, as was his custom. They were met on the shore by the Baroness. She refused Franke's request for accommodation in the old Norwegian buildings which she still frequented at this time, for much of their equipment was still stacked there. What is more, according to Dore's account, she ordered Estampa and Franke off the island, having fallen into a great rage when she heard that Estampa wished to hunt there. Estampa had frequently hunted on Floreana and usually slept in the old Norwegian buildings now occupied by the Baroness's party. He laughed at the Baroness's absurd possessiveness, which only increased her fury. She shouted that the island was now hers and that she merely tolerated the presence of the Wittmers and the Ritters on it.

Estampa and Franke had returned to the ship, but had sent the two Indians up to Friedo where they arrived to awaken Dore and Friedrich with the story of their master's encounter with the Baroness. Dore gave the two Indians breakfast the next morning and they set off to wait at an agreed place for the arrival of Estampa and Franke, who intended to land again on the island.

On the morning of the following day Dore heard desperate shouts from the bush to the south of Friedo. They ran towards the shouting and found Estampa staggering towards them with his clothes torn to shreds and his arms scratched and bleeding. According to Dore, 'there were deep, bleeding gashes on his hands . . . Innumerable scratches criss-crossed on his back. His face was set like iron, and white and drawn as though from superhuman exertion, his breath came in sobbing gasps. He was completely at the end of his strength, and literally fell into our arms.' They took the wounded Estampa back to Friedo where Friedrich tended his wounds and Dore provided tea. Estampa told them that they had shot two calves not far from the Wittmers' caves and the orange grove where the Baroness was camping. They had skinned the two animals, left the hides behind and the Indians had carried the carcasses down to the shore.

Close to Post Office Bay, Estampa and his party encountered the Baroness, Philippson and Valdivieso. She claimed that the calves were hers, and before they could react, her companions had seized the rifles from the Indians. She ordered the Norwegians' raft to be destroyed on the shore. She told Estampa that they must show her the hides, to prove that they were not from her calves, or pay her for shooting the animals. According to Dore, Estampa told the Baroness to go to hell and instructed the Indians to carry the carcasses down to the shore.

The Baroness reacted quickly. She trained a revolver on Estampa. To humour her, Estampa agreed to go and fetch the skins, but with the intention of going to Friedo to seek counsel with Friedrich and Dore. Before he reached the first lava field Estampa saw Valdivieso creeping up behind him with a rifle. Fortunately for Estampa, dusk was falling and he managed to lose his pursuer in dense bush. It had taken him all night to get to Friedo, for he avoided the paths in case the Baroness and her other companions were also hunting him.

Friedrich and Estampa had decided to look for Franke, for they had no idea of his fate. Fortunately, he appeared, before they set out, with reassuring news. The Baroness's men had been up to the Wittmer caves and had found her calves there unharmed. The Baroness, apparently, no longer intended to pursue Estampa and Franke. However, Estampa wanted no more trouble from the Baroness. They discussed their strategy with Wittmer and Ritter. Friedrich knew that Heinz Wittmer had a dinghy concealed in the bushes at Black Beach. It was concealed because the Wittmers feared that the Baroness might purloin it as she had done their rice. They decided that Heinz Wittmer should take Franke in the dinghy from Black Beach round to Estampa's boat at Post Office Bay. Franke would then sail back with Heinz, and the dinghy in tow, to pick up the injured Estampa at Black Beach.

Heinz, and Harry Wittmer, who also went along, managed to get Franke safely to Estampa's boat. Unfortunately it turned out that Franke did not know how to handle a boat – this factor seems to have been overlooked in the plan – and they started to drift dangerously off course. This was a nasty situation for the weather was quite stormy with a high sea running. At risk of their lives Heinz Wittmer decided that he and Harry should go back to Black Beach, pick up Estampa and take him back to the boat where they had left Franke.

Margret Wittmer years later described her fears as she crouched with Lump in front of the fire in the cave. Darkness had fallen and she was desperately worried about her husband and Harry. Even from the cave she could hear the roar of the waves breaking on the shore and imagined Heinz and Harry capsized and at the mercy of the sharks. Eventually Lump pricked his ears, for he had heard a sound amongst the roaring of the wind. It was Heinz and Harry, returned safely after their ordeal. Margret clung to Heinz for several minutes and then brought him and Harry their supper.

Dore at Friedo was also worried for the safety of Heinz and Harry and was relieved when Heinz stopped off at Friedo, on his way back to the caves, to tell her that they were all safe. Heinz Wittmer had behaved with great courage in ferrying first Franke and then Estampa to the boat in rough seas and returning in the stormy darkness.

* * *

About this time the Wittmers received a copy of the Guayaquil newspaper, *El Telegrafo*, the front page of which carried an article, with enormous headlines, describing the Baroness and her plans for Floreana. The article confirmed what the Baroness had earlier shouted at Heinz when he had attempted to collect his bag of rice. She was going to build a spacious hotel, attract American millionaire guests and provide a boost for the Ecuadorian economy. The Baroness, the article announced, was to turn Floreana into something like Miami.

Friedrich Ritter was shown the newspaper article, apparently translated for his benefit by the Baroness. This drove him to write to the Governor of the Galapagos, Major Paredes. Some years later an American journalist, Edward S. Sullivan, obtained and translated a copy of this letter which he published in the magazine *Real Detective*.

> I feel it is my duty, as a physician and a man, to communicate to you the following:
>
> A woman with some men came to visit us, introducing herself as 'The Baroness'. They stayed one night in our house, and the conduct of the lady was not that of a Baroness but of a servant who imagines herself to be a princess.
>
> A week later she sent me a copy of *El Telegrafo* (Guayaquil newspaper). Translating the article regarding the Baroness and her men, I perceived that the newspapermen have been victims of a terrible joke played on them by a woman in the early stages of paralysis cerebri.
>
> I have not examined the woman, but all that I have heard of her confirms my suspicion of a spiritual confusion in the way of megalomania; the adventure of Mr Estampa shows that this woman is gifted for all crimes.
>
> But at this point the joke ends, and the responsibility of the magistrate begins. It would be an ineradicable disgrace to the Ecuadorean government not to realize the crimes of which the woman is capable, who in her megalomania may take seriously her illusion that the whole island is her own property.
>
> Therefore I ask you to take the proper measures to put this crazy woman under observation in a sanitarium.
>
> I have been told that this woman reads all the letters which are left for us in Post Office Bay. Therefore I ask you to put our letters in the Playa Pietra, or entrust them to other persons for us.

7

THE FIRST NATIVE

The Wittmers had plenty to worry about besides the Baroness and her strange friends. They were still building their house, making furniture, establishing their vegetable garden, fighting off large animals and facing the imminent prospect of the birth of Margret's baby.

The season of tropical heat was approaching and thus must have made life very uncomfortable for Margret who was far gone in her pregnancy. They were still greatly annoyed by cattle making nightly forays into the garden. One moonlit night Heinz shot a bull that had broken in, but the other beasts in their flight tore down a great length of the fence the Wittmers had constructed in a vain attempt to protect their crops. They eventually stood nightly guard in the garden: Harry, from eight to midnight, Margret, until three o'clock, and Heinz until dawn. Margret shot a cow which was eating their runner beans on the second night. She remembered the eerie fascination of her nights in the open, usually in total darkness, with the rustling of leaves caused by many unseen animals in the undergrowth and the lowing of cattle, the squealing of pigs and the distant braying of donkeys.

Friedrich, too, was suffering from the destructive intrusions of the wild cattle. On one visit to Friedo at this time, Heinz discovered the vegetarian doctor cutting up, most expertly, a large bull that he had shot in his garden. He offered Heinz a large sizzling steak, and Heinz took it. According to Margret,

Heinz considered it a fitting punishment for a marauding bull 'to land up in a supposed vegetarian's frying pan'.

Like the good Germans they were, the Wittmers made an effort to celebrate Christmas properly, despite the tropical heat, the hard work and their primitive home. Margret was proud that their Christmas fare consisted entirely of food provided by the island. Heinz shot a boar, so that they had Christmas roast pork, home-made liver sausage and even an attempt at salami which Margret smoked in the cave chimney. They had their own runner beans, with some to spare for Friedrich and Dore. They even had a present for Harry, a mouth-organ that he had longed for and which they had brought especially from Germany for him. They went for a Christmas-afternoon walk and looked with pride at their island domain.

Their house was near enough completion for them to be able to move in before the New Year of 1933. The roof was now securely thatched with sugar-cane and seemed to be watertight. Margret was enchanted with their new home, especially as she had a kitchen and, most importantly for the forthcoming birth, a bedroom. The bedroom measured six feet by six. Margret had lined the walls with material she had brought with her. There was a home-made four-poster bed, thick woollen blankets and a mattress stuffed with straw. They used the bed as a divan during the day. There was a curtained shelf on one wall for Margret to keep clothes on and another long shelf above the bed, for books. The living-room was not finished, but the door was in place to lead from the bedroom when it was completed. The kitchen had a stone stove with an oven and wide chimney for smoking meats and sausages. Heinz had made a dresser, several shelves, a table, and two chairs with cowhide seats. The manufacture of the table was, apparently, a great trial for Heinz: he found it difficult to eliminate wobbling. They had no glass for the windows of the new house, but used wire mesh as a substitute.

They were visited by Rudolf Lorenz as they were carrying their belongings from the caves into the house. He was attracted by the smell of freshly made coffee and gladly accepted a cup.

He told them that he was unhappy with the Baroness and that they used him as a sort of man-servant. It was certainly not a partnership, as far as he was concerned, and he told Margret that he was left to carry out the menial tasks whilst Philippson and Valdivieso did all the interesting work. He complained that he had to walk all the way down to the buildings at Post Office Bay, every day, to milk the cows for the Baroness's rice, which she could not take without milk.

* * *

Margret's labour pains started on 30th December. She was of course apprehensive but, characteristically, everything was ready in the new bedroom: 'linen, bandages, cotton wool, scissors, nappies and a tin of talcum powder.' Her bed was prepared and she had covered it first with 'thick layers of paper' and then with 'pieces of linen sterilised by boiling water'. Her pains increased all through that day and went on through the night. Dawn came and Heinz made her some strong coffee. She walked about until her pains abated. She was able to prepare the meals and baked a New Year's cake.

As Heinz and Harry were working hard, she spent the day alone with her pains. She describes how she bit into the pillow to prevent screaming. Night came again and passed without an end to her pains. On New Year's morning she was in extremity, feverishly thirsty and unable to eat.

The pains persisted into the third night. Heinz and Harry were awake and had gone out, perhaps to shoot at a marauding bull. In the darkness she screamed for her husband. She recovered and tried to read. In desperation she ran out into the bush. Then she collapsed calling again for Heinz. There was no answer, except later the bellow of a bull close to her in the darkness. Then she says that she heard the cry of her new-born child and only slowly became aware of Heinz and Harry and Lump running towards her. They brought her into the house and laid her gently on to the bed. Heinz bathed the baby and wrapped it in a towel. Then Margret and the baby fell asleep.

Margret awoke at dawn and Heinz brought her hot coffee

and food. She ate two beaten raw eggs, and stewed pumpkins. Her child was in her arms, but her agonies were still not finished for the after-birth had not come away. Heinz went to fetch Friedrich Ritter. While he was away Margret cradled her son, who had fair hair and brown eyes.

Heinz returned with Friedrich Ritter after about three hours. He recommended quinine and hot and cold compresses. He left Margret to apply the compresses and, she thinks, he went off for an hour to see the Baroness. He returned to perform the painful operation without anaesthetics.

When this last pain was over Margret records her deep gratitude to Friedrich. She felt that she had wronged him in thinking him a boor. Heinz too was full of gratitude and offered Friedrich money. Friedrich refused. After all, he said, what could he do with money on Floreana? However, Friedrich said that he would appreciate a regular, fortnightly, sackful of dried meat for his chickens. Even Margret in her weak condition saw the funny side of that.

Dore was overjoyed when she heard the news of the Wittmer baby. She learned from Friedrich that the baby boy would be called Rolf. She wrote afterwards in her eager and sentimental way: 'The coming of the baby seemed to create an atmosphere almost like Christmas. All differences and quarrels were momentarily lost in a general warmth and goodwill.'

Even the Baroness seems to have been affected by the arrival of the first native of Floreana. Margret describes how she visited her, together with Philippson and Lorenz, without the usual revolver in her belt. She was charmingly effusive and brought presents of a tin of Quaker oats and, incredibly, a little dress and jacket for the baby. The Wittmers gave the Baroness some seeds and vegetables. In the general euphoria, the Baroness had even been moved to give Dore, by way of Friedrich, a present of flower seeds for Dore's garden, something that Dore always longed for.

Friedrich too seems to have joined in the feeling of warmth and friendship that grew up in that strange little community at New Year 1933. Dore was amazed that he made no objection to her planting the seeds and even praised the 'basket of banana leaves' that Dore had made to grow them in.

Dore, in company with Friedrich, visited the new Wittmer house to see the baby. They even stopped on the way to take presents to the Baroness. They took her herbs, ciruela plums, otoi and cabbages. They found the Baroness looking 'most charming, dressed in a simply cut, black and white, check silk dress. The Baroness was in amiable mood, bareheaded and brandishing a riding crop.'

Dore's visit to the Wittmers was quite an event for her, because she had never been to the caves since the Wittmers had arrived on the island. She and Friedrich brought presents of a date palm, and some vegetables and fruit from the Friedo garden. She afterwards wrote that she was 'very enthusiastic' about the new house. Dore considered that it looked 'most picturesque with its well-laid thatch of banana leaves [*sic*] and its neat joinery'. She was particularly impressed with the 'cleanliness and tidiness of the rooms – as immaculate and orderly as that of any German housewife's I have ever seen.' She felt a twinge of guilt at the thought of the untidy house at Friedo. In her blue-stocking way she afterwards consoled herself by recalling the remark of a Floreana visitor: 'The Wittmers' house is very nice, but at Ritters' you can talk!'

Dore approved of the baby and was greatly impressed by the pretty carved cradle which the resourceful Heinz had made from lemon wood. She found Margret looking young and very happy, but she disapproved strongly of Margret's intention not to breast-feed young Rolf in order, as Dore believed, to preserve her figure. 'This on Floreana!' Dore commented.*

In the subsequent conversation, Dore learned of the Wittmers' intense dislike of the Baroness. Margret and Heinz seem to have poured out their grievances, especially in the matter of the purloined rice. Dore adopted a surprisingly detached

*Dore seems to have been more than a little malicious on this point, for Margret Wittmer records that she continued to breast-feed the baby until July 1933, but had to supplement his diet as 'just mother's milk was not enough for him'.

attitude in view of her own previous relations with the Baroness, but nevertheless felt 'bound to admit that their sentiments were not unnatural in the circumstances'. She resolved (now in her role of the lady of the manor visiting some of the local peasants) that she would use all her 'not insignificant powers of persuasion to . . . try and bring the factions to at least an outward truce'.

Friedrich's and Dore's visit to the Wittmers concluded with the ceremonial planting of the date palm, their symbol of friendship from Friedo. Thus they commemorated the unexpected interlude of friendliness among the odd assortment of inhabitants of Floreana which the arrival of young Rolf Wittmer had brought about.

8
CORRUGATED IRON AND SILK

While the Wittmers were completing their house, building operations had also been in progress at the Hacienda Paradiso. The Baroness's hotel for American millionaires had materialized in the form of a large corrugated-iron hut, mid-way between Friedo and the Wittmers' house.

Dore first saw this makeshift paradise when she called with Friedrich to see the Baroness during their pilgrimage to the new Wittmer baby. She was distinctly disappointed at the poor reality after the Baroness's glittering vision. The Baroness told Dore that it had been constructed by 'the Ecuadorian [i.e. Valdivieso] the only one of the men who understood manual labour.' However, the garden at the Hacienda far exceeded Dore's expectations. 'Its arrangement was most excellent, and filled me with surprise, for it was quite the sort of thing one sees in illustrated garden books, and certainly bore witness to the unremitting toil of several hands.'

Friedrich was less impressed. 'Only time will show that the way she arranged her garden is a façade. This is quite obvious to the perceptive eye. Despite the fact the garden only comprises 100m², she lays most importance on flowers. Despite this nonsense, she also wants to find space for a swimming pool.'

The interior of the corrugated-iron building greatly surprised Dore, for the walls were hung with decorative carpets.

> There were two broad divans on which one sat by day and slept by night, as wide as double beds, with covers of bright

silk, and heaped with cushions. The fireplace was framed in an artistic drapery, which caught the light of the flames in shimmering colours, and would make a comfortable and charming effect at night. There was nothing overdone in this decoration; everything was arranged in admirable taste. I could not help observing that the whole house consisted only of this one room with its two couches which serve as beds, a fact telling a great deal of the intimacies of the Baroness' household. At one end a rough door separated the main apartment from a small store-room where the Ecuadorian slept, so we were told.

Friedrich and Dore had been invited for lunch at the Hacienda Paradiso. On that day they found the Baroness to be a charming and entertaining hostess. True she monopolized the conversation, but Dore was entertained by her stories. 'One could only take it in good part, as with an animated and precocious child. She had a most attractive way of bragging, and if one had believed her, one must have thought her an absolute phenomenon.' The Baroness addressed most of her conversation to Friedrich. She boasted that she was highly trained in a wide range of subjects, including arts and crafts, medicine and painting, and had exceptional literary talents.

Lunch was taken in the garden. Dore was impressed with the dainty table setting and noticed that the cutlery was engraved with an initialled seven-pointed star. This surprised Dore, who evidently knew a thing or two, because, she claimed, a seven-pointed star indicated a Countess and not a Baroness. Dore also discovered on her fork to her further surprise the 'tell-tale trade-mark: "Cristoffel", the name of a ware rather less good than nickel plate' – less good, one suspects, than Dore's single set of 'Nirosta' ware. Dore took a rather malevolent satisfaction in her deduction about the Baroness's silver. She was convinced that the Baroness was a fraud. Not that she worried particularly about this, but she determined to find out more when she could get the Baroness to herself.

She achieved this rather sooner than she expected, for

Philippson and Lorenz took Friedrich away to show him around the Hacienda Paradiso. The talk took an unexpected direction, for the Baroness 'plunged into the sort of conversation which I had heard about, but never actually experienced before. It did not take me long to discover that this woman was completely sex-mad.' Poor Dore got more than she bargained for and did not get round to catching out the Baroness in any further social blunders.

The Baroness was apparently interested in Dore's conjugal relationship with Friedrich, but her curiosity was not satisfied by Dore. According to Dore, who must by now have been deeply embarrassed, the Baroness confessed that 'variety was the spice of life' as far as she was concerned and wondered whether she could be satisfied by Philippson alone now that she was tired of Lorenz. Dore strongly suspected that the Baroness had sexual designs on Friedrich. If such an unlikely relationship had matured it would not have been along the lines laid down by the writer of *Thus Spake Zarathustra*. It certainly would not have been a case of the Baroness being used merely for 'the recreation of the warrior'. One suspects that it might have been the Baroness rather than Friedrich who would have wielded the whip which Nietzsche held to be necessary for the warrior to take to his sexual recreation.

Three weeks later, Dore responded to the Baroness's entertainment by organizing a 'grand luncheon party' at Friedo. Dore hoped that she could influence the Baroness sufficiently to bring peace between the three groups of settlers on Floreana.

Dore, who always emphasized her deficiencies as a housewife, took a lot of trouble with the 'grand luncheon party'. There were to be 'rice soup and kohle rabi stuffed with puree of peas, and a salad made of my marvellous cucumbers, which grew like weeds and had an unusually fine flavour'. An important item was otois served with peanut butter, which, interestingly, she included especially for Rudolf Lorenz because she knew it to be a favourite of his. Evidently Dore had got to know Lorenz well enough to be quite familiar with his eating-habits. She made a cake, too, using the dreaded flour of which

Friedrich claimed to disapprove so strongly. She prepared a drink composed of the juice of sugar-cane which she flavoured with fresh pineapple.

Dore was very disappointed when the Baroness and Philippson arrived without Lorenz. She worried that there might be rivalry between the two German companions and that Lorenz had been deliberately excluded by keeping him working that day. She did not believe the Baroness's explanation that 'the poor, unfortunate, dear boy had suddenly been taken with a most alarming sickness'. It was, the Baroness said, a sudden infection which had brought on a recurrence of his tuberculosis. Because of this infection, Lorenz had been banished to the old Norwegian buildings at Post Office Bay. This news infuriated Dore. If he was so ill why hadn't Friedrich been called and why was a sick young man left by himself in a semi-derelict building?

Dore was so cross with the Baroness that she remained silent for most of the meal. Not that this would have had much effect on the Baroness, who was in top form, talking to Friedrich and Robert Philippson about her talents and experiences in various parts of the world.

Philippson too was silent. Dore afterwards wrote that his 'absolutely non-committal calm . . . made him seem horrible to me'. In her quick perceptive way she noticed that Philippson's face was expressionless when the Baroness spoke of Lorenz's illness. She felt that the two men were rivals for the Baroness's affections and that Philippson hated poor Lorenz who, formerly, had been the Baroness's favourite.

At one point in the meal the Baroness's conversation was interrupted by the braying of Burro, Dore's donkey. Dore left the table to let Burro into the corral with the Baroness's donkey. When she returned the Baroness was discoursing on Paris fashions and now, according to Dore, needed her for an audience. The Baroness was clearly displeased when Dore got up again to give the donkey the water with which she had forgotten to provide him. When Dore returned, the Baroness continued to talk of Paris fashions. According to Dore, she said that 'the very latest thing in Paris was white lace. You know, the kind of things they put all the virgins into for their first communion'. She said this 'with unmistakable suggestiveness', which shocked Dore. At this point Burro interrupted once more and Dore again left to attend to him. This was the last straw for the Baroness, who had been interrupted in her monologue three times by the persistent donkey. Dore records that she spoke to her with undisguised venom: 'If you treat your husband as well as you do your donkey, what a happy man he must be!' Dore afterwards believed that poor Burro's interruptions of the Baroness that afternoon cost him his life.

The Baroness next boasted of her marksmanship and spoke of her hunting expeditions on Floreana. Dore was horrified to hear of her cattle slaughter, for she apparently killed only to take the choice cuts from her victims. Worse, she boasted of her treatment of wild dogs. She had tried to capture a pair, but without success, and had then resorted to the strategy of shooting them in the belly. The wounded dogs were then tamed by the Baroness, although one was permanently crippled. 'Men and dogs are all alike, she went on, if they don't come willingly you bring them down by force, and then you make them well again. They will stay then, and it does them good to know who is their master.'

The Baroness further galvanized the others by inquiring of Friedrich: 'Oh, Dr. Ritter – do tell me. Is it true that milk's the antidote for arsenic poisoning?' Friedrich did not have time to answer this question before the Baroness rattled on to further topics, but that sinister question burned itself into Dore's memory sufficiently for her to recall it years later.

For Dore it had been a hideous afternoon. Her well-meaning attempt to bring about reconciliation and peace on Floreana must clearly fail with this appalling woman living among them. Sadly she looked at the pile of gifts that she had intended to give to the Baroness as a gesture of friendship: 'a date palm, otoi and sugar-cane plants, pineapple shoots, aquacate and vine shoots, also seven different kinds of banana plants.' She describes how she could not wait for the Baroness and Philippson to leave Friedo and take these well-intentioned gifts with them.

After their guests had left, Dore seems to have become quite hysterical. She told Friedrich that the Baroness was obviously a criminal, that he must go down to Post Office Bay to discover whether Lorenz was alive or dead and that he must write to the Ecuadorian authorities to tell them that they were all unsafe on the island with that woman there. Friedrich brushed aside her fears and told Dore that the Baroness was just an actress. She was, of course, a fool to attempt to dupe a medical man with her story of Lorenz's tuberculosis, but what would be her motive for ill-treating or murdering the young man? If there had been murder there would be inquiries, which would present difficulties for the Baroness. She was a shrewd woman and would not wish to be involved in post-mortems and the like. Furthermore, if Lorenz was ill, then he was in a good place, down at Post Office Bay, for he might be picked up by a passing ship or boat which could take him to a hospital somewhere. As for writing to the Ecuadorian authorities or the German Consul, this would be useless. He had, in fact, written about the Estampa affair and what good had that done?

By such arguments, Friedrich convinced Dore that there was little that they could do. But he agreed to get Herr Wittmer to ask young Lorenz if he needed medical attention when he next went down to Post Office Bay. But no request came for such assistance.

* * *

Dore's anxieties about the Baroness's behaviour had arisen partly from the odd pieces of information that she and the Wittmers had managed to pick up, largely from Rudolf Lorenz, during his occasional visits to Friedo and to the Wittmer house. She had also attempted to find out about the Baroness's past.

Dore had noticed the graceful Austrian accent when she first spoke in German to her. She had also suspected that the Baroness and her companions must have spent some time in France because this was the language that was spoken at the Hacienda Paradiso. Margret Wittmer had learned from Lorenz that the Baroness claimed to have been a spy during the war and had subsequently become a dancer in Constantinople. She also maintained that she came from an illustrious Austrian family, that she had met an airman during the war in Constantinople and married him there. His name was Bosquet and he was said to have become a wealthy business man. She incorporated her French husband's surname with her own and used the title: Eloise Baroness Wagner de Bosquet.

The details of the Baroness's previous life varied very much in the accounts she gave to different people. She told Hakon Mielche, when he visited Floreana, that she was the daughter of a high Austrian official who was sent to the Middle East to superintend the construction of the Baghdad railway. He took little Eloise with him and later in Syria, not apparently Constantinople, she met the dashing young French Air Force officer who married her 'and introduced her as Baroness Bosquet into the highest society in Paris'. She said that her beauty immediately placed her in the front rank of Parisian society. She described to him the dresses that she wore at Longchamp and Auteuil and maintained that they were discussed in Parisian society at the time 'in greater detail than the last debate on the budget in the senate'. She was, she told Mielche, inundated with invitations to social events and people competed for her to speak at charity bazaars, because of her beautiful voice.

Lorenz made occasional surreptitious visits to Friedo. During close questioning by Dore, he admitted his own doubts as to the reality of the Baroness's aristocratic claims. He told Dore that she had learned her charming manners during her regular attendance at the cinema and then in night clubs. According to Lorenz, she would assume roles which attracted her, to gain poise and confidence. He considered that she could have been a fine actress and that it was a pity she had not gone on the stage.

The possession of her assumed title was evidently an important element in the Baroness's social strategy in Paris. She once told Dore that 'in Paris a lot of men fall for one's title, you know, but if that is what lures them at first, it's something else that keeps them.' It must have been this important secondary quality that had kept Rudolf Lorenz so firmly in her power. He told Dore that he had owned a business in Paris – 'one of those typical Parisian bazaars where knick-knacks are sold for disproportionate prices'. The shop indeed existed and was called 'Antoinette'. It was situated in the Avenue Daumesnil.

The Baroness had, apparently, become Lorenz's business partner. He became deeply attached to the Baroness, 'as many a youth of his age has been by that type of older woman', Dore thought. Lorenz trusted the Baroness with the book-keeping, but, so he told Dore, she entered the expenditure but not the income in the ledgers. Lorenz was unable to persuade her to adopt more orthodox accounting techniques, for she was very ingenious at avoiding any attempted reforms. Inevitably, the business was ruined and Lorenz became bankrupt – though still irrevocably attached to the Baroness.

The Baroness's story of her business relations with Philippson and Lorenz (as given to some American visitors to Floreana in February 1933) differed considerably from Lorenz's account to Dore. She told 'how she had tired of life in Paris, where she ran a successful dress shop and how she left for the Galapagos with Robert Philippson and Alfred Rudolf Lorenz, who had worked for her. Lorenz, an invalid, was to do light jobs on the island.' The Baroness's expressed concern for Lorenz's health is distinctly ironic in view of her subsequent treatment of him.

Robert Philippson apparently entered the Baroness's life when they fell in love, at first sight, at the Colonial Exhibition in the Bois de Vincennes. Philippson was, apparently, an engineer. The Baroness told Hakon Mielche that they walked arm-in-arm through the exhibition looking at pictures of beautiful, faraway islands. Mielche described, in his cynical way, the subsequent progress of the affair as related to him by the Baroness.

> Shortly afterwards the sky went up in flames, as the aviator was not modern enough to tolerate a lover in his household, and a divorce was put through. The two lovers went for

walks in the Bois de Boulogne and amongst the birds, flowers and stinking motor-cars found their way to the beating heart of Father Jean-Jacques Rousseau. They were tired of city life, its alcohol, its evil people and its noise. They were finished with the metropolis. They decided to find their way back to the bosom of mother nature. They spun a globe on its pedestal, stopped it with a finger and lo! a little, red varnished nail pointed exactly to the island of Floreana in the Galapagos group.

This fanciful account differs considerably from that which Lorenz gave to Dore. In the first place, according to Lorenz, the Baroness was never divorced from Bosquet. Lorenz also said that the Baroness hit on the plan to escape shortly after his bankruptcy, when she had read newspaper articles describing Friedrich's and Dore's idyllic life on Floreana. The Baroness quickly hit upon the idea of setting up the hotel on Floreana and had little difficulty in persuading Lorenz and Philippson to fall in with her grandiose scheme.

At this time they seem to have recruited Felipe Valdivieso. According to Lorenz, Valdivieso was an Ecuadorian who had been, until about 1927, a labourer on the neighbouring island of Isabela. He is then supposed to have travelled as a stowaway to Europe and, eventually, to have found work on a railway in France. It was here that he fell in with the Baroness and agreed to join the party that was leaving for the Galapagos.

According to Hakon Mielche, this strange quartet sailed from Le Havre fairly soon after the Baroness had conceived her plan. Their baggage included numerous gardening books, two or three dozen dresses and a swarm of bees. The bees later escaped on board ship and caused a good deal of distress to the other passengers who, Hakon Mielche said, 'gave vent to unconsidered words in several languages. This hurt the Baroness, and when with Baby's [i.e. Philippson's] help she had finally recaptured the swarm from an elderly gentleman's beard, she retired like a whipped dog to her cabin, disappointed against mankind in general.'

Mielche also claimed that on the voyage the Baroness entered a religious phase. 'Her religion included most of the doctrines already known, plus one or two Wagner-Bosquetian dogmas, which were largely concerned with love and more or less with strong drink.' The Baroness's faith seems to have given her at least temporary powers to perform miracles, for Mielche recounts how on Floreana and, in the best biblical manner, she claimed to have struck the hard rock with her fist and caused water to flow from it.

Friedrich Ritter also knew of her claims of miraculous powers: 'the Lord God had appeared to her in Paris in a dream and had told her that she must go to the lonely island of Floreana, that there was no water there, only a wall of rock. All she had to do was to strike this to bring the water gushing forth.'

To Hakon Mielche the Baroness was merely ridiculous. 'The Baroness was small, but one could not say that she was beautiful. In front of her swollen lids she wore strong spectacles and her mouth, though too large, was yet unable to cover her long, yellow, rabbit teeth. She reminded one of a very vicious caricature of Mistinguette. Her hanks of hair were kept in place by means of a pink shoulder strap round her head, and she wore a kind of baby's rompers, like the trunks the ladies of the chorus wear when rehearsing. She moved in that hopping manner which jockeys call a "canter".'

Dore, too, thought the Baroness ridiculous, but also a cruel and sinister presence on the island. Furthermore, she was obviously very much more than a comic figure if she could exert such dominance over her three very much younger male companions.

Dore was particularly shocked at the Baroness's sexual relations with Lorenz and Philippson. She had noticed the sleeping arrangements at the Hacienda Paradiso and claimed that she knew the two men 'were slaves to the woman, even to the extent of sleeping with her together in one bed when she commanded them to do so.'

On her arrival on the island the Baroness clearly favoured

Rudolf Lorenz, even though she introduced Robert Philippson as her 'husband'. At that time, Lorenz was obsessed with the Baroness even to the extent of washing her feet and removing her glasses for her. However, the Baroness quickly tired of Lorenz and seems to have bestowed her favours on Philippson.

Dore seems to have become extremely fond of young Rudolf Lorenz at this time. She was susceptible to good-looking males and Lorenz was an exceptionally handsome specimen. Furthermore, when she knew of his ill-treatment she bestowed on him the compassion that she had formerly reserved for Burro and other ill-treated animals. Margret Wittmer, too, was well disposed towards Lorenz and listened to his troubles with the Baroness and Philippson.

Things had, indeed, gone badly wrong for Rudolf Lorenz at the Hacienda Paradiso. Dore and Friedrich first learned of his troubles when he appeared at Friedo not long after the arrival of the Baroness's party on the island. Lorenz appeared in a hot and flustered condition at Friedo and flung himself down in a deck-chair. Dore thought that he must be ill, for he was very distracted in manner. She noted that 'his pleasant graceful manner was the same as on the first day, but his smile was gone.' She went off to make him 'toy cakes' which she remembered that he had liked on his first visit – a surprising gesture for Dore, who was not fond of cooking. When he had eaten, Lorenz burst out with an account of his troubles at the Hacienda Paradiso. He said that the Baroness was working him to death and acted towards him in a completely despotic manner. Any failure instantly to carry out her orders drove her into an incredible fury. No sooner had he been given one task, he said, than she would find another for him. Lorenz appeared to be exhausted and a mental wreck.

To make sure that Lorenz kept to his tasks, and to prevent rebellion, the Baroness had set Valdivieso to watch him whilst he worked. Valdivieso was apparently terrified of the Baroness and saw to it that he did not earn her displeasure by giving Lorenz an easy time. 'He never lets me out of his sight, and he's sharper than a lynx. He bosses me around, so that it's all I can do not to take whatever tool I'm working with and brain him with it.'

Philippson, on the other hand, was now the favoured lover. According to Lorenz, Philippson hardly ever did any work or, at best, only worked in short bursts to provide a further excuse for the Baroness to compare Lorenz unfavourably with his rival.

Lorenz was in poor condition. His hands were now cut and bruised and not in the well-kept state that the observant Dore had noticed on his first visit to Friedo. He was exhausted, and depressed at being kept virtually a prisoner with no money or means of escape from the island. Later, when Dore showed him articles about the Baroness in Ecuadorian newspapers, Lorenz flew into a great rage. One particular newspaper article represented him in a very bad light and was devoted to an account of the Baroness's grandiose plans for her hotel for millionaire guests on Floreana.

After the failure of Dore's luncheon party, she worried even more for Lorenz's safety and even feared for his life. She felt that Philippson too hated Lorenz and would not hesitate to hurt his rival for the Baroness's affections. Dore knew that Lorenz had been forbidden to visit Friedo or to call on the Wittmers. She feared that Valdivieso was acting as a spy and might have reported Lorenz's visits to the Baroness so as to cause fresh punishments to young Lorenz.

Hakon Mielche's account of his visit to the Hacienda Paradiso provides a similar picture of the Baroness's relations with Philippson and Lorenz. At this time Philippson ('a powerfully built, blond youth') was introduced, by the Baroness, as 'My Baby'. 'Baby looked as though he had been a gigolo in a very cheap restaurant somewhere in Berlin, W. His eyes were watery blue, his hair curly and his smile much too sweet. In private life he was Herr Rudolf [sic] Philippson, aged 28. A German cook, tubercular and with one foot in the grave, smiled sickly from the background and brought tea.' The tubercular cook was, of course, Lorenz.

Before he reached the Hacienda Paradiso, during his short

visit to Floreana, Hakon Mielche had discovered an extraordinary pencilled notice on the shore at Post Office Bay. Both he and Margret Wittmer took the trouble to record it.

WHOEVER YOU ARE – FRIENDS!

Two hours from here is the hacienda 'Paradise'. It is a spot where the tired traveller has the happiness to find peace, refreshment and quiet on his way through life.

Life – this small portion of eternity which is bound to a clock, is so short – so let us then be happy – let us be good!

In Paradise you have only one name – Friend!

With you we will share the salt of the sea, the vegetables of our garden and the fruit of our trees, the cold water which runs down our cliffs and the good things friends brought us when they passed this way.

We will spend one or two moments of life with you and give you the happiness and peace that God planted in our hearts and souls when we left the restless metropolis and journeyed away to the quiet of the ages, which has spread its cloak over the Galapagos!

(Signed) BARONESS WAGNER-BOSQUET

9

STAINLESS STEEL AND SILVER

On Thursday 26th January 1933, the *Velero III* reappeared and anchored off Post Office Bay. This call at Floreana was part of the cruise of the Second Allan Hancock Pacific Expedition. The Baroness did not attempt to prevent a landing, as she had done for some earlier visitors, indeed she positively welcomed it. After all, here was a genuine American millionaire, the kind of man for whom the Hacienda Paradiso had been especially conceived. Dore believed that 'the Baroness would be in a fever of excitement at the arrival of the first millionaire she hoped to bait'.

As the *Velero III* anchored at Black Beach, those on board saw the urgent flashing of a heliograph from Friedo. Allan Hancock and the Chief Officer, Charles Swet, immediately went ashore and walked up to Friedo. They returned at dusk with a wild story from Friedrich and Dore of 'a baroness with three husbands and a machine gun and a Norwegian that had run to their hut for protection, his clothes torn from his body'.

At ten o'clock the next morning Friedrich and Dore came aboard the *Velero III*. Dore was thrilled to be on the ship once again and asked after those members of the previous expedition whom she had known. Karl Koch she particularly remembered, because he had carved his name on one of the trees at Friedo – an action of which she did not approve. Friedrich was very pleased to be given a photograph of himself, by John Garth, and to see a ciné film which had been made of them on the previous expedition.

Dore was discovered to have a particularly bad infection on the fingers of her left hand which the ship's doctor, Dr Harry Wegeforth, pronounced to be a sarcoma. Friedrich agreed with this diagnosis, and said that he was aware of the seriousness, but had not treated the sarcoma. Dr Wegeforth operated immediately. John Garth recorded that 'Dore felt no pain during the cauterization and kept up a rapid-fire conversation under the knife. She is a spartaness.' Dr Wegeforth said that he would continue the treatment when the ship returned.

Friedrich and Dore told Allan Hancock and the scientists of the new arrivals on the island and of the strange goings-on that had occurred there. After their account Dr Waldo Schmitt commented that the island 'seemed to be becoming a modern bohemia', to which Dore retorted, 'the Doctor has set them a bad example.'

Allan Hancock was so intrigued that he decided to take a whole day off from scientific duties to investigate the affairs of the 'free love colonies' of Floreana. Thus on Saturday 28th, Allan Hancock, together with Charles Swet and seven scientists, left at exactly 8.30 a.m. with the intention of first climbing up to Friedo. As soon as they set foot on shore, according to John Garth's diary, 'Dr. Ritter, clad only in a loin cloth and driving a donkey, appeared beside the huge pile of supplies which had been delivered from the *Velero* the day before.' When the party, together with the supplies, arrived at Friedo, they noticed the great changes made since their previous visit. Friedrich had now cleared several acres in front of Friedo to give an unobstructed view of the Black Beach anchorage, a sturdy fence now surrounded the entire garden, and the fruit trees had grown prodigiously. The party were also shown fresh wonders, including Dore's banana-leaf flower-pots and Friedrich's shower bath.

The *Velero* party left Friedo with Friedrich to find the Hacienda Paradiso, passing among blossoming trees and noticing the numerous butterflies and land snails which covered the leaves. On the way they encountered Rudolf Lorenz and were shocked by his appearance. Charles Swet described their meeting:

> A pitiful figure he made as he sat for a moment and rested by the side of the trail. His great sunken blue eyes seem to haunt me yet. Five feet in height and so wasted in frame that I doubt if he would have moved the scale to an even hundred pounds. His clothes were in rags, he was hatless, and burned by the sun to the shade of a native, his skin contrasted strangely with his light blonde hair. Over his shoulder was a pack which in the tropics would have sorely puzzled me to carry. Where was he going, where was he from, I asked him in Spanish, only to be met with a dumb uncomprehending stare. Frankly, I had been amazed to see him toiling up the trail as he had been to see me. Why I tried my halting, stammering German on him, I do not know, but at once he became the most voluble of persons. His unhappiness seemed to leave him for a time. I stood for a new hope, for a chance to escape the drudgery of his everyday life, and the constant reminders of the days when he was well and strong and still the favourite of the Queen. Would we take him away, he wanted to leave so badly. Was there not room for one more? How much would it cost to get back to Paris? Once there he would not have to work so hard, and soon he would be well again. His eyes glowed as he thought of some scenes so far away, the pinkish spots on his cheeks became brighter, he coughed a little, slumped over and in a hopeless, listless tone said, 'I think I am not as strong as I was. Won't you come up the trail with me?' he said. 'I know that the Baroness will be glad to see you. Then too I want you to see our new gate which we have just completed. It is so bright and pretty with the paint which we received from Chatham on the last boat.'

As the party approached the bottom of a large volcanic crater they came suddenly upon the Baroness's retreat. Charles Swet was enchanted. 'Paradise was a beautiful place that day. The great cliffs at the foot of the moss-covered crevices gradually fading into the darker hues of the barren lava rock.'

John Garth, a particularly neat and tidy man, was, however, appalled by the untidiness of the Hacienda Paradiso.

> A tent house revealed the greatest disorder. A clothes line desporting incongruous vari-coloured lingerie and an inadequate fence enclosing the spring and garden are the only features to be mentioned. The water supply comes from the side of a cliff, perhaps fifty feet high, and densely clothed with ferns and vines. The pitch is perpendicular and we were told that cattle frequently fall to their death on dark nights, carrying debris dangerously near the tent. Dr. Schmitt found it an ideal place for collecting isopods and water beetles, fishing them out of the drinking barrel. The Baroness was occupied in showing Charlie Swet through her garden and he missed no embarrassment at having our company discover her clad only in an undergarment. One of her swains [Philippson] (we had met the other bound for Post Office Bay with water) spoke excellent English. He is by training an engineer. The Baroness speaks eight languages, has lived in Vienna, Paris and Constantinople, and, according to Mr. Swet, has good connections in Hollywood. She has, however, no ideas of good house-keeping nor sanitation and we shuddered at the filth in which they live. Her passion for cats and the way in which she fed a kitten by regurgitation of canned milk, which she herself warmed in her mouth before transferring it to the felines, was most repulsive.

The Baroness was in good form on that day. When she had heard the approaching party she hurried, with her hair flying, down the path to meet her visitors and bombarded them with questions. Would they enter the Hacienda? Were they tired from their long walk? She could not serve them tea, as she had none. Had they brought mail for her? They must excuse her appearance, but she had not had time to dress properly.

She told the party that her hair, which was streaked with a

band of white, had gone like that in a single night. 'It happened during the war,' she said. The village in which she had been living had been occupied by Russian soldiers. She had been forced to roll herself in a rug, to hide from them, and had lain there all night in the same room as a group of soldiers who had boasted of what they would do when they discovered her.

She invited the party into the Hacienda and showed them around her corrugated-iron palace. Lorenz was ordered off to make some cakes for the visitors. The visitors rested outside the Hacienda as the Baroness chattered on, even exchanging a few amiable words with Friedrich, and photographs were taken. Eventually the party from the *Velero III* escaped from the Baroness's hospitality.

From the Hacienda Paradiso, Allan Hancock and his party walked the short distance to the Wittmers'. They were met at a gate in a barbed-wire fence, as John Garth described, 'by a great grey dog whose barking brought a woman to let us in. This was Margret Wittmer.' Friedrich, who was still with the party, showed them the caves in which he and Dore had slept during their first nights on the island and which were now part of the Wittmer property. Allan Hancock was impressed by all that the Wittmers had achieved in such a short time, including the production of a healthy baby. According to Margret, he was less impressed by the egg production from her five hens, for just one of his poultry farms produced twenty thousand eggs a day.

Fred Ziesenhenne, a young crewman and biologist, was much taken with Margret Wittmer: 'She was the most beautiful of the three women on the island, blonde, blue eyes and beautifully built. Insect bites on her legs was the only mar on her beauty.' Even the distinguished middle-aged scientist, Waldo Schmitt, appears not to have been immune to Margret's charms, for his close friend, Richard Blackwelder, considers that: 'Waldo's interest in the Galapagos seems to have been 75% in the Crustacea, 24% in Mrs Wittmer and 1% in everything else.' Waldo Schmitt formed a lasting friendship with the Wittmers. He would one day arrive at Floreana with the

President of the United States of America, bearing gifts for the Wittmer family.

Allan Hancock had invited the Baroness and Philippson back to the *Velero III*. The party stopped at Friedo on the return journey for drinks – of lime and cane juice, and papaya. Philippson, apparently wishing to add to the friendliness of the occasion, 'unwrapped some greasy pork from a dingy brown paper' which he offered around. John Garth described how the 'others felt duty-bound to partake of this treat' but that he 'having investigated the method of preparation felt equally bound to refuse'.

The Baroness must have been in a particularly malicious mood at the gathering at Friedo, for Dore mentioned how relieved she felt when the *Velero III* party left for the yacht taking the Baroness and Philippson with them. She had noticed in particular a dangerous 'gleam of sharp resentment in the Baroness's eyes' as she saw the presents which Allan Hancock had left for Friedrich and Dore.

By four o'clock the party had returned to the *Velero III*. There the Baroness enjoyed the customary musical evening. She seemed to have been in excellent form, for she told the company that her great-uncles were Franz Liszt and Richard Wagner. Robert Philippson, again trying to enter into the spirit of the occasion, introduced a jarring note by playing jazz, rather badly, on the piano, which did not go down well with Allan Hancock's highbrow companions. John Garth played a piano solo, especially for the Baroness: the Liszt 'Liebestraum in A Flat'. He recalls that the Baroness was ecstatic at his playing and exclaimed, 'Oh, that's just the way my great-uncle would have liked to have heard it played.'

Later that evening she claimed that she had an uncle who had mastered many of the ancient languages, including Sanskrit, and she asked John Garth to bring her a textbook on Sanskrit on the next voyage of the *Velero III* so that she could learn the language.

When the *Velero III* sailed, Valdivieso left on her. His contract had expired and he had no desire to renew it. Heinz

Wittmer told Dore that there had been a good deal of unpleasantness at the Hacienda Paradiso about Valdivieso's departure. Valdivieso had, Heinz reported, turned upon the Baroness and Philippson to such effect that they were forced to retreat in considerable disorder.

The unpleasantness concerned the termination of Valdivieso's contract. Valdivieso claimed that his contract with the Baroness had commenced when they left Paris and was now terminated. This the Baroness disputed, maintaining that the contract had commenced on their arrival on Floreana. Allan Hancock described how, when he was talking to the Baroness in the Hacienda, Valdivieso burst in, brandishing a revolver. 'But the Baroness, quick as a flash, produced her small revolver, which she usually held in her hand, and the Ecuadorian dashed out of the house like a scared rabbit and hid himself in the bush.'

Hancock refused to take Valdivieso off the island unless the Baroness came down herself to put him on board the *Velero III*. The Baroness evidently relented and agreed to let Valdivieso go, for she conducted the Ecuadorian to the beach and he was taken away to Chatham Island on board the yacht.

Dore was relieved to hear of Valdivieso's departure for she hoped that life would become easier for Lorenz, who had virtually become Valdivieso's prisoner. Dore told Friedrich that she was convinced the Baroness was a dangerous criminal. Again, Friedrich refused to take any action against her. He felt that the best strategy for them to adopt was to keep the Baroness at a distance and not to engage in open war – which the Baroness would probably win. As usual, Dore, who was still totally dominated by Friedrich, tried to obey.

On the Sunday after the *Velero III* sailed, the Baroness appeared at Friedo with Philippson. Dore was alone. According to Dore, her opening conversation was harmless enough. Suddenly, however, the Baroness lashed out: 'Too kind of you to have sent fodder to my donkeys at the Bay! I suppose that Captain Hancock thinks your kindness to animals most awfully touching – it's not a bad trick!' Dore replied that Hancock had asked her to send down some sugar-cane for the half-starved animals at Post Office Bay. The Baroness retaliated by agreeing that the donkeys were in poor condition, but told Dore that she had told Hancock that the animals were Dore's.

Dore seems to have been non-plussed by the Baroness's malice. Before she could reorganize her defence, the Baroness had attacked again, to some effect. She suggested that Dore should confine her kind-heartedness to animals and leave Lorenz's health to her. She further suggested that Dore was in love with Rudolf Lorenz, and then shifted the direction of her attack. 'Your Captain Hancock is very generous to his protégés.' Dore had now gathered her wits sufficiently to protest that she and Friedrich were no one's protégés, but again the Baroness shifted her ground. Hancock, she said, 'was simply charmed with my place, when he comes back we're going to make a film.' The film was to be called *The Empress of Floreana*, and naturally the Baroness was to be the Empress. Dore was rather rude about this, and the Baroness maintained that she, an aristocrat, was the natural ruler of the island. She emphasized, however, that she was 'really very democratic', and had 'always got on excellently with the common people'.

At this point Dore rallied and, disregarding Friedrich's instructions, carried the war into the Baroness's own camp by questioning the authenticity of the Baroness's title. The Baroness, stung, said Dore was insolent and knew nothing of 'aristocratics'. Here, Dore used a long-cherished weapon by informing the Baroness that she, Dore, knew a thing or two about nickel spoons and forks and, in addition, that a Baroness's cutlery would be engraved with five- and not seven-pointed stars. This shook the Baroness, but she held her ground: the silver had belonged to her mother – who was a Countess.

Then Dore produced her ultimate weapon, the glittering 'Nirosta' ware, determined to dazzle her enemy with that fabulous brand-name rather as Perseus turned his shining shield upon Medusa.

Dore used this weapon with cunning. She first mentioned

how difficult it was to keep valuable metals untarnished in a tropical climate and emphasized the superior virtues of 'Nirosta' ware, but added that it was much more expensive than silver. The Baroness rose to this, as Dore had intended, because she could not bear the thought of anyone possessing objects of greater value than hers. According to Dore, the Baroness asked Philippson, 'How much was it, darling, that we paid for our cutlery – not including the engravings, of course?' This indiscretion must have been beyond Dore's wildest hopes: the cutlery was clearly not ancestral, as the Baroness had always claimed, and Dore regarded this as a knock-out blow.

After that the Baroness went to pieces. 'Talking nineteen to the dozen, she plunged into the wildest account of her antecedents, her childhood, her education, her experience at Court where her mother, so she said, had been a lady-in-waiting, of balls and parties and illustrious suitors. But in every other sentence there was a contradiction, and as she forgot one lie before she had composed the next, her tale became a pitiful kaleidoscope of foolish boastings, until I myself would gladly have interrupted her for her own dignity's sake. Philippson was in the throes of dire embarrassment, but she ignored the warning pushes of his foot against hers underneath the table, all easily visible to me; she was so wound up that only the exhaustion of both breath and fantasy could stop her.'

Dore seems to have maintained a fairly calm front in the face of the Baroness's boasting and invective. She must, however, have worried about Friedrich's reaction to her victorious encounter, for he had previously made it clear that they must avoid open war with the Baroness. Fortunately for Dore, as Friedrich came in, the Baroness 'made the mistake of allowing herself to fling an epithet of a kind which is considered even among the lowest of the low a little strong for use in mixed company'. Friedrich very tactfully declared that the Baroness and Dore were quits and suggested that they should take lunch together. The Baroness, very surprisingly, accepted. However, Friedrich got more than he bargained for; according to Dore, the Baroness 'became less careful of the words she used and her

1 Charles Island (Floreana), from Robert Fitz-Roy's account, published in 1839, of the voyage of H.M.S. *Beagle*

2 Dore Strauch and Friedrich Ritter, shortly after their arrival on Floreana

3 Friedrich and Dore on the veranda at Friedo

4 Friedrich and Dore working their sugar press

5 An artist's impression of G. Allan Hancock, his business interests and hobbies

6 The *Velero III* in the Galapagos, 1932

7 Dore and Friedrich aboard the *Velero III*, January 1932

8 Heinz and Margret Wittmer on Floreana, with Harry, baby Rolf and Lump

9 Captain Hancock at Post Office Bay

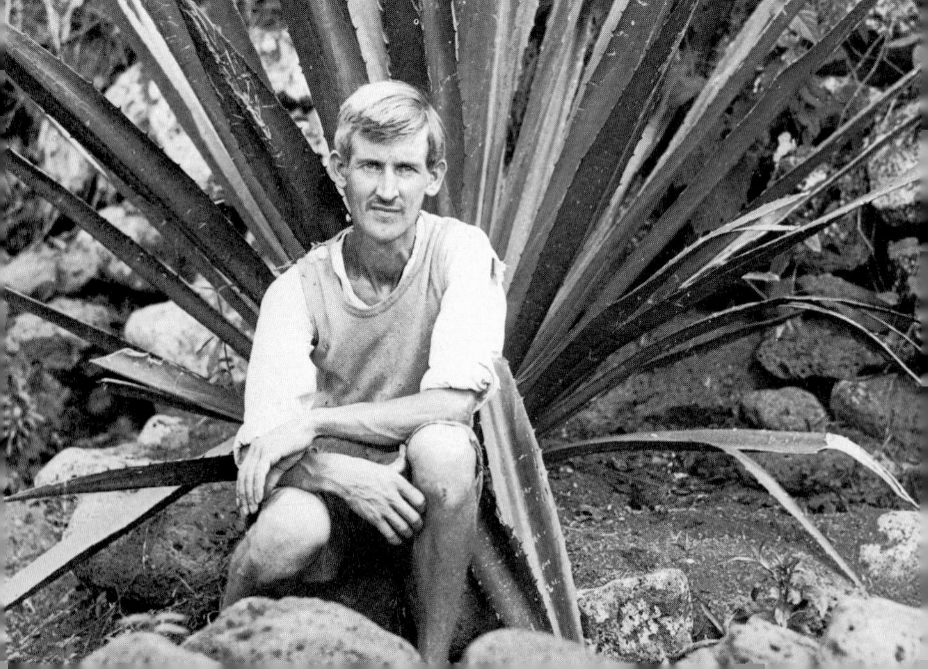

opposite
10 The Baroness and Robert Philippson at the Hacienda Paradiso

11 Rudolf Lorenz

right
12 The Baroness as a young woman

below
13 The Baroness and Rudolf Lorenz, with a friend, at their shop in Paris

left 14 Dore's pride: stainless-steel 'Nirosta' ware, *c.* 1929

above 15 'Christofle' ware, *c.* 1930, the French silver-plated cutlery used by the Baroness

16 Dore Strauch and her pet donkey, Fleck, at Friedo

17 Friedrich Ritter and the Baroness at the Hacienda Paradiso, January 1933

18 The party from the *Velero III* at the Hacienda Paradiso, 28th January 1933, with the Baroness and Robert Philippson

19 Friedrich Ritter, Captain Hancock and Harry Wittmer with Margret Wittmer, during one of her rare visits to Friedo

20 Captain Hancock and the Baroness at the Hacienda Paradiso

21 Fred Ziesenhenne with Rudolf Lorenz, January 1933

22, 23 and 24 The Hollywood film producer Emory Johnson, directing the Baroness in the ciné film made by a party from the *Velero III*, January 1934

25 The Baroness with Robert Philippson during the making of the ciné film

26 The mummified bodies of Rudolf Lorenz (nearest the camera) and Trygve Nuggerud (next to the skiff) on the beach at Marchena Island

27 Dore Strauch sitting at Friedrich Ritter's grave

28 Dore Strauch leaving Floreana on 7th December 1934 with Captain Hancock

29 Dore Strauch on the *Velero III en route* for Guayaquil, December 1934

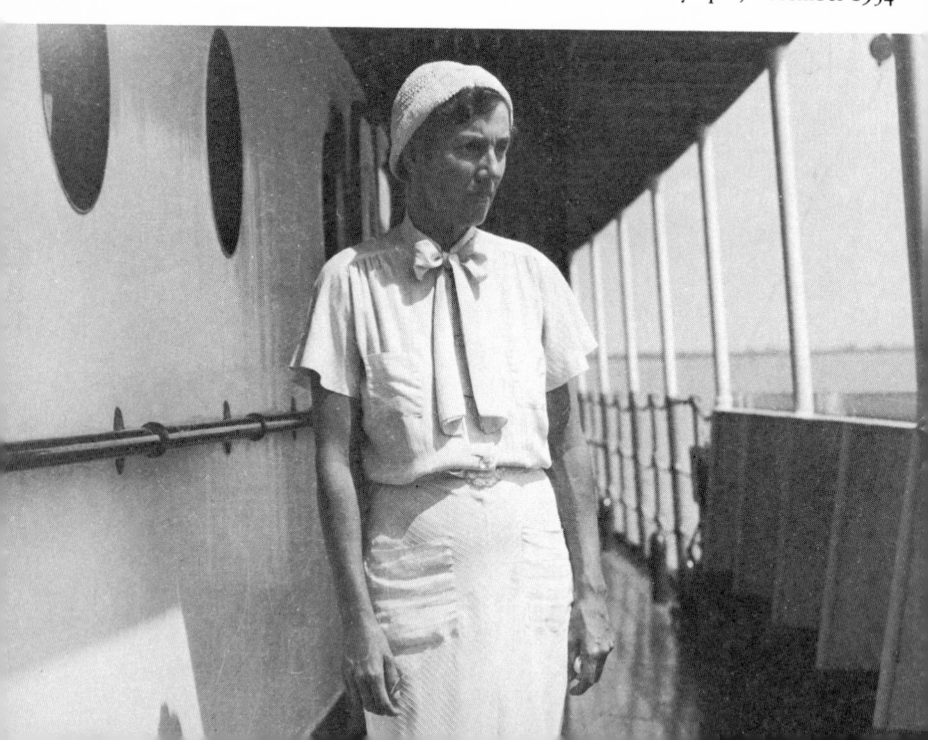

;o Trygve Nuggerud's widow and son

;1 The site of the house at Friedo, which had been dismantled by the other ettlers leaving only the tree trunks that once supported the roof of 'riedrich's and Dore's home

32 Margret and Heinz Wittmer with Rolf and, in Heinz's arms, their daughter Ingeborg Floreanita, who was born in April 1937

33 Margret Wittmer with Rolf and Ingeborg, 1937

talk was after that of a woman of the streets'. Friedrich seemed to be deeply shocked, but Dore was still in good humour, evidently savouring her victory over her formidable adversary.

* * *

The Wittmers were also suffering from the presence of the Baroness. Their home was closer to hers than was the Ritters' at Friedo. Heinz Wittmer had tried to adopt a strategy similar to Friedrich's in his relations with the Hacienda Paradiso. He too was anxious to avoid direct conflict with his difficult neighbours, but he found it a difficult strategy to sustain. He told Dore and Friedrich that he was nearing the end of his patience with the Baroness.

Dore seems to have changed her attitude to Heinz Wittmer completely. By this time he was no longer the rather odd, unattractive figure who had first arrived in the garden at Friedo. 'Both Friedrich and I had formed an excellent opinion of Herr Wittmer now. He had shown himself in many ways to be a thoroughly likeable and honourable person.' Heinz now made regular, weekly visits to Friedo where the three of them seem to have exchanged information and discussed the latest goings-on at the Hacienda Paradiso. Poor Frau Margret, however, was less well thought of at Friedo, even though the two women hardly ever met. 'We thought him [Wittmer] most unfortunate in his partner, who was neither so well-bred nor so kindly a person as he . . . Frau Wittmer was a rather ordinary type of woman and a great gossip.'

For her part, Margret was particularly worried about the feeding of young Rolf Wittmer. They did not have any milking cows and were not anxious to ask for help from the Baroness's animals. It was, for one thing, unlikely that the milk yield of the Baroness's cows would have been sufficient to provide for their baby even if the Baroness had agreed to supply them – which was doubtful. In Dore's opinion the Baroness's cows were in such a poor state that she doubted whether they would 'have produced a cupful between them'.

The Wittmers had made arrangements with Captain

Hancock for him to bring them forty cans of condensed milk, together with some blankets and a bolt of cotton when he next returned. The *Velero III* had in fact called again, but when Heinz went down to the bay the ship had sailed and there was no sign of the expected supplies. Friedrich told Heinz, however, that the Baroness had been invited on board the yacht and had, apparently, left with a number of presents including the canned milk for the Wittmer baby. According to Margret, when Heinz inquired about their supplies the Baroness gave him a can of milk and, according to Dore, also sent some shabby old blankets to Margret.

However, the Baroness may not have been the culprit on this occasion for Fred Ziesenhenne later wrote in his diary that 'we noticed an unusually high number of condensed milk cans in Dr. Ritter's trash dump.'

Nevertheless, the Baroness seems to have headed off some visitors who wanted especially to visit the Wittmers. These were some Americans, the Johnsons, who arrived shortly after the *Velero III* left. Friedrich told Heinz, who related it to Margret, that Mrs Johnson had particularly wanted to see young Rolf, for his birth on a remote Pacific island had received some publicity. Heinz deduced that the Baroness and or Philippson had encountered the Johnsons on the beach and persuaded them that the walk up to the Wittmers' house was far too long and arduous. He was convinced that the Baroness purloined presents that were intended for them. Heinz was so incensed that he wrote to Allan Hancock on the subject, on 26th February 1933. He was not only concerned about the loss of the valuable cans of milk, but also worried by the suspicion that the Baroness had been using the Wittmer baby as a ruse to ask for supplies, which she then kept for herself.

Heinz Wittmer also believed that the Baroness was in some way involved in the loss of his little boat. He had kept it at Black Beach and one day it was gone. It could not have been washed out to sea and it was unlikely that it had been stolen by visiting yachtsmen. The Baroness could not have stolen the boat, because she would have been discovered as the thief if she had used it. It was much more likely that she had ordered the boat to be destroyed. This suspicion was increased by the elaborate rigmarole which the Baroness produced to account for its disappearance. She maintained that the boat had been stolen by English yachtsmen, that it had been bought from them by a Frenchman in Panama and that this man had paddled it all the way to Chatham Island – a matter of some eight hundred miles – where the boat was to be found.

The incident of the stolen boat, which was a very serious loss to the Wittmers, led Heinz, with the help of Friedrich Ritter, to write to the Ecuadorian authorities. In his report he recounted the theft of his boat and then gave a more general description of the Baroness's activities. According to Dore, he requested that a medical expert should be sent to Floreana to examine the Baroness's mental condition. Apparently he believed that, although distressing, 'her infirmity was nothing more serious than acute hysteria'.

* * *

Later in the year, another incident blew up, again concerning a wealthy visitor to the island and, especially, gifts left for the settlers. Not unnaturally, such gifts were greatly valued by the inhabitants of Floreana. Friedrich and Dore particularly had benefited from the equipment that had been left for them by visiting ships. The wheelbarrow that Friedrich had used so effectively in clearing the ground for the garden at Friedo, the dynamite that he had also employed for this task (as well as for attempting to assassinate the demon boar) and the rifle that Allan Hancock had given him, had dramatically changed their way of life. Other choice gifts, such as canned milk, butter and sardines, were saved to be used during the traditional festivals, like Christmas and New Year, which were particularly special for the Wittmers. Even abandoned or forgotten objects could become treasured possessions. A bucket left on the shore by a passing ship would seem like a miracle.

One suspects that Friedrich even advertised some of his wants, for he listed in a magazine article, published in the

Atlantic Monthly in late 1931, some of the items that were still needed at Friedo. One much-desired object mentioned in the article was a cooking stove. The obliging Allan Hancock read the article and brought Dore just such a stove on his visit in January 1932. A later visitor to the island discovered that Friedrich even kept an account book in which he listed his acquisitions and entered items that he would ask visiting yachtsmen to bring for him. The Baroness also used a fairly broad hint in her notice on the shore in which she referred to '... all the good things friends have brought us when they passed'. It is almost as though the Floreana settlers had evolved their own Cargo Cult, with wealthy American yachtsmen in the role of the divine beings that brought the much-desired cargo.

The wealth of some of these visitors made them as near divine as is possible for mortal beings – at least on Floreana in the early 1930s. In addition to Allan Hancock, there was Eugene McDonald: he was founder and chairman of the Zenith Radio Corporation, which achieved annual sales of one hundred and fifty million dollars, as well as being explorer, yachtsman and author. Vincent Astor was another such; he was head of the American branch of the Astor family and was estimated to be worth between one and two hundred million dollars. He too was a keen yachtsman as well as an aviator, racing motorist, amateur zoologist and a director of many companies.

It was, in fact, Vincent Astor, in his luxury yacht *Nourmahal*, who precipitated the next conflict between the settlers. Dore and Friedrich, who had a much better view of the sea than did the Wittmers, first spotted the beautiful white motor-yacht, together with a smaller craft – a fishing boat. The fishing boat dropped anchor first and the watchers up at Friedo saw it put out a rowing-boat which stopped for a few moments at the yacht and then returned. They then saw the yacht move to Black Beach and a motor-boat put ashore. They prepared to receive Vincent Astor and his party within about half an hour – the time for the relatively short climb up from Black Beach. Friedrich walked down to meet the Astor party while Dore stayed behind to feed Burro. They had been sorting papayas when the ship was spotted and Dore was worried that he had not had his breakfast.

Dore was very proud that Burro had been a particular favourite of Vincent Astor's on his earlier visits. He called the donkey the 'Caruso of Floreana' because of the deep bray with which it announced the approach of visitors to Friedo.

Shortly after Burro had made his announcement, Friedrich appeared propelling a new wheelbarrow that had been brought for him. Behind were Vincent Astor himself and his party from the yacht. After greeting Dore, the yacht owner showed his friends around Friedo, for he was an old friend and, according to Dore, 'took a special pleasure in doing the honours in our stead'.

Vincent Astor told Dore and Friedrich that he had received a letter inviting him to visit the Hacienda Paradiso, but did not feel inclined to accept (one suspects partly as a result of some persuasion from Dore and Friedrich). Some of the guests seemed disappointed at this, for a visit to the Empress of Floreana would, no doubt, have been most entertaining for them. Before the matter could be resolved, however, fresh visitors arrived: the *padrone* of Isabela and his young wife. He had come to ask Dr Ritter to attend his wife.

The fresh visitors told the company that as they landed at Post Office Bay a young man approached them, in an agitated state, and asked their boatman if he could take him to the *Nourmahal*. The young man appeared so distressed that they had thought he was in serious trouble and was seeking assistance. The young man appears to have been Philippson. He was frantically waving a letter, which he was most anxious to deliver to Vincent Astor's yacht. Unfortunately, the *Nourmahal* moved off to Black Beach bay before Philippson could hand up his letter. Philippson was in a dreadful state when he realized that he could not deliver the letter: 'if he had been agitated before, he was in a frenzy now'.

The *padrone* told the company at Friedo that Philippson had insisted on being allowed aboard the fishing boat and taken to Black Beach to deliver his letter to the yacht. The letter was obviously another invitation from the Baroness, who must have been particularly anxious not to allow this millionaire to escape as had the previous one.

Vincent Astor and his party did not, it appears, visit the Hacienda Paradiso. Instead they took Dore and Friedrich back on board for an evening meal. The *Nourmahal* left soon after they disembarked. On their way back to Friedo Dore and Friedrich saw the lights of the yacht moving steadily away into the darkness.

Philippson appeared at Friedo early the next morning. Dore says that they were not pleased to see him 'but went towards him with a polite word of greeting, which he scarcely returned'. According to Dore, Philippson pushed past her and walked into the house. He looked around the veranda and even walked into the cage where he stood in apparent perplexity.

Dore and Friedrich evidently thought that Philippson had gone quite mad. His 'face was white with a kind of suppressed fury and he seemed to be holding himself in check with all his strength. Suddenly the bonds of self-control snapped, and gripping the edge of the table tightly with both hands he burst into such a torrent of recrimination against us that it fairly took our breath away.' The substance of Philippson's abuse was entirely predictable. Friedrich and Dore had contrived to keep Vincent Astor and his guests away from the Baroness and, in particular, were responsible for the ignoring of her invitation to the recent yacht party.

Friedrich's denials caused a further avalanche of abuse. The young man's face was contorted with rage and he stepped towards Friedrich with his fist raised. However, Friedrich seems to have had the measure of the man: 'Madame's pimp did threaten me once with violence in a fit of temper because they had been snubbed at Astors.' According to Dore, Friedrich coolly stepped forward and 'took Philippson's upraised arm, looking him so powerfully in the eyes that the younger man, like a cowed animal, wilted before him, and took him to the gate, which Philippson, in his excitement had left wide open. Philippson went without another word.'

Dore's sympathies characteristically went out to the poor defeated young man. He appeared to her 'so dejected and somehow so lost'. Indeed he probably needed her sympathy, for his reception by the Baroness was likely to have been tempestuous, returning as he was, defeated and empty-handed.

The next day Heinz Wittmer called on his regular weekly visit to Friedo. He had heard of the latest goings-on. He told them that after failing to find evidence of gifts of foodstuffs at Friedo, the Baroness had sent Philippson down to the beach to look for the cache that she believed they had hidden. The Baroness, in fact, suspected that Dore and Friedrich had taken for themselves gifts that had been intended for all the settlers.

Margret, with her robust sense of humour, must have enjoyed Heinz's account of the proceedings at Friedo on the previous day. Either Heinz or she seems to have embroidered their accounts by giving the Baroness a part in the events. Margret afterwards wrote: 'After a short and acrimonious interview, he [Ritter] took Philippson by the scruff of his neck and threw him out. The Baroness hastily retreated, as he threatened to apply the same treatment to her.'

Immediately after the encounter with Philippson, Friedrich Ritter got to work with a machete to divert the path from the Hacienda Paradiso which ran past the gate at Friedo. He did this to avoid the necessity of the Baroness or her men passing within sight of Friedo on their way to the beach. Heinz Wittmer seems to have been very interested in Friedrich's path diversion, which no doubt was fully discussed with Frau Margret that evening.

The path diversion took some days of hard work to complete. Dore describes how one day Friedrich saw, as he was working, Philippson sitting in a most dejected manner on a lump of lava 'with his head bowed in both hands and his shoulders bent as though a fearful burden weighed upon them'. Friedrich seems to have felt fatherly compassion for the unhappy young man, but as Philippson did not look up, or move, for a couple of hours, he did not speak to him.

Philippson now was feeling the Baroness's displeasure as had his rival Lorenz before him.

Things were also not going well at Friedo at this time. Margret Wittmer recorded in her diary, on 23rd February 1933, that Lorenz told her that Dore was frequently hysterical and was being beaten by Friedrich Ritter. She also mentioned that Friedrich had hit Dore in the presence of Heinz and Harry Wittmer. Poor Dore would, no doubt, justify Friedrich's behaviour with some high-falutin' rigmarole as she had done in a letter, written in her own curious English, to Allan Hancock, a year earlier: 'Do you know the comedy of Shakespeare, "The Taming of the Stuborn"? Isn't it more than a comedy, isn't it the gate into heaven on earth? That is the truth, Captain, woman likes to be struck as to dominate the man. Shakespeare shows people that it not important who is right, man or woman. But woman must be silent at all and in every time and way recognize her master.'

* * *

Two or three weeks after the throwing out of Philippson, Heinz and Margret Wittmer received a sackful of mail and two crates of presents from their friends and families in Germany. Margret describes this as a red-letter day – certainly something for Heinz to recount on his next visit to Friedo.

Their mail came on the *San Cristóbal*, the old schooner *Manuel y Cobos* under another name, which was now running fairly regularly from Chatham Island to various others in the archipelago. The Baroness did not manage to get her hands on their mail and the Wittmers were overjoyed to receive so many things. There were books, seeds, a razor, cloth, curtains, kitchen knives and a flat iron, as well as Quaker oats, chocolates and some cigars for Heinz.

There were also newspapers in that mail with lots of red lines marked on them. Heinz read the headlines to the impatient Margret and Harry. 'Revolution on Pacific Island ... Woman Proclaims Herself Empress ... Local Opposition Imprisoned', 'Baroness Seizes Control of Galapagos Islands'. Margret read: 'Dr. Friedrich Ritter, the former German dentist who opposed her reign of terror, has been captured and put in chains . . .'

The Baroness was, in fact, successfully eclipsing 'Robinson auf der Galapagos' in the newspaper headlines of the world: by the simple process of anonymously supplying the copy for the fantastic stories about the 'Pirate Queen of the Galapagos' and the 'Empress of Floreana'. This stratagem not only satisfied her megalomania and hatred of Dr Ritter, but also stimulated the curiosity of wealthy yacht owners sufficiently to visit her 'court', bearing longed-for supplies. It even yielded postal marriage proposals.

* * *

The increased hostility of the Baroness towards Dore and Friedrich was swiftly followed by a further deterioration in her relations with the Wittmer family. According to Dore, Heinz Wittmer was involved in a scene at the Hacienda Paradiso about the disappearance of his boat. The Baroness attempted to implicate Dore and Friedrich, and nearly involved them in a quarrel with Heinz Wittmer. Heinz became convinced, however, that it was indeed the Baroness who engineered the destruction of his little craft and was responsible for a succession of thefts of their goods. He forbade Margret to have any further dealings with the Baroness.

Shortly afterwards two notices appeared on the shore, pinned to the famous barrel that had long been used by seafarers to leave and collect their mail. The notices were written in German and signed by the Baroness. One accused both Friedrich and Dore of having slandered the Baroness, and Friedrich of having withheld medical attention when it was requested of him. Dore denied that such a request was ever made. The second notice accused Heinz Wittmer of trespassing upon the Baroness's property and of falsely accusing her, Philippson and Lorenz of purloining his goods.

Beside these notices was a third, advertising a need for four hundred sheets of corrugated iron and forty window frames.

The Baroness was evidently contemplating a dramatic extension of the Hacienda Paradiso.

The Baroness's advertising and press articles did, in fact, produce some effects, for Margret Wittmer recorded in her diary that on 22nd February 1933 'a Herr Rader and a Herr Vinzenz from Santa Cruz' had called at Floreana. 'Rader has actually come here to offer, in all seriousness, Madame his services as architect in the erection of the hotel. Madame falls for it to the extent of examining and discussing plans.'

Dore also referred to Herr Rader's visit in a letter to Allan Hancock, in which she is clearly smarting from some very effective, malicious sallies by her enemy, the Baroness:

Friedo, June 1933.

Dear Captain Hancock!

Hoping that you received our letter meanwhile, I will continue and complete this letter. Maybe you missed the personal details you are interested in. Here they are: My finger healed without any complication without pain; the inflammation of my eyelids is finished, but they rest a little swollen, and my mouth? Well, it is teethless! The toothaches came by eating candy, says the doctor. Who will contradict?

Painful for us rest the affair with the madame. Her hate turned against me (only). She likes to dirty my repute. She read in your book (she tells, she got it from you under the condition, telling nobody of this gift) 'Dore was soiled'. She calls that the biggest idea of your book. Now she believes, she had the right to dirty my repute.

We have been visited by the 'mysterious' man of Indefatigable, Mr Reader, of whom it is said that he founds joint stocks, of which he is the actor. When the money he got is finished, then he goes into another country. So he has been in Argentina, Chile and now he is here. This man offers himself as the architect to build the hotel the madame is planning again.

The whole affair is very painful and I suffer if visitors come who speak at first with this woman and then look for dirt and the soiled Dore and the unhospitality of Ritters. By that I lost my ingenuousness.

But I hope this disturbance will go over soon and meanwhile we do our daily work as usual.

I sent to you 2 stories and with this letter 3 others and – I must confess it, they are written only for intellectual people. What I wrote before, it must be changed.

This I will uphold that one cannot given the mass only candy – and people's desires cannot be the reason to give them what they like, and the task for the intellectual people is to be the master of the others.

But I will admit that it cannot be given to the mass all what is found by thinkers. 'People likes to blacken the radiancy and to drag through the dirt the sublime.' People is like the everyday and 'protect from the everyday all, what is sacred to you, because it would be covered with dust'.

I regret that I have not found a heading for the first 2 stories. I do not like to call them in a sensational manner and therefore I would superscribe the one, only – Gertrud – and the 'Eda-story' – The Route into the Solitude.

How I told you all what press me I must form into stories. By that each one is an insight into my soul, and so I beg for understanding.

In remembering of all your kindness I am

Yours

DORE KOERWEIN STRAUCH

Dore was, in fact, a prolific writer. She wrote frequent, very long letters and a number of short stories – none of which was ever published. Some of them are rather inconsequential tales about the animals on Floreana. The 'Gertrud' to which Dore referred in her letter was one of her favourite fictional creations. 'Gertrud' bears a striking resemblance to Dore. She too served 'harmonic' food from 'Nirosta' ware and, in one story, had her whole life changed by accidentally finding and reading a book on philosophy written by the famous Dr Ritter. This book was also fictional, for Friedrich's philosophical works were never published.

Dore's writings at this time provide a clear picture of her lonely life at Friedo in which she found comfort in writing about the animals that she saw about her and in the fantasy of her intellectual life with her Nietzschean superman. The Baroness too must have been sustained by her fantasies of the grand hotel for millionaire guests, which would, in fact, never materialize. Only the Wittmers in their down-to-earth way were achieving their more limited goal of creating their little Teutonic farm in the wilderness.

10
THE HUNTING OF ADONIS

On 30th May 1933 the Governor of the Galapagos Islands, together with an interpreter and an escort of seven soldiers, landed on Floreana. The interpreter was none other than Knud Arends, the former partner in the fishing enterprises on Floreana who had so impressed Dore by his good looks and who had nearly lost his life in his futile search for Captain Bruuns on Isabela.

The visit of the Governor was in response to the appeals of Friedrich Ritter and Heinz Wittmer for redress against the wrongs they had suffered at the hands of the Baroness. No doubt he also wanted to investigate the source of all the extraordinary rumours that were circulating through the archipelago. The Governor called first at Friedo. He assured Friedrich and Dore of their right to live at Friedo for as long as they wished, and also listened to a long and detailed account from Friedrich of the several enormities which had occurred since the arrival of the Baroness.

When the Governor called at the Hacienda Paradiso he found that the Baroness had gone flamingo hunting. She had apparently conceived the idea of starting a zoo of Floreana fauna and was seeking some specimens of the lovely birds, most probably on a lagoon at the northern end of the island.

The Governor and his interpreter and escort left to visit some other islands and then returned a few days later. Margret Wittmer records her astonishment at the Governor's decision to hold his Court of Enquiry at the Hacienda Paradiso. Margret surmised that the Baroness had probably provided the Ecuadorian authorities with her own version of recent affairs and had probably impressed them with her grandiose plans for the development of tourism of Floreana. Her European title would also not have been without attractions in this remote outpost of South America.

Both Dore and Margret were very put out when they learned that the Baroness had been granted a title to four square miles of land for as long as she lived on Floreana. Dore claimed that she had obtained this grant 'at the price of a more than Arabian night – as she herself afterwards boasted – and the representative of Ecuador had left the next day in high feather'. She had also won her dispute with the Wittmers about access to their spring, which was to be accessible to all of the settlers. The Governor had granted the Wittmers fifty acres, and another fifty to Friedrich Ritter – a far smaller area than that granted to the Baroness. Both Dore and Margret felt that the Baroness had outwitted them and were furious at her easy victory. Their cynicism was increased by the news that the Governor had invited the Baroness to stay with him for a few weeks' holiday on Chatham Island. However, the Wittmers must have been grateful for the peaceful interlude which the Baroness's absence would give them.

The news of the Baroness's departure was, on the other hand, received with some alarm by Friedrich Ritter. He was worried that the Governor would show the Baroness his letter of complaint about the Estampa-Franke affair and that she would return to the island thirsting for revenge. Margret Wittmer wrote in her diary: 'The excitement mounts so high that there are scenes between Dr. Ritter and Frau Koerwin.'

On 7th June the Baroness returned, with Philippson, from her visit to Chatham Island, bringing with her: two dogs, ten chickens, a she-donkey and foals, and Knud Arends, the handsome Danish friend of Captain Bruuns, now acting as the Governor's interpreter. Arends was, apparently, out of work and was to be employed as the Baroness's 'gamekeeper' at a salary of 90 sucres per month. One of his first duties was to call on the Wittmers to inform them that one of the Baroness's donkeys had escaped and to request Heinz not to shoot it. Margret took quite a liking to Knud Arends. She learned from him that he was taking a job with the Baroness to raise enough money to pay his fare back to Denmark.

Dore was excited by the return of the Dane to the island. She had admired the strength of his friendship for Captain Bruuns and, no doubt, looked forward to some enjoyable chats about their early days on Floreana. But Arends did not go to Friedo and Dore could only glean news of him from Rudolf Lorenz during his occasional and surreptitious visits, or from Heinz Wittmer during his weekly call. She no doubt learned from Heinz that Arends was to be the Baroness's 'gamekeeper' and how much he was to be paid for the job.

Despite the breakdown of relations between the inhabitants of Friedo and the Hacienda Paradiso, Dore seems to have been rather well-informed about the Baroness's relations with her three male companions. Knud Arends was the current favourite. Almost every day the Baroness went hunting with him, although, according to Dore, they frequently returned with 'no bag at all, sometimes with only a piece or two'. Philippson, on the other hand, 'retained the position of husband at night ...' Philippson appears to have been still deeply in love with the Baroness and 'would have followed her unquestioningly into the bottomless pit'. He was filled with jealousy at the Baroness's attentions to Arends and on several occasions burst into a paroxysm of rage like the one that Friedrich and Dore had witnessed at Friedo. In one terrible scene the Baroness had cut him across the face with her riding whip. On another occasion she flung a bowl of boiling soup in his face, scalding him badly, and left for a hunting expedition without waiting to discover whether she had injured his eyes.

Rudolf Lorenz was still the labourer at the Hacienda. Life for him had become increasingly horrible. He was clearly ill, exhausted by his toils with little time for rest and no will-power to resist; he appears to have abandoned any hope of escaping from the nightmarish life he led at the hands of the Baroness. Even worse, Robert Philippson too now vented his fury on Lorenz. Dore described how Philippson 'stood over the toiler like a brutal overseer. When Lorenz flagged, he beat him savagely – he allowed him neither food nor drink; he treated him as he must have longed to treat the stranger, Arends.'

In the midst of this turmoil the Baroness still acted out her role as the Empress of Floreana to the visitors who were attracted by her extraordinary reputation and were guided to the Hacienda Paradiso by the notice on the shore at Post Office Bay. She no longer met visitors in the garden of the Hacienda, but had ordered that they should be first received by one or other of her men. If audience was granted, visitors were ushered into her presence in the carpet- and silk-hung room in her corrugated-iron palace. There she reclined on her couch in one or other of her bizarre outfits, most frequently in riding costume with her whip in her hand. She seems to have impressed many of her visitors, as even Dore was forced to admit.

Occasionally, however, things did not go well for the Baroness. Dore recounts, with considerable relish, how one party of visitors to the Hacienda caught her in some disarray and certainly not in her role of Empress of the island. She was, rather unexpectedly, busily engaged in laundering her clothes, presumably because she would not trust her delicate silk garments to the rough male attentions of her entourage. One imagines, however, that the Baroness was equal to this situation and most probably, after a strategic retreat, emerged with the panache that she possessed in such abundance.

Dore derived some satisfaction from the Baroness's apparent shortage of bleach for her hair. By this time she was no longer a spectacular platinum blonde, but had regressed to her natural dark hair. Even so, Dore, who could be surprisingly objective in matters concerning her enemy, was forced to admit that her dark hair suited her at least as well. However, Dore's appreciation of the Baroness was strictly limited. To her, she was the personification of evil, an evil as intense as that portrayed in the book to which the Baroness was inseparably attached: *The Picture of Dorian Gray*.

It is very striking that of all literature the Baroness should have chosen, as her talisman, something so singularly appropriate as Oscar Wilde's study of youth and corruption. It may have been, of course, that for the Baroness it was merely a symbol: sophisticated, beautiful, cruel and trailing a scandalous reputation. But other books could have supplied that kind of image. It is almost as if her obsession with *The Picture of Dorian Gray* was a professional interest. After all, she was in the trade: she knew a good deal about the ruining of handsome young men, and Wilde's portrayal of the character of Lord Henry Wotton must have seemed rather familiar. He too reclined on a divan and had a flair for corrupting the young and beautiful. His cynical wit must have captivated the Baroness and provided her with a model for her undoubted talents as an actress. Furthermore, in Wilde's book she could see evil cloaked in beauty which, for her, perhaps transformed her own squalid cruelty.

The next person on whom the Baroness was to practise her artistry was delivered to her by a humble fishing boat from Santa Cruz. The skipper, Trygve Nuggerud, had brought a young German journalist, Werner Boeckmann. He had come to follow up the numerous stories that were circulating in the world's press about the excitements on Floreana.

Boeckmann landed at Black Beach and, according to Dore, climbed up to Friedo. As it was quite late in the afternoon, Dore and Friedrich asked him to spend the night with them. Boeckmann accepted their invitation and was given the usual conducted tour of Friedo.

While Dore and Friedrich were talking to the young journalist in the garden, Dore noticed, to her surprise, Knud Arends standing at the fence. She and Friedrich greeted him cordially, but Arends seemed very uneasy. Obviously he was there against the Baroness's orders and was anxious not to be discovered by her in such a compromising situation. He asked whether it was Nuggerud's boat that was anchored at Black

Beach. They told him that it was and attempted a friendly conversation, inviting him to come into the garden of Friedo. Before he could reply they heard a cough from the bushes near the fence. It was the Baroness. Dore noticed 'something so sinister in her expression and in her attitude that a cold chill ran down my back'. Without a word the Baroness turned away and Arends followed her silently.

The following morning Boeckmann visited the Hacienda Paradiso – an easy victim. He appears to have succumbed quickly to the Baroness's charms, for Dore (who was becoming quite an expert in this matter), recognized the characteristic signs of infatuation with the Empress of Floreana.

The Baroness apparently tried to prevent Boeckmann from calling on the Wittmers and, according to Dore, directed him not to the Wittmer caves, but to some other ones. The Baroness then invented a story about some recent flooding that made it impossible for them to reach the Wittmers' house at the caves. He got there in the end, because Margret records his visit.

Boeckmann returned to the boat that day (the *San Cristóbal* and not Nuggerud's, according to Margret Wittmer) and left the island. Shortly after his departure Margret and Heinz Wittmer heard the sounds of unusual activity coming from the direction of the Hacienda Paradiso. Each day all had been silence, but at dusk 'everything sprang to life. Trees were felled and wood chopped under the faint light of lamps, to the accompaniment of singing and laughter. The dawn brought silence again, the same strange silence which lasted all day.'

The Wittmers had no idea what was happening at the Hacienda Paradiso. Young Harry Wittmer made the unlikely suggestion that they might be searching for buried treasure, although it is not clear why this could not be carried out by daylight. The nightly disturbances lasted until the return of Boeckmann, when they ceased as abruptly as they had begun.

Herr Boeckmann had returned on the *San Cristóbal*,

bringing with him his brother-in-law, Herr Linde. Accompanying them was an armed soldier who seems to have been their bodyguard. Margret wondered from whom the soldier was protecting Boeckmann and Linde. Had the Baroness warned them against possible violence from the other settlers or had Boeckmann assessed her more shrewdly than Dore had supposed? According to Dore he had merely come to bring the mail.

Dore had watched the *San Cristóbal* put in at Black Beach, from her vantage point up at Friedo. She says, again, that she felt a strong feeling of apprehension. She seems to have had an almost superstitious dread of the ship. This 'ancient, sinful craft', as she called it, had 'a kind of heavy stealthiness that made her look so sinister and guilty'. Dore came to believe that the old *Manuel y Cobos* was a 'bird of ill-omen' that brought with her unhappiness and evil.

Surprisingly, in view of Dore's previous belief that Boeckmann was infatuated with the Baroness, the young journalist came first to Friedo with his brother-in-law and the Ecuadorian soldier. Dore was quite overwhelmed by the masculine charms of Herr Linde. 'I think I have never seen a handsomer young man. I took his age to be about the latter twenties: he was very tall and had wavy, blond hair, and the bluest eyes imaginable.' Here was someone worthy of the Baroness's attentions, although Dore felt that 'he was so much the reverse of the good-looking weaklings with whom the Baroness surrounded herself, that I was sure he would not fall a victim to her wiles'.

The two brothers-in-law and the Ecuadorian soldier accepted Friedrich's invitation to stay at Friedo until the *San Cristóbal* came to pick them up after a few days.

In the morning, which, in September, would probably have been cool and misty, Boeckmann, Linde and the soldier left to visit the Baroness and then go on to see the Wittmers. When the trio arrived at the Hacienda Paradiso they found, as they afterwards related, a scene of domestic harmony. Rudolf Lorenz and Robert Philippson were darning their evening suits, which had attracted the attention of the Floreana moths, Knud Arends was working in the garden and the Baroness was at her washing.

The visitors were invited to lunch at the Hacienda. Afterwards they expressed their intention of calling on the Wittmers and then returning to Friedo for supper. The Baroness seems to have been incensed by this and insisted that the visitors should join her and her party in a hunting expedition. According to Dore's account, the trio paid their call on the Wittmers and then returned to the Hacienda Paradiso at about four o'clock. They left for the expedition, with only a couple of hours of daylight remaining, with the Baroness practising all her charms on Herr Linde and, no doubt, looking forward to showing off her marksmanship to this extremely attractive visitor. Though outwardly calm, the Baroness was probably very cross indeed. After all, she was competing not very successfully with Friedo and the Wittmers, setting off late in the afternoon for a hunting expedition and not, apparently, making great headway with Herr Linde.

Over at Friedo, Dore had spent the day at her usual work and had prepared a splendid supper for her visitors. She was anxious to show just what the garden of Friedo could produce and was determined to give them the best meal that she could. She might also, no doubt, have written some letters. To this day the inhabitants of the Galapagos busily scribble when there is a chance of having mail posted by visitors.

As evening approached and there was no sign of their guests, Dore and Friedrich ate the splendid supper by themselves. They prepared beds for the visitors and, when they still did not appear, went to bed themselves.

Earlier that evening Margret Wittmer was bathing young Rolf when she heard running footsteps outside. Rudolf Lorenz burst in and asked her if he could borrow a water-bag. He told her that there had been a shooting accident and that Knud Arends had been shot by the Ecuadorian soldier. Arends was in terrible pain and the Baroness thought that a cool water-bag might help to ease his pain. Arends had, apparently, been shot in the stomach.

Dore and Friedrich were also surprised from their sleep by the sound of running footsteps. It was Werner Boeckmann. He told them the news and begged Friedrich to come with him to attend to Arends's wounds. According to Dore, Friedrich hesitated because, remembering the Lorenz episode, he was not sure if he would be welcomed by the Baroness. Boeckmann agreed that the Baroness had not wanted to call in Dr Ritter, but, nevertheless, insisted that he should come with him at once to Arends.

Friedrich left with his instruments and limited medical supplies. Dore recounts how she returned to her bed in the 'cage' and lay worrying amidst the clamour of the long Floreana night. She wondered how the accident had happened and worried that Friedrich might be in danger. She contemplated trying to follow him, but realized that with her lame leg they might return whilst she was out by herself in the darkness.

Eventually, Friedrich, Boeckmann, Linde and the soldier returned to Friedo, and Dore learned how the Baroness had persuaded the visitors to join her hunting party on the previous afternoon. When they had arrived on the pampas there were no herds in sight, for in the late afternoon the animals were away on the plain.

Apparently the Baroness arranged the disposition of the hunters in preparation for the return of the herds. Dore was told that 'the three visitors and Arends were to stay together in a group, Philippson was posted at a considerable distance away; she herself [the Baroness] took up a position at an angle from Philippson some fifty yards further down the field. The herd, when it appeared, stood in a compact group at an equal distance from all of them, some hundred yards ahead.'

The hunters were armed with a rather motley collection of weapons. The Baroness had a light-calibre weapon, Arends and the soldier had rifles, the two young Germans had revolvers. It had been agreed that the Baroness would pick out their victim and would give the order to fire. Then: 'The signal came.

Two shots rang out, one from the Ecuadorian's rifle. Meanwhile, the positions of the four young men had altered slightly, Arends having moved up to a position practically abreast of the journalist's friend. Philippson had stayed where he was, well off to one side.'

The herd scattered, with no animal shot, but Arends staggered and fell. The two young Germans and the soldier gathered around the wounded man and Philippson ran up to the group. According to the story that was related to Dore, the Baroness seemed unconcerned and wandered quite calmly towards the group. When she was told it was Arends that was shot she appeared greatly surprised and, after apparently overcoming her astonishment, flung herself on to the ground embracing him and murmuring endearments.

The Baroness then accused Boeckmann of shooting Arends, but he showed that his revolver had not been fired. The Baroness then turned on the Ecuadorian soldier insisting that his bullet had ricocheted. It was at this point that Boeckmann, overcoming the Baroness's objections, ran to fetch Dr Ritter. When he arrived, Friedrich found that the bullet had grazed Arends's arm and penetrated the abdomen; he decreed that Arends could not be moved, due to the danger of peritonitis. The man would have to lie out in the open until his condition had improved enough for him to be moved. The Baroness immediately insisted that she would stay with Arends and would nurse him, never leaving his side until he could be moved.

Friedrich then turned his mind to the question of who had shot Arends. After listening to the account of the incident, Friedrich decided that, from the angle of the shot, it could not have been fired by the Ecuadorian. Furthermore, the wound was not such that it could have been caused by a revolver or a service rifle. When the Baroness heard this, according to the story told to Dore, she flung away her weapon and fell upon Arends with fresh protestations of love and remorse. Her subsequent explanations were so confused and contradictory that they left no doubt in the minds of at least Friedrich and Boeckmann that it was the Baroness who had fired the shot which had wounded Arends. They also believed that it was not her intention to shoot him at all, but to wound the Adonis, Linde.

Margret's account of the proceedings that were related to her, later that afternoon, essentially agrees with Dore's story. She recalls that Linde told her that when walking to the hunt, the Baroness had told him she liked to shoot animals in the legs* and then nurse them – the same story with which the Baroness had so shocked Dore during her disastrous luncheon party at Friedo. Linde then told Margret and Heinz that it was his belief that the Baroness had intended to shoot him. He explained that Arends had been standing near to him and had jumped in front of him to fire, so that the bullet intended for his leg had gone into Arends's stomach. Linde believed that it was he that the Baroness had wanted to nurse, after wounding him, and not Arends at all.

It was five days before the *San Cristóbal* returned to Floreana to pick up Boeckmann and Linde. Dore records that they were difficult days. The party at Friedo were nervous and ill at ease. The two young Germans were anxious to get off the island and the Ecuadorian soldier was worried about the Baroness's accusation that he had shot Arends.

Philippson called each day at Friedo to give an account of Arends's progress. On the day after the shooting, Dore concealed herself behind a curtain, the better to watch Philippson when faced by Friedrich and the three visitors. He evidently assumed the role of a tragic husband and continued to maintain that it was not the Baroness who had shot Arends in the stomach. When the others persisted with the evidence that the Baroness had fired the shot, Philippson became extremely distressed and worried how he would break the news to his 'wife'. From behind her curtain, Dore realized the intensity and sincerity of Philippson's love for the Baroness.

When the *San Cristóbal* was sighted, preparations were made to get Arends aboard the ship. They made a primitive stretcher out of a ladder with a mattress tied to it and took it

* Friedrich, on the other hand, wrote: 'She always shot at a particular part of the belly so as not to injure the intestines and other organs.'

up to the pampas in the moonlight, for it was after dusk and the ship had to sail that night. The officers from the ship accompanied the party to collect Arends. The Baroness had brought along Lorenz, to accompany Arends on board ship and to the hospital in Guayaquil. The officer insisted, however, in taking someone who had been a witness to the shooting, should there be an investigation, and decreed that Philippson should accompany Arends on board his ship.

The Baroness did not wish Philippson to leave. The others could not discover whether this was due to jealousy or to the fact that the Baroness was frightened at being left alone with Lorenz.

Lorenz, too, created a scene, and, according to Dore 'burst into an insane frenzy of protest at not being allowed to go as Arends' escort. He raved as though his life depended upon his getting off the island, and as though this were the only chance of his ever doing so. He wept, he cursed, he implored the man on his knees to take him.' Such was the state to which the domination of the Baroness had reduced this young and handsome man whom she had ruined in Paris and who had been her favourite when she first arrived on Floreana.

There was one moment of farce – when Lorenz had to exchange his suit with Philippson. They were apparently down to only one respectable suit between the two of them.

Dore noticed, with amazement, that the Baroness was completely changed in her manner as they carried Arends down to the beach. 'She was almost humble. She had assumed the expression of a penitent and had adopted every gesture and inflection to the exigencies of this new role ... She came to me with the expression of a holy martyr and held out her hand in silence.' The Baroness looked drawn and ten years older than usual. Her face was lined, for it was not camouflaged with the make-up that belied her forty-four years.

The Baroness seems to have been especially worried about the effects that the news of her escapade might have on Allan Hancock, for she wrote the following letter to him on 2nd October 1934:

Dear Sir,

In contrary of what I asked you in my last letter, please dont make any purchases on my account. An accident has happened, the score of my sufferings seems not yet complete. A young man Mr. Arends, who works and lives with us, has been hurt in the stomach by a bullet, how we dont know, as the shot parted in the opposite direction from where the young man was standing. Dr Ritter who was kind enough to attend him, says that he is out of danger, yet I prefer that Mr. Arends goes to Guayaquil in order to be roentgonized [X-rayed] and if it is necessary the bullet extracted. As this will take all the rest of my resources, we cannot think of our comfort but have to do all to get Mr. Arends right again.

Hoping that this letter finds you in the best of health, with my kind regards to Mr. Swett. I remain

Yours very respectfully

BARONESS WAGNER

* * *

The Baroness assumed many roles during her time on Floreana: libertine, aristocrat, artist, intellectual, martyr and thief. At first sight, she appears a ridiculous but also rather sinister figure in these roles, a bizarre product of the decadence that followed the First World War. It might also be instructive to see her, however, as a figure in a much older tradition which has flowed through the cultural history of Europe like an underground stream, a representative of what Norman Cohn has called 'the élite of amoral supermen'. This élite emerged as long ago as the thirteenth century and subsequently appeared in many guises. In the fourteenth century it crystallized in the form of the heresy of the Free Spirit, a movement which Cohn describes as 'quasi-mystical anarchism – an affirmation of freedom so reckless and unqualified that it amounted to a total denial of every kind of restraint and limitation'.

For historians, the heresy of the Free Spirit is a mysterious and perplexing phenomenon. In the fourteenth century it spread widely in Western Europe and persisted in many different forms, including the Ranters of Cromwellian England and the nihilism of Jean-Antoine Boullan and his sect in the mid-nineteenth century, and was an element, Cohn believes, in the attitudes of the bohemian intelligentsia of the Baroness's time, who were heavily influenced by the writings of Nietzsche.

The Baroness seems to conform exactly to the pattern of those early heretics. Hakon Mielche describes how she spoke to him of her religious experiences during her voyage from France. 'Her religion included most of the doctrines already known, plus one or two Wagner Bosquetian dogmas.' Her claim that she could perform miracles and that, on Floreana, she had caused water to flow from the lava rocks by a single blow of her fist, can be at least partly understood in this context.

Like the followers of the heresy, she was the leader of a group of disciples whom she totally dominated, as did adepts of the Free Spirit such as 'Sister Catherine', Marguerite Porete and Heilwijch Blomart in the fourteenth century.

The Baroness's ill-treatment of Lorenz and, later, of Philippson also paralleled the behaviour of some of the medieval mystical sects. It is recorded that the novices in at least one such sect were forced to dress in rags and to eat revolting food, and flagellation was a common practice in other sects. The disciples or novices were forced to react with blind obedience to the orders of their leader. However, when finally received into the sect they could often live in luxury and were liberated from all restraints; this was presumably a symbolic representation of their union with God or, in the case of the Baroness's followers, their sexual union with her. The Baroness's boast of shooting dogs and men and of afterwards healing and loving them has a similar symbolism.

A recurrent feature of the medieval mystical sects was the wearing of rich and costly costumes. As Norman Cohn emphasizes: 'By adopting noble robes in place of the beggars' rags a heretic symbolized his transformation from 'the lowest of mortals' into an élite which believed itself entitled to dominate the world.' The Baroness clearly intended to rule Floreana, and her various costumes, of which she took enormous care, seem to have been her version of the 'noble robes'. Her silk-covered couch would be the equivalent of the silver chair in which Heilwijch Blomart used to receive her disciples in fourteenth-century Brussels.

Sexual promiscuity was a constant feature of mystical sects, from the thirteenth century to the Ranters of seventeenth-century England, and was certainly paralleled by the behaviour of the Baroness and her followers on Floreana. It was held that by losing her virginity a woman would become more chaste. To the adepts the sexual act had a semi-mystical quality and was 'the delight of Paradise'.

The catechism used by a fourteenth-century mystical sect would have been equally appropriate for the Baroness.

> When a man has truly reached the great and high knowledge he is no longer bound to observe law or any command, for he has become one with God. God created all things to serve such a person, and all that God ever created is the property of such a man ... He shall take from all creatures as much as his nature desires and craves, and shall have no scruples of conscience about it, for all created things are his property ... A man whom all heaven serves, all people and creatures are indeed obliged to serve and to obey; and if any disobeys, it alone is guilty.

It was the misfortune of the other settlers on Floreana that in the eyes of the Baroness they were guilty.

11
THE SATANIC BOAR RETURNS

Soon after the departure of the *San Cristóbal* with Knud Arends and the two German visitors on board, the Baroness appeared with Rudolf Lorenz at the gate of Friedo. Dore was working in the garden at the time and Friedrich came to her with the news of the two callers from the Hacienda. Dore decided that they should remain out of sight, and both retreated into the house. Dore had evidently overcome the impulsive pang of forgiveness which she had experienced when the Baroness gave her performance of grief and remorse. In fact, it was quite a testimony to the Baroness's acting abilities that Dore had experienced this unexpected feeling at all.

As she went into the house, Dore could not refrain from a backward glance. The Baroness stood with Lorenz at her side. He carried a large yellow pumpkin, evidently a peace offering from the Baroness. After a carefully calculated interval, Dore went out to the gate, to find their unexpected visitors departed and the pumpkin left on the ground. She must have guessed, with considerable satisfaction, at the Baroness's displeasure at the rudeness of the inhabitants of Friedo.

However, the Baroness did not let this slight to her unexpected gesture of friendship pass without retribution. She chose an old enemy for her victim: Burro, the donkey which had so ruined her discourse on Parisian fashions during the disastrous luncheon party at Friedo.

Burro went missing shortly after the affair of the Baroness's pumpkin. Dore was surprised at his absence, for at that time of the year Burro usually preferred to spend the nights in his pen at Friedo than with his family out on the pampas.

Dore learned of the likely whereabouts of her donkey when Friedrich told her that the Baroness had waylaid him whilst he was on the way to the orange grove. The Baroness told Friedrich that there had been a stray donkey at the Hacienda Paradiso, and she wondered if it might possibly have come from Friedo. Whilst it was at the Hacienda, she said, they had of course used the donkey. Friedrich suggested that the Baroness should release it. If it was Burro it would find its way back to Friedo.

Burro returned shortly afterwards. Dore found him standing in his pen. He was no longer the Caruso of Floreana; his spirit had been broken and he refused to accept the leaves that Dore offered him. Dore saw that 'his soft grey fur had been literally sweated off, and the skin was raw and broken where the ropes had rubbed him till the blood came.'

It took many days of care and affection by Dore to begin to get Burro back to his former healthy state. Dore could not bring herself to tie him up, for she did not wish to curtail his family life. She later regretted this, because Burro disappeared once more and Dore never saw him again.

On Christmas Day Heinz Wittmer appeared at Friedo with a large tortoise as a present for Dore. It was tame, he told her, and was called Isidore. Dore was convinced by this unusual gift of a pet, and from his previous embarrassed behaviour, that Heinz Wittmer was somehow involved in Burro's disappearance.

Some months later, Dore learned from Heinz of the death of her much-loved old donkey. He told her that he had shot a marauding donkey in his garden one night, for, as Dore observed, 'Wittmer was not sentimental where despoilers of his plantation were concerned.' Only after he had shot the animal did Heinz realize that Burro had been his victim. He was very upset at this mistake and feared to tell Dore at the time. They subsequently learned from Lorenz that the Baroness had, in fact, lured Dore's donkey into the Wittmer plantation to its certain death. Thus did the Baroness avenge herself on Burro for interrupting her discourse at Friedo, and on Dore for her rejection of the Baroness's overtures after Knud Arends's wounding.

Dore seems not to have borne Heinz Wittmer any malice for his part in the death of Burro. Indeed it would have been difficult for her to have done so, for Friedrich himself was also involved in inadvertent donkey slaughter at this time. The cause of the trouble was Friedrich's old enemy, the satanic boar, which had returned to rampage once more through the garden at Friedo. This giant pig, which was nothing if not conservative, kept strictly to his old ways and reopened his previous trail of destruction – as their garden had been extended, this now ran right through its centre. Once again, Friedrich took to plotting the slaughter of this malignant beast. In the middle of the night he blazed away with his rifle into the sugar-canes. Needless to say he did not kill his almost indestructible enemy, but shot instead a female donkey. She had a foal with her, that Friedrich carried back on his shoulders to Dore, who lavished all her affection on the waif. She called him Fleck and adored him. She believed that he was Burro's son and the donkey that Friedrich had shot was Burro's mate, come to find him during his absence from the pampas. Friedrich was apparently very upset at this tragedy and continued with increasing hatred his long battle with the boar. Friedrich eventually triumphed. He devised yet another trap, what Dore called 'a clever and most murderous arrangement', consisting of a rifle with an automatic trip wire. Miraculously, it worked, and in the morning Friedrich discovered the body of his enemy lying in its path of destruction through the garden of Friedo.

Dore seems to have been totally obsessed by the image of this 'devil pig'. She afterwards believed that, having destroyed the demon in its porcine form, it assumed another guise, for 'only drought and misfortune, violence and murder followed the old boar's death ...' She may not have been far wrong in this fancy for, as subsequent events were to show, Friedrich's formidable enemy may have reached beyond the grave to accomplish Friedrich's destruction in a way that Dore could never have suspected.

* * *

The summer of 1934 was exceptionally hot and there was little rain. Drought developed in January and reduced Floreana to an ashen desert. The temperature reached 120°F. Animal corpses lay decaying on the ground, the vegetation was blasted by the intense heat and the island's springs dried almost to nothing.

'Heat such as we had never known on the island', Dore wrote, 'scorched and blasted every growing thing. The sun hung in a sky of brass, and at night the burning earth gave forth a heat as though a furnace blazed beneath its rocky surface. Strong plants withered up; leaves blackened on the trees. The spring that was the source of life at Friedo, had ceased to flow, and had become a thin trickle of water, wearily crawling over its dry bed.'

The rainy season had forsaken the Galapagos that year. The usual winds came, but now dry and hot, withering the plants still further and bringing down the banana trees in the garden at Friedo.

After the winds the island night became strangely silent, no longer filled with the usual cacophony of animal sounds. The thirsty animals remained mute and the dead ones gave off the stink of death amid clouds of flies.

The Wittmers' spring was almost dry and, at Friedo, Friedrich was contemplating distilling sea water and carrying it up for their meagre subsistence. Heinz Wittmer told Dore that things were worst of all at the Hacienda Paradiso. The animals were starving and thirsting and the Baroness's garden was a waste of withered vegetation. Heinz surmised that the Baroness, Lorenz and Philippson, who had returned to the island, must have been surviving on the food stores that they had brought with them.

Rudolf Lorenz was suffering acutely in the hot desolation. His desperation led him to Friedo and the Wittmer house to seek sympathy and help. Dore describes him as being 'terribly thin and gaunt, and ... so starved and ghastly that I wondered whether he had come to us to die.'

Lorenz told both Dore and Margret of fearful quarrels at the Hacienda. On one occasion he had apparently asked for money from the Baroness to enable him to get off the island. This she refused, because her funds were running low. She also refused to let him have his few personal possessions and locked them away from him. Lorenz suspected that she wanted to keep him prisoner to prevent him from revealing the truth about the Hacienda Paradiso. He complained that he was being beaten by Philippson, and Margret described the sounds of these beatings which reached the Wittmers at their new house near Watkins's caves.

It is difficult to understand why Rudolf Lorenz did not ask one or other of the visitors who came to Floreana at this time to take him away on their ships. There were, after all, quite a number of ships and boats calling at Floreana during this period of drought in the early months of 1934. The only explanation must be the total domination of this sick and weak-willed young man by the Baroness. He seems to have submitted to his ill-treatment with an almost fatalistic masochism.

Allan Hancock made two calls at Floreana at this time in the *Velero III* with his party of scientists and musicians. He arrived first in the third week of January 1934.

The party from the *Velero III* visited Friedo. They had with them a particularly important gift – some spare sets of false teeth. Dore was delighted with these and posed for a movie shot in which her broad smile revealed a set of gleaming white teeth. The event was subsequently reported in the American press beneath the headlines: 'Marine Expedition Headed by Dr. Schmitt calls on Dr. Ritter and Frau Koervin, New Teeth for the Pair.' The *Los Angeles Times* recorded: 'Both were toothless, and the Hancock party brought dental supplies with which Dr. Ritter, at one time a dentist, immediately set to provide sets of teeth for himself and Frau Koervin.'

After visiting Friedo, the *Velero III* party walked on to call on the Wittmers. They spent two hours there. They were now able to talk to Margret in English, for she had learned a little of the language, and conversed with Heinz in what Margret describes as 'that droll German of the Americans'. Captain Hancock had brought with him a package of baby clothes for little Rolf Wittmer. Margret was thrilled with the gift. Her happiness was so obvious that Fred Ziesenhenne recorded in his diary that night: 'There were tears in most everyone's eyes when they saw how happy Mrs. Wittmer was about the baby clothes.' Young Rolf was dressed in some of the clothes and 'with Dr. Schmitt directing in German Mr. Swett took a series of pictures about the home showing the attic and front room etc.'

Margret also told Allan Hancock that she was finding it difficult to feed her baby. According to Fred Ziesenhenne she 'showed how the child had sucked her down and that she wore padding in order to wear her dresses.' She also told the *Velero III* party that all she had received of the supplies that Captain Hancock had left on his last visit was three cans of milk and a blanket from Dr. Ritter. This confirmed Fred Ziesenhenne's earlier suspicion that Friedrich as well as the Baroness might have purloined the Wittmer supplies.

During his visit to the Wittmers the kindly Allan Hancock offered to help Heinz in a project which Margret described as 'the thing lying closest to Heinz's heart'. This was the exploration of the eastern side of Floreana. Heinz had long been interested in the possibility of finding a well on this unexplored part of the island, but had been unable to penetrate the dense thorny vegetation. According to Margret, the energetic and resourceful Heinz was contemplating extending his farm on to the eastern side of the island, perhaps to get away from his difficult neighbours.

The next morning Heinz was taken in the ship's motor-boat to explore the eastern side of Floreana, together with Friedrich Ritter and Waldo Schmitt. They discovered that there was no water on that side of the island, as had been reported ten years earlier by William Beebe in his book on the Galapagos.

The Baroness was also not forgotten by the generous Allan Hancock during this visit to Floreana. She achieved a long-cherished ambition – to appear in a film. Allan Hancock had on board a Hollywood professional, Emory Johnson, who, to Dore's astonishment, agreed to make a film about the Baroness. She and Philippson acted out a scenario in which the Baroness appeared as a pirate. The piracy theme seems to have resulted from one of the Baroness's publicity stunts. She had, apparently, engineered a sensational press story involving a honeymoon couple who, while cruising through the archipelago, had been put down on Floreana. According to the story, which even appeared in some European newspapers, the honeymooners were a Peruvian couple, Pablo Rolando and Rosa Fernandez, who had departed from Lima on the steamship *Santa Rosa*. After only a day at sea the ship sank in a severe storm and the newly-weds, together with the crew of twelve, took to the life-boats. One of the life-boats, containing the starving and exhausted Rolando, his wife and three crewmen, was eventually cast up on Floreana where they were taken prisoner by 'some heavily armed men'. According to the story printed in the *Los Angeles Herald* of 24th November 1933, the prisoners were captured by the Baroness, who locked them up, in great discomfort, for four days. On the fifth day they were taken to the beach. The three crewmen were put into one boat and the honeymooners in another and set adrift. Rolando was reported to have subsequently shot the three crewmen when they attempted to board his boat to molest his wife. Rolando and his wife were eventually picked up by a passing ship and taken to Guayaquil.

According to Dore, the Baroness maintained that the story was true. She had, she admitted, behaved in a terrible way, but was full of contrition and promised Allan Hancock that she would mend her ways.* The millionaire seems to have given the Baroness quite a wigging at this time. Fred Ziesenhenne recorded in his diary that Captain Hancock also 'got the Baroness to confess that she shot the Dane in a moment of rage'. After this Hancock 'talked with Philippson' and asked him to 'watch the Baroness and try to be in harmony with the Wittmers and Ritters'.

Before the *Velero III* left, Allan Hancock first invited the Baroness aboard to receive presents from him and then Heinz Wittmer and Friedrich Ritter. According to Margret, 'Mr. Hancock was the very soul of tact through it all – handing out the things to each person from the island himself so that there would be no cause for dissension later.' She also described what she called 'a comical scene on the beach' as the presents were unloaded: 'Frau Korwin is seated on a stone playing with her young donkey; Madame is busy searching for mussels, yet both manage to watch closely in order to find out what everyone received.'

Fred Ziesenhenne, on shore from the *Velero III*, also observed the scene: 'We put the Baroness, Philippson and Lorenzo on shore with supplies of food, tools, cloth and medicine, which infuriated Dore Ritter and she acted up.' In his diary he wrote 'Dr gave Dore hell for coming down etc. It finally ended with all three factions on the beach and the skiff pulled out to let them fight it out for themselves.'

To everyone's surprise the *Velero III* reappeared off Floreana on 30th January. The Wittmers were taking a Sunday afternoon stroll when they spotted the ship. They called at Friedo to announce the return of the *Velero III*, but found that Friedrich already knew of its reappearance off Black Beach. The Wittmers and Friedrich set off to the beach. Margret described the scene. 'The doctor then goes with us towards the beach to meet Mr. Hancock, Frau Koerwin to follow after. On the

* The story was pure invention. Rolf Blomberg found that the Guayaquil police had no knowledge of any such incidents and, furthermore, Knud Arends (who had intimate knowledge of the Baroness and her entourage) referred to it as 'pure fantastics'.

way Dr. Ritter becomes noticeably rude again [the Wittmers' reception at Friedo had not been cordial], running ahead, mumbling to himself etc. and we finally let him go. He sees then that he has been behaving badly and allows us to overtake him. We don't wait to be told a second time, but part company from him at once, while he goes on alone.'

Later, they encounter Friedrich and a party from the *Velero III*, now with Dore in tow. Poor Dore was feeling tired from the walk and Margret describes how she asked if they could take a short rest: 'to which Dr. Ritter snaps out a reply in English that sets her to crying.' Margret drew her away from the angry Friedrich and, in her kind way, tried to comfort Dore. Despite her usually patronizing, and sometimes spiteful, attitude to her neighbour, Dore told Margret of her troubles and asked her to visit her as 'the doctor becomes more and more disagreeable and malicious.' Margret felt it 'painful to have such a scene with the visitors here.'

The party from the ship walked back to the Wittmer house. Waldo Schmitt, who had formed a special friendship with the Wittmers, asked if he could take some more photographs of the Wittmer house.

As they were entertaining their seven visitors, the Wittmers were surprised to hear a call from the garden gate. A cheerful-looking young man introduced himself. He was Hakon Mielche, the Dane, who had just arrived in his gaff-rigged ketch, the *Monsoon*. It turned out that he was on a world cruise with some other young Danes. They were financing their voyage by purchasing 'ethnographic rarities' and selling these to museums and private collectors. Mielche wrote a light-hearted book about his trip, which he called *Let's See if the World is Round*.

The *Monsoon* was moored close to the *Velero III*. The young Danish crew were invited aboard. Hakon Mielche was much impressed:

> The ship was a perfect miracle with its soft-carpeted salons, Steinway piano and luxurious single cabins with real beds

and bathrooms. Modern laboratories, huge aquariums and every conceivable up-to-date accessory were at the disposal of those investigating nature, and in the evenings after the day's work they gathered for a quiet hour in the music salon where famous American virtuosi plied fiddle, flute and piano, while Hancock himself played on a 'cello that had cost a fortune with a bow worth twelve hundred dollars. Hancock was passionately fond of music and the clink of his many dollars was lost in the music he conjured forth.

The next morning Heinz learned from Friedrich Ritter that yet another ship had arrived at the island. It was a large yacht, the six-thousand-ton *Stella Polaris*. She had, in fact, once belonged to Kaiser Wilhelm, as the *Hohenzollern*, but was now used as a tourist ship.* She had brought a party of American tourists who were put ashore for a short time to post their letters in the post barrel at Post Office Bay. Fred Ziesenhenne watched the tourists from the deck of the *Velero III*. One of his pals suggested that 'we set up a lemonade stand or sell hot dogs' but Ziesenhenne felt that 'Captain would not approve of his idea.'

The Floreana settlers were one of the tourist sights. Both Friedrich and Dore as well as the Baroness were invited on board the *Stella Polaris*, so that they could be seen by the tourists. Friedrich seems to have completely abandoned his much-vaunted contempt for and rudeness to the visitors who called to see him on Floreana. That afternoon the three settlers were taken down to the ship's saloon to meet the tourist passengers, who must have been intrigued to meet the famous Dr Ritter ('*Der moderne Robinson auf Galapagos*') and the notorious Empress of Floreana. Dore seems to have enjoyed

* Evelyn Waugh was a passenger on the *Stella Polaris* during a Mediterranean cruise in 1929, when his new wife almost died of double pneumonia. Waugh wrote in a letter to Henry Yorke: 'All the sailors on the ship took to seamanship late in life. The Captain was a bank manager until a few years ago, the Purser the editor of a humorous Norwegian weekly, and the First-Engineer taught dancing.'

the conversation and interest of the tourists. 'They made much of Friedrich and me, and plied us with a thousand questions. They were extremely friendly and some of them we found so agreeable, that we were sorry that they would be sailing away too soon for us to ask them up to Friedo.'

Dore noticed that, while she and Friedrich were the centre of interest, the Baroness stood by herself in a corner of the saloon. She was dressed in green-velvet knee-breeches and an embroidered blouse. 'It was a most peculiar costume, certainly designed to attract attention. But if it did so one could only regret it, for those garments did not suit her.' She felt sorry for the Baroness, standing alone in the crowded saloon in her garish costume.

After they disembarked from the *Stella Polaris*, Dore and Friedrich joined Allan Hancock on board the *Velero III*. Dore was surprised to find Philippson already on the ship. He had come aboard to borrow medicine, although Dore believed that this was a subterfuge to enable him to ingratiate himself with visiting yacht owners. Philippson left soon after the arrival of Dore and Friedrich. Dore watched him being rowed towards the shore. She did not realize, as the boat disappeared into the gathering dusk, that she would never see either Philippson or the Baroness again.

* * *

Hakon Mielche visited the Hacienda and Friedo and was not impressed. However, he hit it off with the Wittmers and, years later, Margret remembered his visits to their new stone house with considerable pleasure. Mielche seems to have been an excellent mimic and the Wittmers were no doubt entertained by his imitations of the other settlers. For his part, Mielche was relieved to find such a perfectly normal family as the Wittmers on Floreana. 'Wittmer was quite an ordinary person living in an uncommonly beautiful stone house set in a large, well-cultivated garden. He had a charming natural wife, and two children quieter and better behaved than children usually are.'

Trygve Nuggerud had accompanied the young Danes to

Floreana in his boat, the *Dinamita*, in the hope of picking up some orders for supplies from the settlers. He too climbed up to Friedo and told Dore and Friedrich of some curious goings-on at the beach during the previous night. He had seen, from the deck of the *Dinamita*, the Baroness and Philippson dancing on the shore in the flickering light of a large bonfire. Nuggerud believed that they were both drunk and quite oblivious of their surroundings.

12
DROUGHT AND DISAPPEARANCES

With the departure of the ships from the bay, the settlers were once again left to themselves in the appalling heat. Margret Wittmer was particularly sorry to see Hakon Mielche sail away on the *Monsoon*. 'Mielche's visit to Floreana was all too short for our liking, but soon all the ships had gone, and we were back to our solitude and daily cares, including the drought, for it was the dry season.'

Rudolf Lorenz's suffering was the greatest of all. He called much more frequently at Friedo and at the Wittmer house. He told Dore that he was desperate to get off the island and 'lived in terror lest a passing boat might call and go away without him'. He had formed the plan to wait at Post Office Bay until a boat came to take him away, but he needed money, or if not that, then at least water and food to exist in the terrible heat. Lorenz pleaded with the Baroness to let him have these basic necessities. According to Dore, the Baroness answered: 'Get out of my sight, you spawn - you dog - you low-down bastard - ! Go to your damn bay and rot there for all I care.'

At this, Lorenz completely lost control and seized a chair to smash in the flimsy cupboard in which the Baroness had locked his few possessions. He was knocked unconscious, presumably by the stronger and better-nourished Philippson, no doubt assisted by the Baroness with her riding crop. Perhaps as on previous occasions, as recounted by Hakon Mielche, 'he was beaten, while the Baroness looked on and encouraged her gladiator [Philippson] with wild shrieks.'

When he recovered, Lorenz seems to have crept away and fallen unconscious again out in the open during the long, hot night. Dore said that he roamed the island for two days and eventually called at Friedo, but did not ask to be taken in. According to Margret Wittmer, Friedrich refused to let him stay, for fear of retribution from the Baroness. Dore and Friedrich agreed, however, to write a notice and post it on the barrel at Post Office Bay asking any calling ship to take off a German settler.

At this time Lorenz also wrote letters to his family to seek help. These letters were subsequently found in circumstances which no one could have predicted. One was to his brother, Carl Lorenz, in Dresden. 'Things are not going so good. The Baroness has hidden all the money and won't give me any. She has kicked me out and has taken in Philippson, who beats me up. I'm sick of it all and want to get to Germany.' In another he wrote: 'Please help me get off this island. Send my money care of the German Consul at Guayaquil. He will come and get me. I am still fighting with Philippson.' Lorenz also wrote to the Baroness's legal husband in Paris. He asked Bosquet to find him a job and, in return for help to quit the islands, offered to assist the Baron in gaining a divorce.

When he called at the Wittmers', in the new stone house, Lorenz pleaded with them to give him asylum. Like Friedrich, they were not anxious to attract the Baroness's wrath by helping him. However, they did eventually take him in, on 19th March, and Margret recalled, years later, that 'with Lorenz in the house I found it hard to sleep that night. The Baroness and her "husband" must both be insane, there was no telling what they might not do against the protectors of their chief victim.'

When the Baroness did appear, she did not seem to be annoyed at finding Lorenz living with the Wittmers. The Baroness called for Lorenz: 'Lori, do come out a moment please. Please come, dear Lori, I've got something I *must* say to you.' She succeeded in enticing Lorenz away and Margret watched them walk along the path until they disappeared from sight. When Lorenz reappeared, Margret thought that he looked cheerful and relaxed. Soon afterwards, however, he began to weep. Like Dore, Margret was worried about Lorenz's health, for he was clearly a very sick man.

The drought on Floreana dragged on. The heat was intense. On several occasions the Baroness called for Lorenz at the Wittmers'. Each time he went off with the Baroness and each time returned to the Wittmer home alone.

On 26th March, a Monday, the Wittmers heard a great deal of animated talk coming from the direction of the Hacienda, and supposed there were visitors to the Baroness. The following morning, the Baroness appeared, as before, at the Wittmers' gate. She was wearing riding breeches, shirt and riding boots, with a scarf tied round her hair. She did not enter the garden but asked to speak to Rudolf Lorenz. Margret told the Baroness that Lorenz was not in the house, but was away working with Heinz and Harry. In considerable excitement, the Baroness announced that a party of friends had called in a private yacht and were to take her and Philippson away with them on a cruise.

'We're going to Tahiti with them,' Margret was informed. 'I hope that'll be a better place to realize my plans. Lorenz is to look after the things I've left behind, till I either return or send him word.'

Margret told Dore later that the Baroness had said she had suffered terribly in the drought and was pleased that, by leaving the island, she would not take more of the precious water from their shrinking spring.

When Lorenz returned, with Heinz and Harry, and heard of the Baroness's visit, he at once suspected a trap. He convinced Margret that Philippson, who had frequently threatened Lorenz and latterly had promised to kill him when they next met, would be waiting for him at the Hacienda. Margret prevailed on Lorenz to delay going there and to have his midday meal before doing anything further. She had been told that the Baroness and her party expected to be gone by noon. It would be as well if Lorenz arrived at the Hacienda Paradiso some time after the departure.

According to Margret, Lorenz stayed away for two days. In fact, she and Heinz began to think that he might have been captured by the Baroness and that the whole story of her departure had been merely a device to decoy Lorenz from their house. When at last he reappeared, Lorenz told the Wittmers that the Hacienda was deserted and the donkeys missing, as were most of the Baroness's and Philippson's belongings. He had gone down to Post Office Bay and found some footprints in the sand, but no other trace of the Baroness or Philippson.

Margret found Dore jubilant at the news. It was a rare event for Friedo to receive a visit from Margret, who had taken Rudolf Lorenz with her to report the dramatic turn of events – first to Friedrich, who then turned to call Dore out of the house.

'She danced for joy, almost forgetting her bad leg. She made us some hot chocolate and fetched all sorts of delicacies from her store-room. We had never seen her so cordial, but Ritter was strikingly silent, and seemed far from his usual self. We were spared all philosophical discourse.'

Margret went on to relate in her account that Friedrich then turned to Lorenz and advised him to get away from Floreana. 'Sell what you don't want to take with you, and then make tracks to get yourself back to Germany as quick as you can.'

Friedrich, Heinz and Rudolf Lorenz went together to the Hacienda. Margret describes how Ritter opened up the crates and boxes with complete assurance. He seemed quite sure the Baroness and Philippson had gone for good. 'Whatever he may have been like as a philosopher, he was certainly a good businessman, and excelled in bargaining, paying far less for his purchases than Lorenz asked.' There would be no denying now that Friedrich had money and knew how to put it to good use.

Margret questioned whether they had any right to dispense the Baroness's possessions in this way. Lorenz reassured her by saying that the things had been bought with his money in the first place. Heinz then took what was left, including the corrugated iron.

Friedrich seemed to be in a great hurry to draw up a formal report of the events surrounding the departure of the Baroness and Philippson. Margret felt that he was putting in writing what was, after all, far from proven fact. When she tried to suggest that the Baroness might return, he shook his head. 'She won't come back. Take my word for it.' He did admit that he had not seen any sort of boat, but told Heinz that he would not have seen one anyway unless it had put in at Black Beach. 'Anyhow, they're gone – gone for good.' So Margret Wittmer wrote.

* * *

A quite different story is told by Dore Strauch. She and Friedrich had been finding it difficult to work and impossible to study in the overwhelming heat of the day. Breaking with their usual routine, they had taken to lying down in the midday hours. On one such day the hot wind had died down so that not even the movement of a leaf disturbed the noon-day stillness at Friedo.

Suddenly, according to Dore, the silence was shattered by a long-drawn shriek. To her it seemed 'an outcry of such panic-terror that it was hardly human. It froze the marrow in our bones and momentarily paralysed us. It sounded neither near nor far. It seemed like no earthly sound at all; and almost before it had been uttered, the silence closed about it once again . . .'

Dore, who subsequently placed great stress on this incident, says that they heard the shriek at noon on 19th March. She describes how Friedrich walked to the gate, expecting to hear running footsteps or a call for help from along the path to Friedo. But there were no footsteps and there was no call. Surprisingly, they did not investigate further. They resolved to ask Heinz Wittmer what he knew of the incident when he made his weekly call on the following day. Heinz did not appear.

On the day after that, 21st March, Lorenz turned up at Friedo. To Dore he was totally changed in manner and appearance. 'His fearful load of hatred and despair seemed to have lifted. He still looked very ill, but was in good spirits . . . he seemed to have regained something of his former youthfulness.'

Dore surmised that Lorenz had made it up with the Baroness, but Lorenz said that he had not. He told Dore that he had broken with the Baroness and had been staying with the Wittmers for three days when the Baroness had come for him.

Dore's account of Lorenz's story goes on to describe how he had been working with Heinz and Margret when the Baroness arrived and refused Margret's invitation to come through their gate. Margret did not want Lorenz to leave the garden, for he had told her that Philippson intended to shoot him the next time they met. Eventually the Baroness changed her mind and entered the garden to ask Lorenz if he knew the whereabouts of a spanner that she and Philippson needed but could not find at the Hacienda. Having told her where to find the spanner, Lorenz then refused to return and help her make some bread and resisted her further blandishments.

Dore did not believe that Lorenz had the will-power to resist the Baroness, and she was probably right to be suspicious, for Lorenz's story also conflicts with Margret Wittmer's account of the Baroness calling for him. Lorenz then told Dore that he had captured a mother and two young donkeys. This interested Dore because she was finding it difficult to bottle-feed Burro's orphaned son. Lorenz did not allow her to follow up the matter and left abruptly, telling Dore and Friedrich that Heinz would call on them on Sunday.

25th March was Dore's birthday and she baked a cake for the occasion, no doubt offering a slice to Heinz when he called at Friedo on that day. Heinz produced a letter to someone called 'Alec', which contained a brief description of life at the Hacienda Paradiso and referred to a recent book which described Friedrich and Dore in unflattering terms. Enclosed was a newspaper article which also represented the Ritters in a very bad light. Dora believed it originated from the Baroness. The letter was signed 'Antoinette,* Robert and Lorenz'.

Friedrich not unnaturally wanted to know how Heinz had come by the letter and was told that Lorenz had taken it from the table at the Hacienda. If this were true, either Lorenz had lied when he told Dore that he had not been back to the Hacienda or else he had been there after 21st March when (Dore had said) he last called at Friedo. Heinz began talking himself into 'a raving fury' against the Baroness, and afterwards Dore placed great emphasis on the fact that he shouted that they would have to take the law into their own hands, for they could get no protection from the Ecuadorian authorities.

The next visitor to Friedo was Margret Wittmer, with news of the disappearance of the Baroness and Philippson, which Dore says she listened to calmly, merely asking a few questions. Friedrich remained silent. After Margret Wittmer and Rudolf Lorenz left Friedo, Friedrich told Dore that she had 'played [her] part extremely well' but was surprised that she had believed the tale about the Baroness's and Philippson's disappearance.

Dore's account of the episode clearly meant to imply that the Baroness and her lover disappeared on 19th March, while Margret firmly places their departure on, or after, 27th March. Dore claimed that Margret and Lorenz arranged to take her down to the Hacienda the following Sunday, 1st April, on which day Rudolf Lorenz and Harry Wittmer called for her punctually with a donkey, for her lame leg made it difficult to walk along the rough paths to the Hacienda. She and Friedrich were to lunch with the Wittmers before inspecting the Baroness's domain. She wrote that they passed the Hacienda at noon in the burning summer heat. 'The whole place looked inviting, cheerful and well-kept, a smiling mask that hid confusion, evil memories and crime.'

At luncheon, Dore was again impressed by Margret's food and skilful cooking, and noticed particularly the beautiful pink

* The name of the shop that the Baroness had run with Rudolf Lorenz in Paris (see p. 98).

damask tablecloth and the very handsome tea-set that replaced the plates at the end of the meal. Dore claimed that she had seen both the cloth and the tea-set before – at a luncheon party at the Hacienda during the earlier brief attempt at reconciliation with the Baroness. Margret was infuriated by Dore's suggestion when she heard about it and said that she bought the tea-set in Guayaquil and that the cloth was a gift from her sister in Germany.

After lunch, Dore recounts, Friedrich produced a well-drawn-up document describing everything that they had heard from Rudolf Lorenz and Margret Wittmer, which Lorenz protested was quite unnecessary, though Friedrich persisted that they must have the record straight. Dore goes on to describe the visit of the settlers to the Hacienda and her own reluctance to set foot in the place. As they passed through the gate, 'all at once a sudden scorching wind swept up and rustled horribly through the parched and straw-like leaves of the bananas.'

Rudolf Lorenz led the way into the Hacienda, followed by the Wittmers and then Dore and Friedrich. The first thing to catch Dore's eye, she claims, was the Baroness's hat upon the table. In a corner stood her baggage, stacked up as it always had been. The Hacienda was perfectly neat and tidy, the Baroness's family photographs, including one of her grandmother, still in their places. Most surprising of all was her copy of *The Picture of Dorian Gray*, her talisman, which she always treasured and kept close to her. It was inconceivable to Dore that the Baroness would have left this most treasured possession behind during a cruise to Tahiti.

13
DEATH IN EDEN

The drought continued into April of that year. Dore afterwards wrote that the days following the visit to the empty Hacienda Paradiso were 'haunted and uncanny'. She was worried that she and Friedrich would be implicated in some way, should there ever be an investigation of the disappearance of the Baroness and Philippson.

Rudolf Lorenz too seems to have been anxious and uneasy. Margret Wittmer later told Waldo Schmitt that, during his stay with them, Lorenz was in the habit of going off by himself 'for hours at a time'. When asked by Heinz Wittmer where he had been, 'he would always say that he had been on the "heath",' presumably meaning the large stretch of level land on which the wild cattle lived.

No ships came in the days that followed the disappearance of his two tormentors from the Hacienda. It was as though the island was isolated by a silent wall of heat.

On the 21st April it rained at last. The Wittmers heard signals from a ship's whistle and Rudolf Lorenz and Harry Wittmer walked down to Black Beach to intercept it. But the ship had anchored at Post Office Bay and shortly after they had departed several men appeared at the Wittmer gate. One of the men introduced himself as Mr Howell, the owner of the yacht *Thalia*. He was, in fact, Thomas Howell, a wealthy Chicago grain-broker. He had come to see the notorious Baroness and was very surprised to learn of her disappearance.

It was already five o'clock and, as darkness would fall in an hour, Heinz Wittmer offered to guide the visitors back to Post Office Bay. On their way down to the bay they encountered Lorenz and Harry. Lorenz said that he would like to go aboard the ship, but had some difficulty in communicating with Mr Howell and his visitors as they spoke only English. However, Lorenz learned that the *Thalia* was to depart early in the morning and decided that there would be insufficient time for him to collect together his belongings, which he valued so much.

Mr Howell gave Heinz Wittmer a packet, containing seeds: 'half for you – half for Dr. Ritter.' The next morning Rudolf Lorenz took the packet down to Friedo and, in Margret Wittmer's words: 'There is the devil to pay.' Friedrich demanded to know why Mr Howell had not called on him. He suspected that the visitors had been side-tracked from visiting Friedo and, furthermore, accused Heinz Wittmer of breaking open 'his' packet of seeds and of withholding other mail intended for him.

Later in the day, Heinz Wittmer walked down to Friedo to 'straighten things out'. According to Margret, Dore became very abusive towards Heinz and refused to believe that half of the seeds were intended for the Wittmers, even though Rudolf Lorenz vouched for the truth of Heinz's statement. Friedrich Ritter attempted to be reasonable about the affair, but Dore continued with her tirade to such an extent that Heinz Wittmer told Margret that he would have nothing more to do with Dore.

Lorenz too seems to have fallen out with Dore at this time for Margret wrote: 'It's the same with Lorenz. He and Frau Koerwin used to be good friends; now, because of this last affair, they've become enemies. A sad state of affairs – only Germans on the island and all enemies.'

* * *

Life at the Wittmer house continued uneventfully. Heinz had to plant another crop of corn, because the seed planted in

January had been killed by the drought. Heinz's second birthday on Floreana was duly celebrated with the two Wittmer children and Rudolf Lorenz each giving him a cake. Heinz tried to construct a raft from some old oil drums, but failed because they were too rusty. The Wittmers were pleased to see that the island animals were beginning to recover from the devastating effects of the drought, for the donkeys were again engaged in their noisy mating ritual.

Margret Wittmer's diary describes the continuing routine of their lonely island life. In July she welcomed the rain which came in torrential cloudbursts, reviving both plants and animals. Their garden once more became productive and she felt satisfaction that they could survive the rigours of such a terrible drought. She regretted that there was no way of storing the rainwater on Floreana. The energetic and ingenious Heinz must have considered a number of projects but was probably defeated by the highly permeable volcanic soil.

Margret seems to have been quite content with her life on Floreana at this time. She had a new house and young Rolf was sitting up and taking an interest in his surroundings. Margret records that she even had time to spare in the long equatorial evenings to read once again, although Heinz's reading habits were disturbed by Lorenz wanting him to play cards. She and Heinz were giving themselves lessons in English and Spanish. Margret kept a small dictionary with her as she worked and looked up the names of all the familiar objects. She would then repeat the phrases in English and Spanish.

Margret was also pleased that Harry had adapted to life on Floreana. His eyesight, unfortunately, had not improved, as she and Heinz had hoped, but he seems to have inherited his father's practical abilities, for Margret remarked on how expert he was at chopping down trees.

Only Rudolf Lorenz was unhappy in the comfortable atmosphere of the Wittmer home. He had tried to live alone at Post Office Bay, but could not stand the solitude, and had asked to come back to the Wittmer family again. He left his trunks in the old buildings at the bay, but they were forced open, he suspected by the crew of a passing ship. His dinner jacket and dress shirts were stolen, although Margret wondered whether he would ever have worn them again, for Lorenz looked very ill. 'Fever spots on his cheeks, coughing spells that leave him spent – in short, a deathly sick man.'

Margret felt the deepest sympathy for Lorenz. 'Hours on end he sits in one spot, crying softly to himself, saying not a word – a heart-rending picture. Outside these spells of despondency, however, he always behaves very well with us and not infrequently he has guarded the house when Heinz and I were gone. He can even be trusted with Rolf.'

* * *

In mid-July (Dore and Margret are for once agreed on this) Trygve Nuggerud appeared off Floreana in his small fishing-boat, the *Dinamita*. Nuggerud had on board his negro crewman, Trivino, and two passengers: Rolf Blomberg,* an energetic and adventurous young Swede who was exploring the archipelago to seek material for a book, and Artur Wörm-Muller (Captain Bruuns's friend who had stayed with him at Post Office Bay), who had come along for the trip. Before sailing to Floreana, Nuggerud had taken his dark-eyed Ecuadorian wife from their home on Santa Cruz to Chatham Island. She was eight months pregnant and there was a midwife there. Blomberg said that Nuggerud was 'happy as a lark' at the prospect of fatherhood, but he was 'worried and did not know how to pass the time awaiting the big day.' To kill time he decided to sail across to Floreana to deliver some coffee bushes that he had promised to give to the Baroness. Blomberg and Wörm-Muller were pleased to accompany Nuggerud on the *Dinamita*, for they were both eager to discover the truth about the extraordinary stories that had been circulating among the islands about the Baroness. Wörm-Muller also wanted to renew his acquaintance with Friedrich Ritter.

The *Dinamita* anchored at Post Office Bay. When they came

* Rolf Blomberg, then in his early twenties, subsequently became a distinguished writer and explorer in South America.

ashore the visitors found a notice pinned to the wall of the old Norwegian building.

> A young man on this island is forced to leave as he has no longer anything to live on. Therefore, he asks for an opportunity to go to Chatham or Guayaquil. I live by the track marked with red approximately 2 hours walk from here. 27th May 1934. Rudolf Lorenz.

Leaving Wörm-Muller at the old Norwegian house, Nuggerud, Trivino and Blomberg walked up the skull-bordered track (a memento of the Baroness's wanton animal slaughter) towards the Hacienda Paradiso. After an hour's climb they reached a grove of wild orange and lemon trees. There they branched left and walked for another hour along the track to the Hacienda. Blomberg describes how they glimpsed a clearing in the trees ahead of them on a small plateau close to the steep mountainside. He saw 'several huts and beneath them ... a plantation of banana trees, atoi plants, guavas and large golden sunflowers.' But there was no sign of the Hacienda, 'only the place where it once had stood. Not a living soul to be found anywhere.' They shouted in case anyone was within earshot, but 'the only answer we got was the echo.'

The three men then walked back along the track and turned towards the Wittmer home. Lorenz and Wittmer were standing at the door of the little stone house. They rushed forward together, shouting in considerable excitement, 'Oh, you have brought the mail ... please come, hurry, hurry.' Blomberg noticed that Lorenz looked thin and ill. After being introduced to Margret, the visitors asked where the Baroness was. 'Disappeared' was the simple answer from Lorenz.

The visitors were told of the Baroness's message, about a visiting English yacht that was to take her and Philippson to the South Pacific. Lorenz told Blomberg that he was surprised to receive the message and hurried over to the Hacienda to find it empty. To make sure that they really had left he went down to Post Office Bay, but found only some footprints in the sand. And that was all that Blomberg and his companions could get from Lorenz.

Nuggerud, Trivino and Blomberg spent that night in the hospitable Wittmer home. Blomberg liked his hosts: 'nice discreet people, who did not want to be photographed or written about.' The visitors left early the next morning to visit Friedrich and Dore at Friedo. Lorenz was their guide. Blomberg recalls that it was a pleasant walk and that they listened to Lorenz telling them about the Baroness.

As they approached Friedo Nuggerud suggested that they should call out: 'as they always walk about with no clothes on. We must give them time to make themselves decent and put in their false teeth.'

They spent the rest of the morning and most of the afternoon at Friedo. Friedrich told them of his life in Germany, of his escape from civilization with Dore and of his philosophical works. Blomberg considered that 'modesty came in rather short supply' with Dr Ritter and was amused at the eagerness with which Friedrich posed for photographs showing him digging, working the famous sugar-press or adopting various philosophical poses.

Blomberg noticed that Dore was 'trained to say certain things and if she ventured further in the conversation she received an angry look from Ritter and perhaps even a reprimand.' When Trygve Nuggerud offered them the coffee bushes intended for the Baroness, Dore clapped her hands with delight at the prospect of drinking coffee once again. But Friedrich intervened with a severe lecture on the harmfulness of such stimulants. Blomberg describes how poor Dore, realizing her error, 'hurriedly explained that, of course, under no circumstances were they to have coffee. It was just a whim.'

Friedrich prepared the dinner of egg nog and bananas, which Blomberg considered quite delicious.

Trygve Nuggerud had agreed to take Rudolf Lorenz off the island in the *Dinamita*. After dinner, Trivino and Nuggerud left for Post Office Bay to collect Wörm-Muller and sail the boat round to Black Beach from where it would pick up Rolf Blomberg and Lorenz.

Such was Dore's enmity for Lorenz at this time, that she had to be persuaded by Friedrich even to bid him farewell. As she looked at Lorenz she could not refrain from comparing him, ill, tired and embittered, with the good-looking, cheerful and healthy young man who had come to Floreana with the Baroness nearly two years before. She seems to have suspected him of having been involved somehow in the disposal of the Baroness and Philippson, for she spoke of him as 'a man with blood on his hands'. But with characteristic spontaneity she relented and tried to cheer Rudolf Lorenz before he parted from them. She recalled that she told him that he had many years before him and that he would one day look back on his years on Floreana merely as a bad dream.

Lorenz and Blomberg walked down to Black Beach, accompanied by Ritter. When asked by Blomberg what he thought of the Baroness's disappearance, Friedrich looked pleased and replied: 'Oh, it is wonderful that that scheming, peace-disturbing, that ... – I don't know what to call her – has left the island.' He also advanced his own theory about her disappearance. 'When the Baroness realized that her dream of a Paradise hotel was not feasible, when she understood that she could not act a pirate Queen for the rest of her life without making a fool of herself, and when she realized that after a long drought on the island, it was not always so easy to survive – especially as Lorenz no longer worked for her – she decided to commit suicide and Philippson followed her to death. That is the obvious explanation.' Friedrich's theory was, in fact, not improbable because the Baroness had apparently spoken of the possibility of suicide (see p. 204).

The *Dinamita* was riding at anchor when Blomberg, Lorenz and Ritter reached Black Beach. Lorenz took his farewell from Margret and Heinz Wittmer, who had come down to see him off. Margret recalled: 'I can still see Lorenz saying "good-bye" to us that day on Floreana, putting our letters in his pocket and then, swinging his little bundle of smoked meat, depart after saying to us in a high voice, full of joy because of the trip before him: "Until September, then I'll be back." '

The four visitors together with Rudolf sailed back round to Post Office Bay. Lorenz also had with him several letters which Friedrich had asked him to post when he reached the mainland.

One of the letters from Friedrich, written on 10th July, contained a paragraph that sheds an interesting light on his state of mind at that time. 'Should it ever be announced that either myself or both of us have disappeared, you can be sure that it was a bullet out of the bush which is responsible – even if there is no more baroness here. Do not be frightened by this – it is only a whim, and I do not believe I shall meet my fate so quickly and painlessly.' This is a very curious thought, for if the hated Baroness and Philippson had committed suicide, as Friedrich had just suggested, then what had there been to fear from Lorenz and the Wittmers with whom he had lived with some semblance of amity?

* * *

Nuggerud, his companions and Lorenz spent an uncomfortable night in the old Norwegian buildings, tormented by the formidable Galapagos mosquitoes. They were no doubt glad to sail very early next morning, bound for Santa Cruz.

During their voyage, they spotted the old *San Cristóbal* beating her way back from Isabela through a choppy sea, bound for Chatham Island with a load of sulphur. Rolf Blomberg said that it was at this moment that Lorenz saw an opportunity to get back to the mainland. When the *Dinamita* reached Academy Bay on Santa Cruz, Lorenz tried to persuade Trygve Nuggerud to take him on to Chatham, where the ship would remain for another day or so before sailing to Guayaquil. The superstitious Nuggerud was not keen on this idea, for it was Friday 13th July and, furthermore, there was quite a heavy sea running. But Lorenz persisted and finally persuaded Nuggerud by offering him what was then the large sum of fifty sucres. As Blomberg, Wörm-Muller and Trivino wished to remain on Santa

Cruz, Nuggerud got a twelve-year-old boy, José Pasmino, to act as his crewman.

Rolf Blomberg recalls that he said farewell to the elderly Norwegian and the young boy in the early dawn, on the shore at Santa Cruz, then watched Nuggerud's single-masted motor-boat gradually disappear into the distance.

A few days later, Blomberg was very alarmed when he learned, from a fishing-boat that sailed into Academy Bay, that the *Dinamita* had not arrived at Chatham Island. Blomberg was a staunch friend and spent several weeks searching among the islands for Nuggerud, Pasmino and Lorenz or any sign of the *Dinamita*. The *San Cristóbal* also searched for the *Dinamita*. No trace could be found of the missing boat.

Blomberg eventually abandoned the search assuming Nuggerud had drowned, and prepared to leave the Galapagos. He said that he never forgot his parting from Mrs Nuggerud: 'Her large, black eyes were full of tears and on her arm she held her baby son, an image of Nuggerud.'

* * *

About a month later Heinz Wittmer found a letter from Rolf Blomberg in the barrel at Post Office Bay. Blomberg had given the letter to the skipper of the *San Cristóbal* to leave on Floreana when it next passed the island. The Wittmers learned that Lorenz had eventually persuaded Trygve Nuggerud to take him on to Chatham Island, but that the *Dinamita* had failed to arrive there. Blomberg said he feared that the *Dinamita* might have come to grief, for she had no sail and would have been helpless in the treacherous Galapagos currents if her engine broke down.

Dore's 'sinful craft' had appeared, according to her, on 20th August bringing letters and newspapers for her and Friedrich. They too learned of the loss of the *Dinamita* and also discovered that the story of the disappearance of the Baroness and Philippson had spawned numerous press articles.

Two months later the *San Cristóbal* reappeared at Floreana. Rolf Blomberg was on board but had no news of the fate of

Lorenz and Nuggerud or of the whereabouts of the Baroness and Philippson.

On 26th August the inhabitants were surprised by the arrival of three Germans, later called by the Wittmers the 'globe-trotters' because they seem to have been much travelled. Herr Heinlein was a jockey from Brandenburg, Herr Senff a mechanic from Hamburg and Herr Tremel a salesman from southern Germany. They had all previously worked in the Galapagos or at Guayaquil and had come to Floreana to revive the cattle-slaughtering business which Captain Bruuns had run on the island. They had an arrangement with the part-owner of the ship the *Esperanza*, who was to export the animal hides from the island.

Heinz doubted that the enterprise would prosper. He reckoned that there were not more than a hundred and fifty cattle left on the island and the situation was hardly better with the pigs and donkeys. However, Heinz was pleased that the *Esperanza* would be making fairly regular calls in connection with this business, for she could bring supplies and mail to the island.

Following the island tradition, the 'globe-trotters' settled into the pirate caves and soon made themselves comfortable there. They were also introduced into the social life of the island, for Friedrich invited them to Friedo together with the Wittmers, on Sunday 10th September, provided that they brought their own rice and meat. Heinz shot a calf and contributed a roast ham while the visitors brought a pound of rice. They all seem to have enjoyed the occasion, despite the recent feud between Heinz and Dore. Dore was much impressed with Herr Tremel when she learned that he wrote for American newspapers.

In the midst of the proceedings two more visitors appeared. They were a Mr Taylor and his friend who had arrived on the yacht *Aldebaran*. Their hosts positively blossomed with the arrival of these two guests. According to Heinz, 'Frau Koerwin related her life's history and Dr Ritter, though at first reserved, finally brought out his various writings.' Friedrich gave Mr

Taylor an article of his in which he supported the views of Dr Bartels, of Cologne, that the Earth is not merely a small sphere in the Cosmos; Herr Tremel was also honoured with copies of some of Friedrich Ritter's articles but, according to Heinz Wittmer, was unable to follow them, especially 'the writings dealing with Dr Bartel's theory of the point-curvature and zero-curvature of the earth's surface.'

It turned out that Mr Taylor's motives for visiting Floreana were far from philosophical. He had come to the island to meet the Baroness, whose exploits he had read about in some sensational magazine articles. Before he departed he gave the 'globe-trotters' some fish and three bottles of whisky, the Wittmers received vegetables and salt meat, and the Friedo inhabitants some groceries.

The 'globe-trotters' seem to have got on well with the Wittmers. On 16th September, Heinz recorded in his diary that they came to Harry's birthday party and that Herr Tremel was giving Margret lessons in English – in exchange for fresh vegetables and meat. On 11th October, Herr Senff and Herr Tremel fetched Friedrich Ritter to attend to baby Rolf when he developed a high fever.

Friedrich, on the other hand, was distinctly irritable about them. In a letter he wrote:

> The simultaneous presence of the three German visitors and the settlers in the interior is making the situation in our garden somewhat uncomfortable – we feel strongly how much we exist outside of the diligence of these people. The last settlers seem to have appreciated that they cannot remain here for ever although, just like the baroness, they have fallen to the depths of modern piracy. To be brought into contact with these people is distasteful.

The 'globe-trotters' did eventually realize, as Heinz Wittmer had predicted, the difficulty of making a living by shooting the island's cattle. In fact, Heinz maintained that they only managed to shoot a total of five *duck* during their stay on Floreana.

They left the island in early November 1934 very much in Heinz Wittmer's bad books: 'Those two slick customers [Senff and Heinlein] had taken a large tank and some fishing tackle of mine away with them. One can't depend on anybody anymore. We fed and cared for those three fellows as well as we could and as thanks for it they have made off with things belonging to me. Just wait until the next one comes . . .'

At about this time, according to Margret, Dore told the Wittmers that she intended to leave Floreana. Friedrich also seems to have been depressed. He told the Wittmers that 'the island has not given me what I hoped.' Heinz recorded in his diary that 'Dr. Ritter seems to be suffering deeply himself; he looks old and broken and says he'd like to leave the island, for his life here is just one disappointment after another.' Margret also maintained that Friedrich told her that Dore was ill, that he and Dore were constantly quarrelling and that it was all getting on his nerves. If Margret's account was true, then Friedrich's relationship with Dore must have deteriorated very badly for previously, despite Dore's descriptions of her hatred for him, Friedrich seems never to have deliberately revealed the truth of their relationship. Friedrich apparently expressed the hope that Allan Hancock would take Dore to the mainland when the *Velero III* next came to the island. The *Velero III* was, in fact, scheduled to leave Los Angeles on the Fourth Allan Hancock Expedition on 23rd November 1934, and was expected in the Galapagos archipelago in January 1935.

Dore's account of her relationship with Friedrich was totally different from that which the Wittmers related. According to Dore 'a strange mood came over Friedrich'. He apparently worked unceasingly at his philosophical studies and left the gardening, the care of the animals and the household chores entirely to her. This behaviour would be consistent with a deteriorating relationship with Dore, a relationship which she, subsequently, might well have represented as resulting from an unusual burst of creative activity by Friedrich. However, Dore specifically claimed that she and Friedrich 'had found perfect harmony and peace together. All differences had been smoothed out, and we had reached the infinite understanding of each other which no words can tell. Friedrich had become considerate and tender. All storms had ceased ... A stillness and a happiness that we had never known before united us in that last month in more than human happiness.'

* * *

On 6th November the American broadcaster Philips Lord sailed into Floreana on his four-masted schooner, the *Seth Parker*. He had encountered Rolf Blomberg at Chatham Island and had no doubt learned of the events on Floreana. Lord was at that time at the height of his popularity as a radio broadcaster, having created the Seth Parker series (about a homespun family in Jonesport, Maine), which had a regular audience of ten million listeners. At this time, Lord was producing a highly publicized radio programme for the National Broadcasting Company: *The Cruise of the Schooner Seth Parker*. The programme was broadcast weekly in the United States and told of Lord's experience during his world cruise. The 'Adam and Eve of Floreana' and the disappearing 'Queen' of that island would have made excellent material for his programme. Lord was thirty-two years old, six feet tall and athletic, with attractive wavy brown hair. Dore, characteristically, noted his handsomeness.

Philips Lord visited Friedo and talked with Friedrich on philosophical matters. Dore afterwards recalled, with considerable pleasure, that Friedrich told Lord that she was the only woman who had ever understood his work. However, this was not particularly high praise from Friedrich, for as a disciple of Nietszche he was likely to have had an extremely low opinion of the philosophical understanding of women in general.

Philips Lord seems to have made quite a hit with the Wittmers. Margret describes 14th November as a 'memorable day', the first time that she had left Floreana since setting foot on the island two years before. She and Heinz were taken out to the *Seth Parker* in a motor-boat. The Wittmers had never before been invited on to one of the larger ships that called at Floreana;

they seem to have been totally overshadowed in this respect by the inhabitants of Friedo and the Hacienda.

As the Wittmers were eating a meal with Philips Lord in the saloon, some of the sailors returned from a visit to Friedo. They told the company that Dr Ritter's chickens were all dead, apparently as a result of eating poisoned potted pork (from the 'satanic boar'?). According to Margret, Philips Lord confirmed that while he was at Friedo on the previous day, Friedrich had opened a jar of potted pork and found that it was bad. Dore threw the meat to their chickens. The returning ship's officers also carried a message asking Heinz and Margret to spare a couple of hens and a cock so that Friedrich and Dore could start to build up their stock again.

Two days later, Margret and Heinz took the rooster up to Friedo. Friedrich told them of his bad luck and then took Heinz and Margret into the house. To Margret's astonishment, they saw that Friedrich had been busily potting the chickens that had been killed by the poisoned pork. However, Friedrich assured the Wittmers, according to Margret, that he could destroy the poison by boiling the potted chickens. He offered them some of the boiled chickens, but Margret and Heinz refused.

Before they left Friedo, the Wittmers promised Friedrich several more chickens. On the following day he came up to collect them. Heinz recorded that 'the price Grete [Margret] asked was the return of some books that we gave him once in exchange for three hens, which didn't seem to please the doctor too well.'

Some days later, on 20th November 1934, Margret heard rapid footsteps at the gate of their new house. It was Dore, who had limped along the rough path from Friedo. According to Margret, Dore disregarded her greeting and burst out: 'Something terrible's happened, Frau Wittmer. Dr. Ritter has got meat-poisoning. He's extremely ill, in fact I think he's dying.'

Margret took the exhausted Dore into the house. Dore collapsed into a chair and, according to Margret, told her: 'The day before yesterday we opened some of the jars, with the meat from the dead chickens ... We realized at once the meat was bad, but Friedrich said I only needed to give it a good boiling, then it would be quite safe.' Dore said that she had boiled the jar and had eaten some of the contents. Friedrich had felt ill on the previous morning, as a result, he believed, of eating the potted chicken meat. Dore herself had been sick directly after eating the meat, but had felt no lasting ill-effects. Friedrich, however, was in a very bad way, his tongue was so swollen that he could no longer speak. Margret records that Friedrich's last comprehensible spoken words were to the effect that it would be ironic if a vegetarian should die of food-poisoning.

With her usual practicality, Margret found some thin rubber tubing to use as a stomach pump, scribbled a note for Heinz (who was turtle hunting) to tell him to come on to Friedo when he returned, and walked slowly down to Friedo with the tired and limping Dore.

When she saw Friedrich, Margret realized that it was probably too late to save him by stomach pumping. She wrote afterwards that although he could not speak, Friedrich could understand everything that was said and was able to write messages on a piece of paper.

Friedrich was clearly in great pain, but, even so, would not allow Dore to attempt to give him an injection of morphine which, despite his earlier objections to the drug, he had now evidently acquired. Dore failed to dislodge the mucus in his windpipe that was obstructing his breathing.

Just before dusk, at five o'clock, Heinz Wittmer arrived. By this time, but with great effort, Friedrich scribbled a last message. Years later Margret described the scene: 'He made an immense effort, felt for the pencil and wrote his last sentence: "I curse you with my dying breath." Then he looked up at Dore, his eyes gleaming with hate.' Dore avoided Friedrich's hatred-filled eyes. But when she came near to him he made 'feeble movements as if to hit or kick her.'

Friedrich became restless and then quietened as the darkness gathered outside, and Dore left him to rest a while. When the Wittmers were alone with him, Friedrich suddenly put his hands together and lifted them towards Margret. He did not appear to want to pray and they could make nothing of his gesture.

Margret sat with Friedrich, mopping the sweat from his face, until nearly nine o'clock, when Dore returned from her rest. When Friedrich heard Dore's voice, Margret wrote, 'he sat up, looking like a ghost as he tried to pounce on her. His eyes flashed with a wild feverish flame. Dore shrieked, and drew back in horror. Then he collapsed soundlessly, falling back on the pillows. He had gone.'

Heinz left Friedo soon after Friedrich died, to go back to the children. Margret stayed on to keep company with the distraught Dore. Margret did not get much sleep that night for Dore talked incessantly. She apparently kept referring to a secret that had existed between Friedrich and Rudolf Lorenz. Margret was not able to discover what the secret was.

During that long sleepless night Margret learned from Dore that Friedrich probably held his hands together to ask Margret's forgiveness, although Dore did not know why he should have done so. Dore rambled on about leaving the island and how, if she stayed, she would be murdered. She told Margret that she would spread Friedrich's fame so that his writings would be acknowledged as great masterpieces of philosophy. Margret must have been grateful for the dawn and relieved to walk in the early-morning sunshine with her husband, who had come to fetch her back to their little stone-built house, and to be greeted by Lump and then by Harry and Rolf.

* * *

Dore's account of Friedrich's death differs totally from Margret's. She wrote of their closeness during his last days and of the 'reunion of their souls'. She described how he awoke feeling ill. She said that he had a stroke and was paralysed on the right side: '. . . as he lay there immobile he told me again what he often told me: "In reality I have fulfilled my task on earth. In the material world I have built Friedo; in the psychical world I obtained control of my affections and emotions; in the mental world I have thought out and written my philosophy; but the task in the religious world, the ultimate reality, the mingling of the ego with the ALL – that only can be solved by death." ' As she sat with Friedrich she read to him some of their favourite passages from *Thus Spake Zarathustra*.

When Friedrich realized that death was near, Dore claimed, he asked her to give him his revolver, but she refused.

Dore described how the Wittmers came to Friedo and shared her vigil with the suffering Friedrich. She also described how she rested and how when she awoke 'he was violently twitching. He was seized with convulsions – it was the agony of death – but I did not know it. Suddenly he opened his great blue eyes and stretched his arms towards me. His glance was joyously tranquil, and he seemed actually to say to me: "I go; but promise you will not forget what we have lived for." '

Heinz and Harry walked down to Friedo the next day to bury Friedrich Ritter. When they lifted his body they found that the underside was bluish-red in colour. Thick, dark blood oozed from his nose. They wrapped the body in linen from the roll that Dore and Friedrich had brought with them from Germany and carried up from Post Office Bay when Dore was so full of hatred for her lover. Heinz and Harry loaded the body on Friedrich's wheelbarrow and wheeled it to the shallow grave that they had previously dug among the stones that Friedrich had so laboriously levered from the ground. Margret brought flowers from their garden and lined the grave with them. Dore did not, according to Margret, attend the burial.

14

BABY CLOTHES AND CORPSES

Friedrich Ritter died on 21st November 1934. On the same day on the other side of the world Robert Philippson's father wrote this letter to Allan Hancock:

Berlin, W15, Germany,
Hantener Str. 6
November 21st, 1934.

Dear Sir:

Referring to the tragedy which seems to have happened on one of the Galapagos Islands, known to us by recent newspaper publications, I take the liberty of addressing this letter to you, known to have a good knowledge of many things on those islands.

My son Robert Philippson, probably personally known to you as having resided on Dr. Ritters Island, seems to have left Floreana in July 34.

The last news I had from him, are dated Dec. 33; since that date I have not heard the least from my son, so my wife and myself are most anxious to know what has become of him since.

You surely will understand parents helpless situation and deep sorrow about this, and therefore excuse my request to your kindness, dear Captain, – I do not know whom else I could address to – whether it is possible for you to inquire on my behalf, if anybody could inform unfortunate parents of the fate of their only son.

Whatever you will be so good to communicate to me in this matter, will be accepted with sincere thanks.

Apologizing once more for the trouble I might cause you – and for my bad English,

I remain, dear Captain
Every yours sincerely,
ERNST PHILIPPSON

Two days before Herr Philippson had written his letter, the world's newspapers had exploded with news from the Galapagos. On that Monday morning, at breakfast tables from Los Angeles to London, people were reading of two bodies that had been found on a Galapagos island. 'Two Found Dead on Lonely Isle in a Tragedy of the Galapagos', 'Island Deaths Cause Stir. Two Continents Aroused', 'Dead Couple Found on Tropical Island'.

The *Los Angeles Times* deemed it 'most likely that the victims of slow death were Mr. & Mrs. Arthur Wittmer'. Philips Lord, quoted in the *New York Times*, 'expressed the belief that the bodies might be those of Baroness Eloise Bosquet de Wagner who went to the lonely archipelago three years ago, "and her companion".' *The Times* in London dwelt with commendable caution on the difficulties of the situation. 'Where the Baroness and Herr Philippson are now nobody seems to know. Nobody seems to know either where M. Lorenz is, or why, if it is the two Wittmers who are dead on Marchena beach, M. Lorenz's passport and papers were found on their bodies.'

A few days later, the *New York Times* advanced the theory that 'the bodies are those of Arthur Estampa, 34 years old, a Norwegian resident of Indefatigable Island and Alfred Rudolph Lorenz, 40 years old, a former Parisian ...' Eventually the newspapers got the truth of the matter. On 6th December, *The Times* reported '... one of the bodies was that of Rudolph Lorenz, the third member of the household of Baroness de Wagner Wehrborn and Robert Philippson, and the other that of Trygve Nuggerud, a Norwegian "yachtsman", with whom Lorenz had left Charles Island.'

The bodies of Nuggerud and Rudolf Lorenz had, in fact, been found on Marchena Island, by the crew of a tuna clipper, the *Santa Amaro*. The discovery was described by the captain, William Borthen, in the *New York Times* of 13th December 1934:

> It was 4 p.m., Nov. 17, as I swung the Santa Amaro around to anchor off Marchena Island, that I glanced ashore and spotted a mast with remnants of cloth at its top. With four crew members, I went ashore and found the bodies, about seventy five feet from the water-line and twenty feet apart.
>
> Near the bodies I found about thirty letters, scattered helter skelter. Also I found hundreds of burnt matches and a small pile of wood with charred paper beneath it, evidence that the men had failed in their effort to start a fire. Nearby was the carcass of a seal. The men apparently had captured the seal, killed it with a rock, drunk its blood to allay thirst, and then torn the animal apart with their bare hands and eaten some of it for food. Several safety razor blades also were found.
>
> Both men undoubtedly died of thirst and starvation. Wittmer [i.e. Nuggerud] perhaps died first, and Lorenz covered him with the skiff. Indications were that the men had been dead several months.

There was no sign of the Ecuadorian crewman, the twelve-year-old boy José Pasmino, or of the *Dinamita*; neither his body nor the boat was ever seen again.

Captain Borthen left the two bodies on the beach at Marchena, but collected up the scattered letters. He also gathered up some baby clothes – a present from Margret Wittmer to her sister that she had asked Lorenz to deliver for her. Borthen also radioed the news of his discovery to Chatham Island and thus started the furore in the world's press.

The letters which had been found lying on the beach at Marchena included some from Lorenz to his brother in Dresden, others from the Wittmers to friends in Germany and also one from Friedrich Ritter to Allan Hancock. In this letter Friedrich had written: 'the Baroness and Philippson have vanished to the South Seas ... we hope you will come once more to the island. Then I will tell you what I cannot write, for I have no proof of it.'

In Los Angeles the *Velero III* was preparing to leave for the Fourth Allan Hancock Pacific Expedition. She sailed on the morning of 23rd November 1934. In addition to his plans for the scientific expedition, Allan Hancock also intended to call at Marchena Island, to identify the bodies, and then to sail on to Floreana.

On board the *Velero III* with Allan Hancock were three biologists who had visited the Galapagos before and knew the settlers on Floreana. These were: Waldo Schmitt, the distinguished expert on crustaceans, and the two younger men, Fred Ziesenhenne, who collected sea urchins and starfish, and John S. Garth, also an expert on crustaceans.

The *Velero III* dropped anchor off the northern end of Marchena at midday on Sunday 2nd December 1934. On the following day, a party from the ship found the bodies on the beach, just as they had been described by the captain of the *Santa Amaro*. There was the tiny skiff and beside it the mummified body of Nuggerud. A short distance away lay the body of Lorenz, weighing only twenty pounds. He was dressed just as John Garth had last seen him on Floreana: 'knit sweater, grey vest, overalls cut to shorts and hand stitched at the knees.' As he gazed at the body Garth 'could not help but wonder if I were looking into the face of the murderer of the Baroness and Philippson.'

Exactly what happened to the *Dinamita* and her crew and passenger will never be known. However, it seems most likely that somewhere between Santa Cruz and Chatham Island the engine broke down. She was an old boat, with no sail, and would have been helpless in the strong ocean currents that sweep through the archipelago. These currents would have tended to carry the boat northwards, towards Marchena. It

DEAD COUPLE FOUND ON TROPICAL ISLAND

FROM OUR OWN CORRESPONDENT

NEW YORK, Nov. 18

A wireless message has been received in Los Angeles from the American fishing vessel Santa Amaro stating that the bodies of a man and woman had been found on Merchena Island, one of the Galapagos group. The island is uninhabited and without water or vegetation. The bodies lay on the beach, and on the cliffs above stood a pole with a few rags fastened to it. Apparently the couple had sought to attract the attention of some passing ship and afterwards died of thirst. A broken skiff also lay on the beach.

In the pocket of the man's shirt was found a passport with the name Alfred Rudolph Lorenz and a Paris address. There was also a letter addressed to Captain G. Allan Hancock, who lives in Los Angeles. It is known that a man named Lorenz arrived at Charles Island about two years ago, but Captain Hancock said that the brief description he had received suggested the couple might be Germans, Mr. and Mrs. Wittmer, who with their two children were also members of the colony on that island.

Fig. 4 Article from *The Times*, 18th November 1934

could have been that near this island the crewman was swept from the *Dinamita*, perhaps as it sank, and that Lorenz and Nuggerud escaped in the skiff. It could also be, as Margret Wittmer suggested, that Pasmino may have refused to leave, preferring to take his luck on the boat, which was swept into the vastness of the Pacific. Even a three-masted sailing ship, the *Alexander*, had suffered such a fate, in 1906, when it was becalmed near the Galapagos, abandoned by its crew, and carried away empty and helpless by the powerful oceanic currents that flow through the Galapagos archipelago.*

Other theories were also advanced to account for the presence of the bodies on the beach at Marchena. Captain William Borthen, the discoverer of the bodies, attributed to the hard-working Heinz Wittmer the additional duties of postman for the entire archipelago. He wrote in the *New York Times*: 'How did the men get on the island? My theory is that Lorenz was with Wittmer, the postmaster, as Wittmer visited the islands of the Galapagos group to pick up mail ... Their boat may have sprung a leak, forcing them to abandon ship hurriedly. This may explain why the skiff on Marchena Island had no oars or oar locks.' A 'graphic chart' published in the *Los Angeles Times* also has a picture of three men rowing a boat, which would have been crowded even on the river at Maidenhead, towards Chatham Island and then being swept northwards to Marchena. This theory presumably had the advantage that there was no need to account for the disappearance of the motorboat.

Hakon Mielche even managed to inject a further note of excitement by later writing that Lorenz and Nuggerud had been treasure hunting.

*This story was told to William Beebe in 1923, by a New York taxi-driver who had been a crew member of the Norwegian barque, and was also reconstructed from the ship's log by Wolfgang von Hagen in 1935. One of the ship's boats landed on Santa Cruz. The occupants also tried to keep alive by drinking seal-blood and eating turtles. Two of the party died before the rest were picked up by a passing sloop.

That would account for the curious voyages of the *Dynamite* which were observed by the other settlers during those three weeks and would also explain why the three inhabitants of the boat landed on an island which otherwise had nothing of interest to offer.

Did Nuggerud and Lorenz then quarrel about the imagined treasure and kill each other, or were they wrecked and driven ashore on the island? If so, where is the boat and native sailor? It is not impossible that he stole both the boat and the secret and abandoned his employer to die of thirst under the merciless sun! Then where is he now?

Where indeed? Mielche was more to the point in concluding that 'the whole affair is shrouded in a veil of impenetrable mystery'. Certainly Allan Hancock was unable to penetrate the mystery, despite press reports of his intention to solve it.

* * *

The *Velero III* arrived off Floreana at four o'clock on Tuesday 4th Decmber 1934. As the ship anchored at Black Beach the crew saw the urgent flashing of a mirror from the direction of Friedo. Allan Hancock, Charles Swet and three members of the crew went ashore to investigate.

Margret Wittmer recalled that she was up at Friedo with Dore Strauch when they saw the ship sailing towards Black Beach. Dore also describes her excitement at the sight of the white, twin-funnelled yacht. She had earlier written a telegram to be sent to Allan Hancock: 'Friedrich is dead, please help me.' Heinz had taken it down to Post Office Bay but a passing fishing boat had not called at the island.

Margret recalled that Allan Hancock asked the whereabouts of the menfolk. 'I am afraid there's bad news,' she told him. 'Dr Ritter died three weeks ago. It's been a great shock to Miss Dore, and I'm looking after her a bit.'

'My God!' Hancock exclaimed. 'And he said something terrible might happen. What a series of tragedies.' Hancock told Margret of the deaths of Nuggerud and Lorenz and then explained that he had received the letter from Ritter telling him of the disappearance of the Baroness and Philippson, and also of things that were too terrible to write about. Surprisingly, Dore in her account made no mention at all of Friedrich's letter to Hancock. This is odd, because it might have been expected that the message from her dead lover would have been intensely interesting to her. Furthermore, she never mentioned any of the accusations that Friedrich made.

Dore told Allan Hancock that his timely arrival was 'an act of providence'. According to John Garth, she told the *Velero III* party that Friedrich 'had been very abusive of her in the later days'. This testimony thus fully confirms Margret Wittmer's story of Friedrich's and Dore's deteriorating relationship.

On the following day a party from the *Velero III* landed, at eight o'clock in the morning. John Garth describes how, as he walked up to Friedo with his friend Fred Ziesenhenne, he noticed that the island was greener than he had ever seen it before, with most of the plants in flower. Leaving Mr Swet and another member of the party to keep company with Dore at Friedo, Garth and Ziesenhenne walked on to the Hacienda Paradiso, on their way collecting butterflies: sulphurs, blues, skippers and fritillaries. When they arrived, they too were surprised to find that Lorenz had completely dismantled the home of the Baroness and sold it to Friedrich and the Wittmers. The corrugated-iron roof now rested on top of the Wittmers' house. Garth and Ziesenhenne stayed at the Wittmers' long enough to hear Margret tell Waldo Schmitt, who could speak German, of the disappearance of the Baroness and Philippson and the death of Ritter. Fred Ziesenhenne had brought some candy for the Wittmer children which was much appreciated. The Wittmers returned the kindness with a gift of fruit.

The news of Friedrich's death was radioed from the *Velero III*, and reactivated the worldwide press interest in Floreana. On 2nd December the *Los Angeles Times* had carried the headlines: 'Hancock at Galapagos. Yacht Believed Anchored. Mystery of Island Tragedy Expected to be Solved when Party Lands'. Four days later there were more headlines: 'More

Deaths Reported in Galapagos Mystery. Capt. Hancock Reports Dr. Ritter and Unidentified Native Boy Victims of Enigmatic South Sea Isles'.

Allan Hancock was enjoying a fresh role to add to his many others: that of newspaper reporter. He was quite secretive about the messages that he radioed to the press and had as his confidant only his Chief Officer, Charles Swet. However, John Garth kept abreast of developments by giving his cabin mate, Stirling Smith, who typed the messages, a sheet of carbon paper to obtain a copy of the regular radio messages from the ship.

Allan Hancock had not thought of the possibility of being scooped in his role as 'newshound'. He realized this danger when a suitcase with initials M. L. was found in the Norwegian buildings at Post Office Bay. At first it was thought to have belonged to Lorenz, but it contained papers which showed that it was really the property of a representative of *El Universo* News Service, who had actually arrived on the island and was on his way to the Hacienda Paradiso in pursuit of news. Hancock ordered that all pictures of the Floreana inhabitants should be hidden and that no one should give information to the unfortunate newshound, who turned out to be a Señor Luna from a Guayaquil newspaper. However, there could have been little danger that Hancock would have been scooped by Señor Luna, because his sole communication with the outside world was the old *San Cristóbal*, hardly comparable to Hancock's powerful radio transmitter.

15

DEPARTURE FROM PARADISE

On Friday 7th December, Dore left Floreana. Allan Hancock had come ashore in the early morning and walked up to Friedo to collect her. She took a last look at Friedrich's grave and posed for the photographer that Allan Hancock had brought with him. She looked frail and tired, but still showed glimpses of characteristic animation as she talked with Allan Hancock. They returned to Friedo. There Dore broke down and wept bitterly.* Margret Wittmer was there and also in tears, holding a handkerchief to her face.

Allan Hancock took Dore's left arm and led her gently through the gate of Friedo and down the path to Black Beach. Her limp was pronounced even with her stick and she frequently staggered over the rough ground. Her young pet donkey trotted up to her on the way down, and romped with her for the last time, nearly knocking her to the ground in his boisterousness.

Heinz Wittmer was there too and had loaded another donkey with several bags and boxes of her possessions. When they reached the beach Dore, again in tears, bade the Wittmers farewell and Allan Hancock helped her into the dinghy which was drawn up on the beach. He sat by her side in the stern as the dinghy moved away towards the launch waiting to take her to the *Velero III*.

* This description is based on the ciné film which was shot at the time by the Hancock Expedition.

Waldo Schmitt was astonished at the amount of baggage that Dore took on board with her. He described it as 'a great assortment of trash', for it even included half a can of the sugar which she and Friedrich had so laboriously refined from their own cane. However, these possessions were precious to her: the only tangible mementoes of the island paradise that she had dreamt of with Friedrich on the Berlin rooftop six years before.

This was how Dore concluded her account of her life on Floreana:

> I said good-bye to Friedrich's grave, but did not feel as if I was leaving him there, cold in the hostile Floreana earth. In some strange way that I cannot find words for I did not feel that he was dead, but simply bodyless.
>
> And as the thought came to me like a great illumination I knew that the great task which I had found in him had only just begun. That look with which he died had told me that our experiment had not failed.
>
> That Floreana was only one stage in my life's work I can never doubt again. The gods of Floreana slew Friedrich but can have no power over him! He must live on through me.

Dore stepped on board the *Velero III* at quarter-past five on an overcast December day. She had been on Allan Hancock's great yacht before, but its carpeted saloons, luxurious cabins and bathrooms must have overwhelmed the sad limping woman after five years in the solitude of Floreana.

Poor Dore's mountain of possessions was distinctly unpopular, not only with Fred Ziesenhenne and Waldo Schmitt, but, particularly, with the crewmen who had to carry it. The ship's Purser, Bob Irwin, was in charge of the moving and stowing of Dore's belongings in the fo'c's'le head. He was greatly incensed at having to deal with such 'old garments and rotted cloth' and contrived to 'lose' some of them on the way down to the beach. According to Fred Ziesenhenne, Bob Irwin disposed of the remainder, 'little by little', 'until it all went into a large packing case.' Among the possessions that were stored in that packing case Fred noticed 'Dr. Ritter's shopping list ledger, with the names of the yachts and what he was going to ask the yacht owners to supply for his use.'

After leaving the Black Beach anchorage the *Velero III* sailed for Academy Bay on Santa Cruz. During the following days she moved along the north coast of Santiago and then down the western shore of Isabela, regularly stopping and dropping anchor offshore for the scientists to go about their work of collecting specimens from the unique Galapagos fauna.

Dore was given Cabin 1 in the crew quarters of the *Velero III*, thus displacing its occupant to the cabin of Fred Ziesenhenne, who became, in effect, Dore's attendant. 'With Dore Ritter occupying Cabin No. 1 ... the guests wanting to contact Dore 'phoned me in Cabin 4 and I would have to relay the message or have Dore use my 'phone. Then Dore would ask me to get cold water, fruit, writing paper, pens etc. for her. Dore had one crippled leg and did not walk too well in a rolling sea.'

Dore spent much of her time leaning on the ship's rail, gazing at the sea. When Fred Ziesenhenne asked her whether she was lonely she would reply that she loved and enjoyed the sea. He noted in his diary on 7th December that 'she would not speak about Dr. Ritter or her experiences on Charles Island.' She did eventually tell her attendant about Friedrich eating poisoned chicken meat and how she had warned him not to eat it. Fred Ziesenhenne also noted that 'another story being heard [presumably from gossiping crewmen] was that Dr. Ritter would take his temper out on Dore when upset. During the dry season Dr. Ritter's temper really flared and poor Dore could not take any more punishment and decided to kill the Dr. and leave Charles Island.'

On 8th December Ziesenhenne wrote: 'Dore is now becoming more sociable with the guests ... cleaning up and dressing up in clothes she has not worn for years.' On 11th December Dore watched the traditional fun and games of 'Neptune's Equator Crossing'. By this time young Ziesenhenne's diary was more concerned with this important event, his work, the Paul

Whiteman and Fred Waring orchestras heard on the radio, and card games with his friends. But on 14th December he described his surprise at finding that the *Velero III* was returning to Floreana where Waldo Schmitt was put ashore with one crewman. 'Ray and Dr. Schmitt made a mysterious trip to the Wittmers for more information. It seems Dore may have given some information implicating the Wittmers in the disappearance of the Baroness and Philippson. Mrs. Wittmer thinks that Dr. Ritter had a hand in the killing of the Baroness and Philippson.'

Heinz Wittmer also described the events in his diary.

> On the day after the departure of the *Dar Pomorza* [a ship which anchored at Floreana], to our astonishment, the *Velero III* drops anchor again in the bay. Dr. Schmitt and a young man come to us in Friedo to get oranges and prepare an account of the disappearance of the Baroness. This account is to be signed by Frau Körwin as well as myself for she has been telling all sorts of things on board the ship – things it is difficult to make head or tail of. I then go along on board and after the evening meal the document is brought out and signed by Frau Körwin and myself [see Appendix].
>
> The thing we enjoy the most on the ship is an after-dinner concert. Mr. Hancock himself plays cello. It is wonderful and almost overpowering to hear such music after long years. We are also shown a film, taken by the Baroness. Mr. Swett points out to me that the film does not deal with an actual happening but with a comedy.

* * *

The *Velero III* got under way again at six o'clock on the following morning, 15th December, and headed for Chatham Island. She arrived there at half-past eleven and anchored at Wreck Bay, in cold and windy conditions. The crew seem to have been quite busy that day. Fred Ziesenhenne made no mention of Dore in his diary. He spent the morning writing eight letters. In the afternoon, he cleaned 'all the dried echinoderms ... out of the stack', went out in the ship's boat to dredge for specimens, 'had a bull session' in his cabin after dinner, then cleaned up in the fish room and finished the day listening to the radio, while the rest of the crew played poker in their mess hall.

The wind blew hard that night and it was still cold and wet when Dore left the ship on the following morning, to face the ordeal of the official inquiry into the death of Friedrich Ritter. She was apprehensive as she was taken in the ship's launch at one o'clock to meet the newly-arrived Governor of the Galapagos, a short, sharp-featured man with a five o'clock shadow, who was waiting for her on the shore. Dore was accompanied by Waldo Schmitt and John Garth. The four of them walked to what John Garth describes as the 'Governor's tin palace'. Dore spoke mostly in German at the interview. John Garth acted as her interpreter and translated her halting sentences into Spanish for the Governor. She told the Governor that Friedrich had died from 'eating spoiled chicken'. John Garth felt that this was a strange death for a supposed vegetarian but said that 'there was nothing to be gained by sharing any of these suspicions with the Governor of the Galapagos Islands' and confessed that he 'left out a good deal in the translation'. The *Velero III* party were clearly anxious to get Dore out of 'what was an impossible situation for her' and to get her back to her family in Germany. The Governor quickly wrote out the death certificate: John Garth felt that he too was relieved to 'get Dore off his hands'.

The *Velero III* sailed from Wreck Bay at dawn on the next day, 17th December 1934, bound for Hood Island. The ship stayed there, anchored at Gardner Bay, for three days, while more photographs were taken, specimens collected, and mud samples dredged up.

On the morning of 20th December the ship left for Ecuador to take Dore to Guayaquil to find a passage back to Germany. They had a smooth crossing. An Ecuadorian pilot took the *Velero III* upriver on a fast flooding tide to Guayaquil harbour. The crew and guests on the ship were astonished to see that the quayside was crowded, in John Garth's words, 'with an army of newspapermen'. There were also plenty of curious spectators for the Guayaquil newspapers had been full of stories and photographs about the missing Baroness and her lover, Friedrich's poisoning and the two mummified bodies found on the beach of an uninhabited island. All had come to see Dore Strauch, the mistress of the nudist Dr Ritter of Floreana.

Captain Hancock had decided that the *Velero III* should be anchored away from the quayside and that Dore should be kept on board until the first German ship arrived that could take her back to Germany. She could then be directly transferred to the German ship without setting foot on Ecuadorian soil, thus avoiding the possibility of any further questioning by the Ecuadorian authorities.

However, Hancock's strategy did not isolate Dore, for the people watching from the *Velero III* saw what Fred Ziesenhenne described as 'a dozen small metal boats' making for their ship. These contained the Grace Line Agent, the German Consul and Equadorian officials, but there were also water-taxis full of excited journalists and press photographers, all determined to get Dore's story. But they did not succeed, for Dore managed to stonewall and the newspapers of the world could print only her evasive statements that she was withholding all details about life on Floreana to incorporate in two or three books she intended to write.

Fred Ziesenhenne went ashore with the Grace Line Agent. In the city market he encountered Frau Wörm-Muller who was waiting in Guayaquil for the *San Cristóbal* to take her back to her husband on Isla Santa Cruz. He also met Knud Arends, 'who had recovered from his gunshot wound'. Rather surprisingly, Arends told Fred that 'he had a good time living with the Baroness. If he had the chance, he would return' – an arrangement that might not have been to the liking of Arends's English-speaking wife whom Fred met when he was taken home by Arends.

Dore was left to spend Christmas on board the *Velero III* while Captain Hancock and his party travelled to Quito to give

WOMAN IS LEAVING GALAPAGOS 'EDEN'

Survivor of Nudist Idyll Going Home to Germany After Death of Companion.

LOS ANGELES, Dec. 8 (AP).—Her Garden of Eden life shattered by the death of her companion after six years in the Galapagos archipelago, Frau Dore Strauch Koerwin is going back to her home in Germany, word from the old convict colony of Charles Island disclosed today.

This news was flashed from the Smithsonian Institution scientific party at the island headed by Captain G. Allan Hancock of Los Angeles.

"Hysterical over the death of Dr. Friedrich Ritter, her mate, Frau Dore is packing up to go back to Berlin," Capain Hancock reported.

The lonely survivor of this internationally famous nudist couple, both of whom deserted their marital companions in Berlin in 1928 to go to the old haunts of buccaneers in the Pacific, 500 miles off the coast of Ecuador, will be taken to Guayaquil, Ecuador, and there transship to Berlin.

A year ago a plea was received by Captain Hancock from her mother beseeching him to bring back her daughter. "Never will I leave here," was the answer at this time, but the death of Dr. Ritter on Nov. 21 has led her to change her mind.

Fig. 5 Article from the *New York Times*, 8th December 1934

some concert performances and show films of the Galapagos.

The party from Quito returned to Guayaquil in time for Fred Ziesenhenne to take part in a lively New Year's Eve Party in Guayaquil. When he came aboard the *Velero III*, at three o'clock in the morning of 1st January 1935, he learned that the local papers had carried 'big stories about the *Velero III*'s departure from Guayaquil' and that 'the German ship, S.S. *Cali*, had finished loading and was ready to take Dore Ritter Strauch back to Germany to her relatives and that all her earthly and smelly possessions were crated and sent on a freight boat to the *Cali*.' With all the unfeeling exuberance of youth, Fred recorded that 'Ray rejoiced he could return to the privacy of Cabin No. 1, once it was thoroughly cleaned. My days of telephone messenger boy and personal waiter to Dore had come to an end and she never told me what actually happened.'

The next morning the *Velero III* sailed on the outgoing tide from Guayaquil, bound for Peru, leaving Dore to face the long sea voyage back to Nazi Germany.

16

THE SURVIVORS

When Dore left Floreana on the *Velero III*, the Wittmers honoured their promise to Dore to look after Friedo. Margret took Rolf with her to Friedo, leaving Harry in charge of their home, while Heinz 'ran back and forth'.

Heinz was appalled by the untidiness at Friedo. 'Pots and pans lie around everywhere and there are tools of all kinds. Heaps of empty shells speak eloquently of frequent hunting ... We have tried to clean the living room a bit.' One suspects that the house at Friedo was cleaner after the attentions of Frau Margret than during the bohemian regime of Dore Strauch. Heinz erected a simple cross to mark Friedrich's grave and then, on 28th December, they turned their backs on Friedrich's and Dore's desolate Garden of Eden.

With Dore gone, the press turned its attention to the Wittmers. Floreana was invaded by some American newspapermen, eager for the scoop that would solve the Floreana mystery. They seem to have gleaned little from the Wittmers and, according to Margret, garbled mercilessly what information they did extract.

After this the Wittmers faced a worse ordeal: investigation by the Governor of the Galapagos. On 2nd January he landed on the island with an interpreter, an armed escort and Señor Luna, the newspaper reporter from Guayaquil. It was then that Margret learned of Friedrich Ritter's statement, made in the Ecuadorian newspaper article, that it was Heinz who had killed the Baroness and Philippson. The Wittmers successfully rebutted the accusation. The Governor stayed for lunch with the Wittmers (he apparently enjoyed a leg of chicken cooked by Margret) and departed in an amiable mood.

The Governor had brought with him a sack full of mail for the Wittmers and also a cable from a Cologne newspaper asking for a written account of the recent events on Floreana. They were also asked to make a pre-paid reply of up to seven words. The words were selected and the Governor radioed them when he returned to his ship. Margret afterwards learned that, seven hours later, their carefully chosen words were displayed, in huge letters, outside the newspaper office: 'WE ARE ALIVE RITTER DEAD WILL WRITE'.

Shortly after this, Heinz suggested that Margret would benefit from a holiday in Germany. She could use the money that they had set aside for their return fare to Germany, should their enterprise have failed on Floreana. As they had clearly succeeded the money could be used for Margret's fare and, while in Germany, she could live from the lucrative offer of the Cologne newspaper for a serialized account of their life in the Galapagos.

On 17th February 1935 the *San Cristóbal* arrived at the island. On board was the Governor from Chatham Island who had come to introduce his successor and a painter from Munich, Siegfried Neumann. Herr Neumann agreed to take Margret under his protection during the trip to Guayaquil and, after some very rapid packing, she sailed that afternoon, with Rolf, on the old schooner bound for Chatham Island and then Guayaquil.

Margret had to run the gauntlet of the assembled newspapermen when the *San Cristóbal* docked at Guayaquil. She found them 'harder to keep away than the bulls on Floreana.' But none of the persistent newshounds got the scoop that they were so desperately seeking.

The considerate Herr Neumann had booked a hotel for Margret and a berth on the S.S. *Cerigo*, of the Hamburg-American Line, which would take her and Rolf to Panama, from where she could catch the S.S. *San Francisco* to Hamburg.

Before she sailed, Margret was summoned to the German Consulate to be questioned by a court of six men, including a judge, about the recent events on Floreana. 'From 5 until 8 there were questionings about writings and translations. Rolf began to cry and was given a ruler to play with and by the time we finished the poor little fellow had reduced it to splinters. All questions that had been asked on Floreana and of which they already had a report, were repeated and towards the end they questioned me regarding the relations that existed between Frau Dora Korwin and Dr. Ritter. But at last this too was finished...'

Having successfully acquitted herself Margret sailed down the Rio Guayas aboard the German steam-packet on 1st March. She eventually reached Cologne in late April 1935. Margret was delighted to meet her father again, but was repelled by the recent changes, especially the treatment of the Jews, that had been wrought in Germany by the Nazi regime.

In Cologne Margret wrote her newspaper articles and prepared the public lectures that she illustrated with a ciné film sent by the kindly Allan Hancock. Her lectures seem to have been successful, for in a letter to Allan Hancock she wrote that all the 1,200 places in the lecture hall were taken and 'there was still a crowd of men outside'.

When Margret's articles were published the Editor of the Cologne newspaper was bombarded with angry letters from Dore. She was then living in Berlin and writing her own account of her life with Friedrich on Floreana, which was eventually translated and published as *Satan Came to Eden* in London and New York in 1935. Margret later commented that Dore's book caused only 'a minor stir' and 'was not very successful'.

Dore did not succeed in getting Friedrich Ritter's philosophical works published, despite her avowed intention, expressed on Floreana, of spreading his fame so that 'his writings would be acknowledged as great masterpieces of philosophy'. It was Ritter's nephew, Dr Heiber, who tried to undertake the task. He had no success for he wrote, in a letter to Allan Hancock: 'Even though I would like to immediately publish the great philosophical works of Dr. Ritter, it has not yet been made possible because I have not been able to find a publisher who would do it. I have now to be satisfied with the book of experiences.'

Dore seems not even to have been involved in the publication of this 'book of experiences', *Als Robinson auf Galapagos*, which was published in 1935, for Ritter's nephew wrote: 'The net proceeds from the book will go to the lawful heirs of Dr. Ritter, his wife and sister, after it was found impossible to get the assistance of Frau Strauch-Körwin'. He also revealed that 'Frau Dr. Ritter had the intention, upon the request of Dr. Ritter, to come to the islands this year, while Frau Strauch-Ritter desired to return to Germany. Unfortunately, his untimely death stopped that.'

Another of the old Floreana animosities was transplanted to Germany at this time. The Baroness's brother was apparently a big-shot in the Nazi Party and had power in the Ministry of Propaganda. Margret believed that it was his influence that led to the censoring of the book that she had decided to compile from her press articles.

Margret and Rolf Wittmer left Germany early in November and eventually landed from the *San Cristóbal* at Black Beach in mid-January 1936. Margret described the joy of her reunion with Heinz on the beach with Rolf calling to his father and Lump excitedly barking. When she climbed up to their home she was astonished to find that Heinz and Harry had added a fine new bedroom with concrete floor, six windows and other undreamed-of luxuries.

Life continued peacefully for the Wittmer family in their island solitude, relieved only by the visitors from occasional passing yachts and ships and the irregular arrival of the mail from Germany and from some of their American friends. In April 1937 Margret produced the second native of Floreana, a daughter: Ingeborg Floreanita Wittmer.

Soon after this momentous event, there arrived the first settlers to come to Floreana since the departure of Dore Strauch. They walked up to the Wittmer house early in the morning of 31st May: a tall middle-aged Ecuadorian, Don Ezekial Zavala, his dark-skinned wife Maria, his sixteen-year-old daughter, Marta, and a black-eyed Indian boy, José, who was to work for Don Zavala.

Zavala was to act as the Governor's agent on the island and to supply him with meat and hides from the island's wild cattle. He was given the proprietorship of Friedo by the Governor.

Some six weeks after the arrival of Don Ezekial Zavala two more families came to settle temporarily on Floreana. Captain-Engineer Humberto Goya Rico had been banished to the Galapagos for his involvement in a bomb-explosion in Guayaquil and so brought to Floreana his wife and eight children. Two Americans, Frances and Ainslie Conway, arrived to build their own farmstead in the wilderness and were later to write a book about their adventures. Frances Conway was strongly moved by the garden at Friedo, 'quiet as oblivion, except for the soft trickle of water and the rustling of wind in palm leaves', with the ruined house and Friedrich's grave, obscured by weeds, in the abandoned garden.

The Conways became good neighbours and friends of the Wittmers, despite their antipathy to the large portrait of Adolf Hitler which then adorned the wall of the Wittmer living-room, a gift from a visiting German Admiral. They were naturally keen to discover as much as possible about the disappearance of the Baroness and Philippson, but drew a blank with Margret. 'We have so much trouble with the Baroness that we like not to talk about her.' Despite their years on the island, the Conways got no nearer to the truth of these matters than anyone else who had tried.

Even the curiosity of the President of the United States remained unsatisfied when the cruiser U.S.S. *Houston* anchored off Black Beach with Franklin D. Roosevelt on board in July 1938. The 8th August issue of *Time* magazine said that 'the official news report from the *Houston* announced that the landing parties tried to pump the settlers about Baroness Eloise Wehrborn, the queer German woman who, wearing silk panties and a pearl-handled revolver, sought to rule the island several years ago until she and her retinue of young men came to mysterious ends. The settlers would not tell, and the whereabouts of the Baroness have been unknown for four years.' But she still stole the news, for dominating the President's column of *Time* magazine was a picture of the Baroness showing the familiar buck teeth and sagging bosom.

When the Second World War came, the Conways left Floreana, Ainslie to work at the American air base at Baltra (North Seymour Island) and Frances to do war work in California. A detachment of Ecuadorian soldiers was stationed on the island. The Wittmers were allowed to stay despite their German nationality. After the war they were given one of the timber buildings that the Americans had erected at their base on Baltra. This was dismantled, towed to Floreana and erected at Black Beach to become the new Wittmer home and the nucleus of the little village that would grow up on Floreana.

In 1951, after nearly twenty years on Floreana, Harry Wittmer was drowned when his fishing-boat capsized. But five years later Heinz and Margret derived much happiness from the marriages of Rolf and Ingeborg, and later from the appearance of the third generation of Floreana Wittmers.

In the 1960s Floreana lived up to its sinister reputation when two more people vanished from the island. The first was an American woman, a tourist, who was lost without trace in 1964. Four years later Ingeborg Wittmer's husband, Mario, also disappeared. These events led to much speculation and gossip in the archipelago. Once again an indignant Margret Wittmer was summoned to an official inquiry and, again, there was no conclusive verdict. One of the mysteries was however solved, in 1980, when the skeleton of the American tourist was found in circumstances which left no doubt that she had become lost and died from exhaustion and exposure.

Heinz Wittmer died in 1963. He had fulfilled Hakon Mielche's prediction, that when the other settlers had 'turned to dust' Heinz would smoke his pipe in his cosy house and 'forget to count the days'. And it was true: Dore Strauch had died in Berlin in 1942.

The indomitable Margret Wittmer still lives with her family at Black Beach, steadfastly refusing to talk about the events of fifty years ago – the last survivor of the strange collection of people who fled from twentieth-century civilization to seek their own versions of paradise in the wilderness.

17
POSTSCRIPT

I heard about the strange events on Floreana during a series of visits to the Galapagos to carry out biological research. These events had been an international sensation in the 1930s but were obscured by the Second World War and are now only remembered by some older settlers on the islands.

My original intention was to solve the Floreana mystery, to explain the intricate links between the disappearance of the Baroness and Philippson and the deaths of Ritter, Lorenz and Nuggerud. But, as I found, the critical evidence is fragmentary and contradictory, and the mystery remains. Yet the temptation to produce a satisfying hypothesis is irresistible.

The most intriguing thing about the whole affair is, of course, the fate of the Baroness and Philippson. There are several possible explanations for their mysterious disappearance.

It could be that there was no foul play. The Baroness and Philippson might really have been picked up by a passing boat, never to be heard of again, and Ritter's death may have been quite accidental. Lorenz's death, in any case, appears to have been purely coincidental.

How feasible is the theory that the Baroness and Philippson left the island? Two possibilities have been advanced.

It was claimed, in at least two newspaper reports, that the Baroness was seen on a Galapagos island a year after the events described above and, what is more, had even threatened the Governor of Pennsylvania with the famous pearl-handled revolver (see Fig. 6). However, almost as surprising, the claim was later admitted to be a hoax on the part of the Governor. Another newspaper article, published in December 1935, reported that the Baroness had built a fort on Isabela Island: 'There were two-foot high walls of rock, four-foot towers studded the angles and brass cannons peeped over the parapet.' This report of course was never substantiated. It is difficult to imagine how she and Philippson could have existed, undetected, without either equipment or supplies (which would have required contact with other people in the archipelago).

The alternative theory, that the Baroness and Philippson had been taken off on a ship and subsequently lived on a South Sea island, is also difficult to sustain. Firstly, no ship was seen at Floreana at the time of the disappearances, neither were there reports of such a ship being seen elsewhere in the archipelago. Secondly, it is unlikely that the Baroness would not have sought maximum international publicity for her activities, wherever she lived. Thirdly, there was no later substantiated news of her, or reports from the crew of the supposed ship, despite the fierce international publicity and occasional press reports that she had been seen on other Pacific islands.

The possibility remains that the Baroness and Philippson were picked up by a passing ship which was subsequently wrecked. This must, however, be highly improbable, for it is unlikely that a ship would have been in the waters of the Galapagos without someone's knowledge, and its loss would have been the subject of inquiry. Certainly the claim that a skeleton found at Tortuga Bay, Santa Cruz, in November 1935 was that of Philippson was not substantiated. Dr V.W. von Hagen, an American scientist, subsequently identified the skeleton as that of a seaman from the becalmed Norwegian barque, *Alexander* (see p. 182).

In addition, it is extremely improbable that the Baroness would have left her hat, luggage and her talisman book behind, as Dore claimed, if she was going on a South Sea cruise or leaving Floreana for ever.

Furthermore, it should be borne in mind that the story of the

GALAPAGOS VISITOR TELLS OF 'EMPRESS'

Cruise Conductor Says Baroness Wehrborn Pointed Pistol at Ex-Gov. Pinchot.

ST. PAUL, Minn., March 14 (AP). —The belief that she had seen the missing Baroness Eloisa de Wagner Wehrborn, "Empress of the Galapagos Islands," and that the Empress had pointed a gun at former Governor Gifford Pinchot of Pennsylvania, was expressed in a letter received by a St. Paul friend today from Miss Marguerite Davis.

Miss Davis, a former tennis player of St. Paul, is conducting a group of prominent persons on a world cruise. The party landed at the islands in February. In describing the visit, Miss Davis said in her letter:

"We saw signs of wild animals, but went on. Mr. Pinchot, who was leading us, was quite a way ahead. He rushed on, leaving us behind, for he had found a piece of white silk.

"'Stop!' shouted a voice. Then he felt something on his shoulder. It was a pearl-handled revolver held by the steady hand of a woman who was dressed very much the same as the women on our cruise boat.

"The woman was the Baroness, who gave him a very cold look and said: 'I don't like you. Go!' He went.

"Another man with us had quite a conversation with the Baroness. She told him that she had more than just two admirers; that they fought for the honor, but that the new one always won. The discarded ones she locked up in a cabin not far from her own. She supposed that they eventually escaped, for she never saw them again."

Fig. 6 Article from the *New York Times*, 14th March 1935, based on the hoax by the former Governor of Pennsylvania, who claimed to have discovered the missing Baroness

passing ship that picked up the Baroness and Philippson rested only on the evidence of one person, Margret Wittmer, and could not be corroborated by any other witness.

If the Baroness and Philippson were not taken from Floreana by a passing ship, then only two possibilities remain: suicide or murder.

Friedrich Ritter at first advanced the suicide theory, because, he proposed, the Baroness could not face the prospect of the failure of her dream of the millionaires' hotel on Floreana. This theory is not totally impossible. Rolf Blomberg, for example, quotes a remark that the Baroness is supposed to have made about herself and Philippson: 'One day we shall smoke a last cigarette, drink a last whisky and together swim out into the big sea.' The Baroness, with her strong dramatic sense and considerable talents for publicity, would certainly have realized the furore that her unexplained disappearance would cause and just conceivably could have attempted this means to achieve posthumously even more notoriety.

On balance, however, the possibility of murder seems more likely than suicide, for the following reasons. Firstly, Dore Strauch stated categorically her belief that murder had been done: 'The Baroness has been murdered, Philippson has been murdered.' Secondly, Friedrich later abandoned his suicide theory and made a direct accusation of murder in an Ecuadorian newspaper. Thirdly, the inhabitants apparently made no concerted attempt to search the island for the bodies of the Baroness and Philippson. This is surprising, for when two people vanish on a remote island (with no evidence of a ship to take them off), it might be reasonably expected that an intensive search would have been made for them – even if for no better reason than to establish right of claim to abandoned property. Finally, there is the curious disparity between Margret Wittmer's and Dore Strauch's account of the events that occurred between 19th March and 1st April 1934. If the Baroness had committed suicide secretly, then why was it necessary for one or other of the two women to fabricate an obviously false version of the events?

If, as seems likely, the Baroness and Philippson never left the island, then what happened to them, and, more to the point, who disposed of them? All of the remaining settlers had motives for getting rid of the objectionable Baroness Wagner de Bosquet. To the Wittmers she was a considerable nuisance, but they had nevertheless established themselves on Floreana, and had built a comfortable home with an obviously happy family atmosphere. To the inhabitants of Friedo the Baroness was an uncongenial and difficult neighbour, but, more importantly, she threatened Friedrich Ritter's role as the philosopher and '*der Robinson auf Galapagos*'. For Rudolf Lorenz, however, the Baroness and Philippson were a threat to his very existence. The Baroness had ruined him, financially, morally and physically, and reduced him to a wretched fugitive.

Lorenz, therefore, obviously had the strongest motive for disposing of the Baroness and Philippson. But could Lorenz, a weak-willed man in very poor physical condition, have single-handedly overpowered and killed the Baroness, who was quite able to look after herself, let alone the stronger and more powerful Philippson? Certainly Lorenz had reached such a desperate state that he was driven to use physical violence at the Hacienda Paradiso. Furthermore, he seems to have been able to move in a quite stealthy way, for Margret frequently describes him slipping out suddenly from the undergrowth: 'Lorenz had often scared me with his way of creeping through the bush followed by sudden jack-in-the-box appearances.' It is, therefore, conceivable that Lorenz could, for example, have surprised the Baroness and Philippson or, perhaps, have disposed of them by some other subterfuge. There were, for example, poisonous substances on the island which Lorenz might have obtained and used. Friedrich certainly possessed something with which he attempted to poison the 'satanic boar' and Dore placed great emphasis on the question that the Baroness once addressed to Friedrich: 'Oh, Dr. Ritter – do tell me! Is it true that milk's the antidote for arsenic poisoning?'

Margret Wittmer's theory was that Lorenz might have

sneaked into the Hacienda Paradiso in the Baroness's absence and taken her revolver. She speculated that Lorenz could then have murdered the Baroness and Philippson at Post Office Bay. There were, according to her, footprints in the sand. The lack of blood stains suggested to Margret that 'if there *was* foul play, it took place on the beach, not in the chalet'. According to this theory the tide, which came within a few yards of the Norwegian chalet, would have washed away any traces of blood and the sharks in the bay would have quickly disposed of the bodies.

John Garth and Fred Ziesenhenne both mention another possibility, which also appeared in a magazine article, namely: that the bodies of the Baroness and Philippson were in a large box, kept at Post Office Bay, that Lorenz took on board the *Dinamita* when he left the island. Fred Ziesenhenne wrote in his diary in December 1934: 'Many believed the bodies of the Baroness and Philippson were in the box and enough rocks were added to sink the box and bodies in very deep water.' This must, however, be a remote possibility for a number of reasons, not the least being that it would have involved four complete outsiders (Nuggerud, Travino, Wörm-Muller and Blomberg) as accomplices. Furthermore, Rolf Blomberg, who gave a detailed description of his visit to Floreana and his voyage on the *Dinamita*, made no mention of any such happening.

The important thing is that the consensus of the people directly involved was that Lorenz was the murderer. The only uncertainties are the methods of his dispatch of the Baroness and Philippson and the disposal of their bodies. The major question remaining is whether Lorenz had an accomplice or accomplices.

There are grounds for suspicion. Firstly, as already emphasized, Rudolf Lorenz was a weak-willed young man, in very poor physical condition, and it seems doubtful that he would have had the means or the courage to directly overcome the Baroness and Philippson by himself. Secondly, there are the strange discrepancies between the accounts of the Wittmers and the inhabitants of Friedo concerning the events surrounding the disappearance of the Baroness and her lover.

At first sight Margret Wittmer might appear to be an obvious accomplice, or confidante, of Lorenz, for the story of the ship that had come to collect the Baroness and Philippson was, as Frances Conway also believed, merely a 'clumsy invention'. There was no ship and, in any case, the subsequent accusations and counter-accusations concerning the Baroness's murder, by Friedrich Ritter, Dore Strauch and the Wittmers, indicate that they all believed that the Baroness had not left the island.

The critical point is, who was responsible for the 'clumsy invention'? This message appears to be a crude attempt by Margret Wittmer to provide an alibi for the murderer of the Baroness and Philippson, presumably Lorenz, perhaps in collaboration with Heinz Wittmer. After all, according to Dore, Heinz Wittmer had once maintained that they should take the law into their own hands. In this case the alibi would have been concocted for the benefit of the Friedo inhabitants and, later, for the outside world. But Margret would have had plenty of time to devise an alibi before her visit to Friedo and it is very difficult to see why she, an obviously intelligent and practical woman, should have produced such a crude story. She could, to choose just one example, have concocted a much more effective story based on the Baroness's drunken escapade with Philippson on the beach, an escapade that was witnessed at the time by several people in the anchored ships. Such a story would have assigned the intoxicated Baroness and her companion to a watery grave with no awkward questions.

The story of the South Sea cruise was quite out of character for Margret Wittmer, but exactly what the Baroness might have devised to lure Lorenz back to the Hacienda Paradiso to claim his longed-for possessions. Lorenz did, in fact, according to Margret, specifically mention the possibility of a trap before he left for the Hacienda Paradiso. According to this interpretation Margret Wittmer was unwittingly passing off the Baroness's lie as the truth.

It is, indeed, quite impressive that Margret Wittmer should

have unwaveringly maintained the truth of the Baroness's story of her leaving the island on a visiting yacht, for Margret had nothing to gain by sustaining such an improbable story. Furthermore, the Wittmers appear to have been truthful witnesses, for their accounts of the events on Floreana correspond at a number of points with those of other people, notably on the date of the disappearance of the Baroness and Philippson and, also, concerning the subsequent death of Friedrich Ritter. It should also be borne in mind that the Wittmers later survived a rigorous inquiry by the Governor of the Galapagos on Floreana and that Margret satisfied an investigating court, at the German Consulate in Guayaquil, without any of the protection that Dore Strauch received from the members of the *Velero III* expedition during her interview on Chatham Island.

Dore Strauch and Friedrich Ritter, on the other hand, both appear to have been less than truthful on a number of occasions. This can be said not only of their way of life at Friedo and of their personal relations, but also of their accounts of the events associated with the disappearance of the Baroness and Philippson. A particularly telling example is Dore's behaviour on the *Velero III*, which led Captain Hancock to return to Floreana and make her produce a joint, witnessed account with Heinz Wittmer of the events on the island. And yet Dore deliberately made great efforts in her subsequent writings to imply that the Baroness and Philippson had disappeared a week before the date ('around 28th March') that she had agreed in the statement to Captain Hancock.

Dore's description of the 'long-drawn scream' at midday is also difficult to relate to events at the Hacienda Paradiso, for it would have been impossible for her and Friedrich to have heard such a noise at a distance of three miles, separated from the spot as they were by a substantial mountain slope. Furthermore, it is odd that, according to Dore's account, she and Friedrich did not leave Friedo to investigate the cause of the terrible shriek – if, as she implies, someone had been injured or killed within earshot. It is, in addition, difficult to imagine that the shriek could have resulted from the weak and ill-nourished Lorenz dispatching the Baroness and/or Philippson close at hand, in broad daylight, by a violent attack that did not involve shooting – for there was no description of shots preceding the shriek. Her description of the midday scream also conflicts with Friedrich's claim, printed in an Ecuadorian newspaper, that he heard shots and a woman's scream at night.

It is distinctly odd that, of all the settlers on the island, Dore was most certain of Rudolf Lorenz's involvement in the killing of the Baroness and Philippson. She spoke with certainty of Lorenz as 'a man with blood on his hands', but gave no reasons for her certainty.

This could be because it was Friedrich Ritter who was Rudolf Lorenz's accomplice. Dore might have been aware of this and have falsified her account of the events to protect the reputation of the famous Dr Ritter of Floreana. Friedrich's violent hatred of the Baroness was well documented. Contrary to Dore's description, Friedrich was, as witnessed by Margret Wittmer and Rolf Blomberg, delighted that the Baroness had disappeared from Floreana.

Certainly Friedrich's behaviour after the disappearance of his neighbours was distinctly odd and inconsistent. At first he sustained the story about the Baroness's departure on a visiting yacht. For example, in a letter that he gave to Lorenz when the young man left the island, he wrote: 'The Baroness and Philippson have vanished to the South Seas.' Yet he told Rolf Blomberg at this time that he believed that the Baroness and Philippson had committed suicide. Subsequently, he wrote to the Ecuadorian newspaper directly accusing Heinz Wittmer of assisting in the shooting of the Baroness. It may be significant that he produced this accusation only *after* Lorenz had disappeared and could not, therefore, dispute the charge.

The involvement of Friedrich Ritter as Lorenz's accomplice might also explain the extremely odd sentences in a letter written on 10th July 1934, stating that he feared: 'a bullet out of the bush ... even if there is no more baroness here.'

He wrote these words at the time he was writing to Allan

Hancock that the Baroness had gone on a 'South Sea cruise' and telling Rolf Blomberg that he believed she had committed suicide. If he accepted either of these explanations then why should he have feared 'a bullet out of the bush' which could only have been fired by Rudolf Lorenz or Heinz Wittmer, with whom he had no serious quarrel? The most obvious explanation would be that he feared that his accomplice might dispatch him in this way, so as to silence Friedrich in case he should ever reveal the truth. If this was the case then it could be that it was Friedrich who had supplied one of his rifles (of which Heinz said there were a number stacked at Friedo) to Lorenz to enable him to shoot the Baroness or Philippson or, perhaps, had given Lorenz poison (which it is known that he had) to kill them by, say, surreptitiously putting it in their food or drink at the Hacienda Paradiso.

If Friedrich had been Lorenz's accomplice in the murder, then this would represent an even stronger motive for Dore to attempt to falsify the chronology and other details connected with the disappearance of the Baroness and her lover in the terrible heat of that Galapagos summer of 1934. For even if Dore's love for Friedrich had died, she would still want to preserve the fiction of her relationship with the great philosopher of Floreana, who could not be implicated as a squalid accomplice in murder.

* * *

There is also the mystery surrounding the death of Friedrich Ritter. Dore wrote, some years later: 'One morning he awoke feeling ill. He had a stroke, and was paralyzed on the right side.' Yet Margret Wittmer described Friedrich as dying of food poisoning.

Here again, Margret Wittmer's story is by far the more plausible. Firstly, it involved other people. Philips Lord, and his crew, for example, knew of the poisoned chickens. This is also the story that Dore told the members of the *Velero III* expedition. Furthermore, an Associated Press report from Guayaquil (published in the *New York Times* on 12th December

1934) specifically stated that Dore herself, again, 'related that Dr. Ritter, who went to the islands to put into practice his theory of raw food diet and natural living, had died after eating poisoned meat and had been buried in a shallow grave near their primitive dwelling.' Secondly, Margret Wittmer's description of Friedrich's end is consistent with the symptoms that would be expected of death by botulin poisoning. She described how his sight had deteriorated, that his tongue was affected so that he could not speak and that he had respiratory difficulties – all typical of botulism. Both Margret and Dore described how Friedrich lifted both his arms, which would certainly not be expected of someone who, according to Dore's later account, was supposed to be dying of a stroke.

Dore's account of her relationship with Friedrich before and during his poisoning conflicts with Margret's description and, very importantly, with the account of the party from the *Velero III* who collected Dore from the island. Far from the idyllic relationship which Dore related, in romantic and unconvincing terms, there seems to have been positive hatred between them. This was probably far worse than that of which she wrote during their early months on the island, for Friedrich was in such an extremity that, according to Margret, he told her of the personal difficulties which he was earlier at such pains to conceal. He had also written to Germany to ask his wife to come to live with him on Floreana and was arranging for Dore to be shipped back to Germany.

The essential truth of Margret Wittmer's description of Friedrich's death, and the quite independent evidence (from the *Velero III* party) of Friedrich's hatred of Dore, adds conviction to Margret's description of Friedrich's dying enmity for Dore: his 'hate-filled eyes', 'the feeble movements as if to hit or kick her', his attempt 'to pounce on her' and his last written sentence, 'I curse you with my dying breath.'

Dore Strauch made no reference in her written account to poisoned chicken, despite the evidence of Margret Wittmer, Philips Lord, her own press statement in Guayaquil or that of the party from the *Velero III*. This could have been because of her unwillingness to reveal Friedrich's carnivorous habits. However, she wrote about them several times in her account of their life together on Friedo. Furthermore, she knew that there were several direct, and indirect, witnesses as well as a number of press reports about Friedrich's death. And yet she later suppressed any mention of poisoned chicken meat. This is very odd indeed, for it not only flaws her account but indicates that she must have had a very particular reason for the suppression.

Now, according to the Wittmers, Friedrich Ritter told them that the potted meat would be safe to eat provided that it was boiled, and Dr Ritter was quite correct in saying this. According to Margret, Dore said that she gave the potted meat 'a good boiling'. And yet Friedrich died of food poisoning and Dore did not, despite the fact that, according to Margret, she too ate the potted meat. Dore claimed, again according to Margret, that she was sick after eating the boiled meat, and hence was not poisoned.

However, this explanation leaves one critical question unanswered. Why had Dore not boiled the potted meat sufficiently to destroy the toxin in the first place? It is unlikely that Friedrich, a physician, would not have given her precise instructions as to the length of time that the pots of meat should have been boiled. Furthermore, the short time necessary for the heat-destruction of botulin toxin (three minutes' boiling for home-canned foods, according to one authority) makes it difficult to believe that Friedrich's poisoning was accidental.

In addition, there are three curious aspects of Dore's and Friedrich's behaviour at that time which give cause for doubt. Firstly, there was the fact that, according to Margret, Dore waited for a whole day, until Friedrich was far gone and virtually speechless, before she sought help. Secondly, as already noted, there was Dore's suppression of any mention of food poisoning in her final version of the events surrounding Friedrich's death. Finally, there was Friedrich's hatred of Dore, which was independently confirmed, and, especially, his extraordinary death-bed behaviour when, according to Margret

Wittmer, he wrote his last sentence cursing Dore 'with his dying breath'.

There could be several reasons for Friedrich's appalling death-bed hatred of Dore. It might have been merely a final lash of the hatred that had built up as his relationship with Dore deteriorated. The extraordinary intensity suggests, however, that there could be more to it than that; namely, that he knew that Dore had poisoned him. But would Dore, normally so gentle and kind, have been capable of destroying her lover? She was clearly an emotional person, with strong feelings – whether of love or of hatred. She was also impulsive: she even had occasional spasms of sympathy for her enemy, the Baroness. It is easy to imagine a situation in which Friedrich had ordered Dore to boil the meat, because of the danger of botulin toxin. Dore could have ignored this by serving cold, unboiled meat and abstained from eating it: either from mere contrariness or as a spontaneous act of malice.

It is far less easy to imagine that Dore used the opportunity provided by the tainted meat to carry out a premeditated act of poisoning. However, from Dore's standpoint there were two Friedrich Ritters. There was the Dr Ritter whom she had first seen in the ward of the Hydrotherapeutic Institute in Berlin: philosopher, disciple of Nietzsche and noble seeker of truth in the wilderness. The other was Friedrich the pigeon-toed destroyer of her cherished flowers, the cold indifferent lover who had left her exhausted on the lava slope during the agonizing climb to Friedo with their belongings and who struck her in front of Heinz and Harry Wittmer.

She could perhaps dispense with the second Friedrich, for their love had shrivelled to hatred. But the myth of Dr Ritter the noble philosopher was essential to Dore. Without it her life had no purpose or dignity. Indeed, the living Friedrich threatened the myth. But with him dead, Dore could devote all her life and love to the idea of him. 'The gods of Floreana slew Friedrich, but can have no power over him. He must live on through me.'

Dore's imagery of divine wrath not only veiled Friedrich's

squalid death, but also obscured her own involvement in his poisoning, whether it was accidental or intentional. This was not a new attitude for Dore. Since her first days on Floreana, she had developed a double life in which she compensated for the desolate reality of her life with Friedrich by fantasies of their closeness on the 'spiritual and intellectual plane' and her role as the disciple of a man of 'more than ordinary human stature'.

But would these fantasies have been sufficient to sustain her in her desperate loneliness, hated by Friedrich Ritter? She would surely have longed for the comfort of another human contact. The only person for such a contact would have been Rudolf Lorenz, also lonely, unhappy and, no doubt, desperate for love and affection. Dore clearly found him physically attractive. She was also intimate enough with him to know his favourite foods, to go to considerable lengths to prepare them for him when she expected him to visit Friedo and to become extremely upset when he did not appear at her party with the Baroness and Philippson. Dore was, in addition, capable of astonishing duplicity in her human relationships, as was shown by her behaviour in Berlin before her flight to the wilderness with Friedrich. Rudolf Lorenz was himself a stealthy, secretive man who would have been capable of concealing a clandestine relationship with Dore.

A secret friendship between Dore and Lorenz could also account for her certainty that Lorenz disposed of the Baroness and Philippson. After the event she might well have felt revulsion for Lorenz. This could explain her strange words on his departure from Floreana: 'Suddenly all the recoil which I had felt against him as a man with blood upon his hands subsided, leaving me filled with sympathy for this wrecked life which might have been so different.'

* * *

As we have seen, it is difficult to trace with certainty the truth of the events that led to the disappearance of the Baroness and Philippson and the poisoning of Ritter. However, the following hypothesis is feasible. The Baroness, together with Philippson, really did call on Margret Wittmer, and told her that they were about to depart on a yacht for a cruise. This story was a subterfuge to lure Lorenz back to the Hacienda Paradiso. Lorenz was not fooled, but, instead, managed to kill the Baroness and Philippson, by unknown means, most probably on 27th or 28th March 1934. Friedrich Ritter would have been his most likely accomplice. Dore Strauch's relationship with Friedrich had deteriorated to such an extent that she sought Lorenz's company and, therefore, knew of his dispatch of the Baroness and Philippson, or alternatively, learned from Friedrich of his own involvement. Dore poisoned Ritter: most probably as a result of a culinary accident or an unpremeditated act of malice or, very much less likely, as a calculated act.

* * *

Despite my original intentions, the most fascinating thing for me has been to follow the lives of the strange collection of settlers as they sought their own versions of paradise in the solitude of the Galapagos half a century ago – for Dore and Friedrich to discover the truth of existence, for the Baroness to fulfil bizarre imperial ambitions and for the Wittmers to establish a farmstead in the wilderness. All of them were trying to escape from the stresses and constraints of early-twentieth-century civilization. Instead, they brought with them the seeds of conflict that grew to the jealousies and hatreds which, as with the castaways in Schnabel's Utopian version of 'Robinson', destroyed the inhabitants of the Hacienda Paradiso and Friedo.

The tragedies on Floreana in 1934 primarily resulted from the hatreds that sprang up *within* two of the households rather than from competition *between* the three groups of settlers. It was not only the Wittmers' normality and resourcefulness, but also the love that existed in their home that ensured their survival. At the time of the birth of young Rolf Wittmer, at Christmas 1932, this love touched all of the island's inhabitants and showed how things might have been. The good-will that was generated by the appearance of the first native of Floreana died after a few brief days and left only the enmities that caused the destruction of Friedrich, the Baroness, Philippson, Lorenz and the innocent Nuggerud.

APPENDIX

The document that Dore Strauch and Heinz Wittmer jointly produced and signed in the presence of Captain Hancock

APPENDIX

Joint Statement by MR. HEINZ WITTMER AND DORE STRAUCH RITTER as given to Captain G. Allan Hancock of the Velero III on Dec. 14th/34 REGARDING THE DEPARTURE OF THE BARONESS WAGNER AND ROBERT PHILLIPSON AND RUDOLPH LORENZ FROM CHARLES ISLAND.

Troubles on Charles Island between the Baroness and Lorenz seem to have come to a head during the long period of drought which lasted from Oct. 1933 to April 16th, 1934. At the height of the drought water ran short at the Baroness's place, so that they got scarcely a pitcher-full a day. There was neither enough to eat nor to drink and Lorenz, who had been ill treated for a long time was finally driven out. He came to the Wittmers' for food and shelter. It was early in March when they took him in. He slept upstairs with their son Harry. Some days after he arrived at their place, the Baroness came to the fence and asked for him. Lorenz went off for a time with her that day. Practically each afternoon thereafter, she would come for him and often the two went off for a walk together, or else she would leave a note for him.

Around the 28th of March the Baroness, in her usual island garb, came and called for Lorenz, and when she learned that he was out, asked that he be told to come down to see her. She added that she was going away and told Mrs. Wittmer 'goodbye', saying that she was leaving on a vessel lying in Post Office Bay at the time, the name of which she did not give. When Lorenz returned, some hours later, he departed in the direction of the Baroness's house, but came back that evening to sleep at Wittmer's.

Following the Baroness's departure, Lorenz continued to eat at the Wittmers', off and on, at irregular intervals, but slept at the Baroness's house. This continued for the next two or three weeks. Even before the departure of the Baroness, he had wanted to leave the island and had put up a notice to that effect at Post-Office Bay. He asked to be taken by the first vessel calling, to Chatham Island, and was willing to pay 50 Sucres for the passage. After those two or three weeks he moved down to Post-Office Bay for a period of 5 weeks, hoping to contact some vessel or boat, but without success. He came up to Wittmer's about twice a week for water and food supplies, and on two occasions when he had gone upland for food and water he missed boats. Also his belongings had been broken into on two occasions when he was away. Prior to this, on April 20th, a vessel owned by Thomas Howell Sr., of Miami, Florida, did call. Mr. Howell, seeing Lorenz's sign, came up and offered to take him away, but he refused because it was raining and he could not get his belongings packed in time. It was following Howell's departure, that Lorenz moved all of his things down to Post-Office Bay.

Finally, on July 11th, Lorenz went off with a Norwegian, Nuggerud, from Academy Bay on Indefatigable Island, who had with him two other men from that place, who had come over on a visit to Charles Island. Lorenz took with him letters from both the Wittmers and the Ritters, together with the money that Ritter and Wittmer had paid him for supplies which the Baroness had left behind and which they needed.

So far as we know, Lorenz got to Academy Bay on the 12th and left the next day, Friday July 13th, with Nuggerud and an Ecuadorian for Chatham. He was not seen again until an American fishing boat discovered the bodies of Nuggerud and Lorenz on Marchena Island about November 21st. We know nothing of the Baroness's whereabouts, dead or alive, and only know about her what Lorenz imparted to us before his departure.

BIBLIOGRAPHY

Much useful information was gleaned from the following books, which describe the events that occurred on Floreana between 1929 and 1935:

Allan Hancock Pacific Expeditions. Volume 1, Parts I, II, III (1943), University of Southern California Press, Los Angeles.

BLOMBERG, Rolf. *Underliga människor och underliga djur; strövtåg på Galapagos och i Amazonas* (1936), Geber, Stockholm.

CLOVER, Sam T. *A Pioneer Heritage* (1932), Saturday Night Publishing Co., Los Angeles.

CONWAY, Ainslie and Frances. *The Enchanted Islands* (1948), Bles, London.

HOWARD, Sidney. *Isles of Escape, Being the Adventures of Roydon Bristow* (1934), Bell, London.

MEREDITH, De Witt. *Voyages of the Velero III*, published privately.

MIELCHE, Hakon. *Let's See if the World is Round* (1938), Hodge, London.

PINCHOT, Gifford. *To the South Seas* (1931), Hutchinson, London.

RITTER, F. *Dr. Ritter auf der Galapagosinsel* (1931), Verlag von M. Willahn, Berlin.

RITTER, Friedrich. *Als Robinson auf Galapagos* (1935), Grethlein & Co. Nachf., Leipzig.

STRAUCH, Dora. *Satan Came to Eden* (1935), Jarrolds, London.

SWET, W. Charles. 'Floreana' (1935), unpublished manuscript.

WITTMER, Margret. *What Happened on Galapagos? The Truth of the Galapagos Affair as Told by a Lady From Cologne*, manuscript, n.d., commissioned by and dedicated to Captain G. Allan Hancock, translated by Sydney Skamser.

WITTMER, Margret. *Floreana* (1961), Michael Joseph, London.

The following magazine articles proved useful:

RITTER, Friedrich. 'Adam and Eve in Galapagos' (1931), *Atlantic Monthly* 148, pp. 409–18.
RITTER, Friedrich. 'Satan walks in the garden' (1931), *Atlantic Monthly* 148, pp. 565–75.
RITTER, Friedrich. 'Eve calls it a day' (1931), *Atlantic Monthly* 148, pp. 733–43.
STRAUCH, Dore (as told to Walter Brockman). 'Satan Came to Eden' (1936), articles in *Hearst's International Cosmopolitan.*
WITTMER, Greta [Margret]. 'Death Over Galapagos' (1937), articles in *Liberty*

I have, in addition, had access to a film and the papers of the late Captain G. Allan Hancock and to the personal diaries and papers of Dr John S. Garth and Captain Fred. C. Ziesenhenne. I have also consulted and used a collection of photographs in the possession of the Allan Hancock Foundation at the University of Southern California. Some information has been obtained from articles and reports published in the following magazines: *Time*, *Liberty*, *Detective Tabloid*, *Wide World* and *Real Detective*. The following newspapers have also been consulted: the *Los Angeles Times*, the *Los Angeles Herald*, the *New York Times*, *The Times*, *El Universo* (Guayaquil), *El Telegrafo* (Guayaquil).

The following books provided useful background information:

BEEBE, William. *Galapagos: World's End* (1924), Putnam's and Witherby, London & New York.
BLACKWELDER, Richard E. *The Zest for Life or Waldo Had a Pretty Good Run. The Life of Waldo La Salle Schmitt* (1979), Allen Press, Lawrence, Kansas.
COHN, Norman. *The Pursuit of the Millennium* (1957), Secker & Warburg, London.
COLNETT, Captain James. *A Cruising Voyage Around the World* (1978), London.
CONWAY, Ainslie and Frances. *Return to the Islands* (1952), Bles, London.
COWLEY, Ambrose. *Voyage Round the World* (1699), London.
DAMPIER, William. *A Collection of Voyages* (1729), London.
DARWIN, Charles. *Journal of Researches into the Natural History and Geology of the Countries Visited During the Voyage of H.M.S. Beagle Round the World* (1852), John Murray, London.

EIBL-EIBESFELDT, Ireanaus. *Galapagos* (1960), MacGibbon & Kee, London.

FITZ-ROY, Robert. *Narrative of the Surveying Voyages of His Majesty's Ships Adventure and Beagle Between 1826 and 1836* (1839), Colburn, London.

VON HAGEN, Victor Wolfgang. *Ecuador the Unknown* (1939), Jarrolds, London.

MELVILLE, Herman. *The Encantadas* (1854), published in *Billy Budd, Sailor and Other Stories* (1971), Penguin Books, London.

PORTER, Captain David. *Journal of a Cruise made to the Pacific Ocean* (1822), New York.

SCHNABEL, Johann Gottfried. *Die Insel Felsenburg* (1731–1743), ed. Volker Meid and Ingeborg Springer-Strand (1979), Philipp Reclam, Stuttgart.

WILDE, Oscar. *The Picture of Dorian Gray* (1891), Ward Lock, London.

I consulted the following works to educate myself about botulism:

HUGHES, J. M. *et al.* 'Clinical features of Types A and B food-borne botulism', *Annals of Internal Medicine* 95 (1981), pp. 442–5.

SALLE, A. J. *Fundamental Principles of Bacteriology* (1972), McGraw-Hill, New York, p. 902.

WILSON, G. S. and MILES, A. *Principles of Bacteriology, Virology and Immunity* (1975), 6th edition, pp. 2099–119, Edward Arnold, London.

About the Author

JOHN TREHERNE is a fellow of Downing College, Cambridge, and edits the *Journal of Experimental Biology.* He is director of a team of seventeen research scientists and author of numerous papers, monographs and books on biological subjects. This is his first nonscientific book. He lives in England.

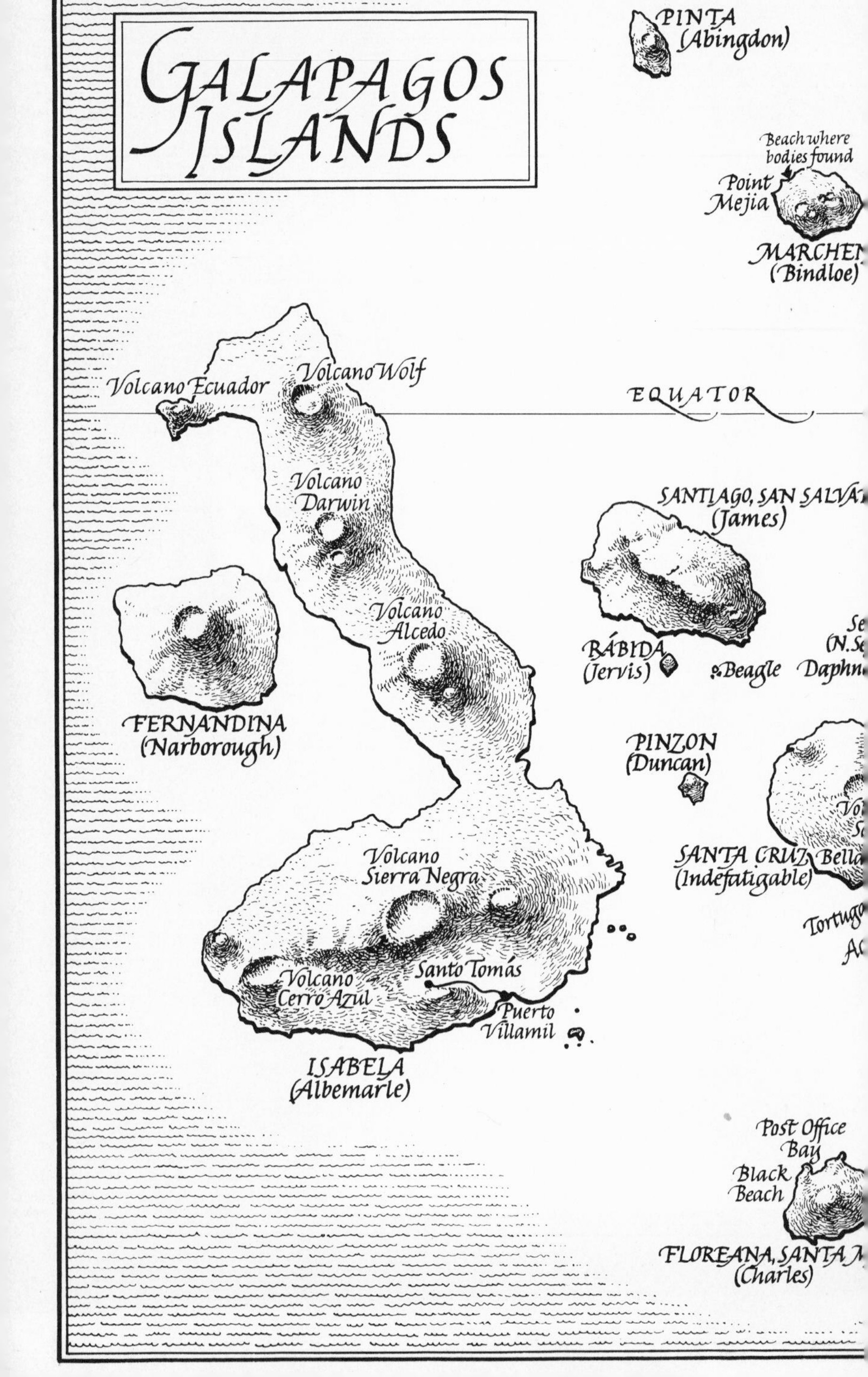

GALAPAGOS ISLANDS
PINTA
(Abingdon)
Beach where bodies found
Point Mejia
(Bindloe)
Volcano Ecuador
Volcano Wolf
EQUATOR
Volcano Darwin
(James)
Volcano Alcedo
RÁBIDA
(Jervis)
Beagle
FERNANDINA
(Narborough)
PINZON
(Duncan)
Volcano Sierra Negra
SANTA CRUZ
(Indefatigable)
Santo Tomás
Volcano Cerro Azul
Puerto Villamil
ISABELA
(Albemarle)
Post Office Bay
Black Beach
(Charles)

GALAPAGOS! On these islands 600 miles off the coast of Ecuador, goodies for the amateur naturalist: booby dances, swimming lizards, giant tortoises

Story by Lynn Ferrin/Photography by Frans Lanting

In a composite photo, Golden Gate Park's playground with its carousel forms the backdrop for the (left to right) Buick LeSabre, Mazda 929S, Pontiac Bonneville SSE and the Chrysler Town & Country. For more on carousels, see San Francisco's Small Museums *in this issue.*

to make certain that you do not step off the trail or harm the natural environment in any way. (When we got off the plane we were greeted by our naturalist, a blond blue-eyed Guatemalan named Patsy Topke. Said she forthwith: "You may not touch any animal. And you may not ride the giant tortoises.")

I was a long time coming to the Galapagos. Perhaps it was the dread of seasickness—alleviated in recent years by the new drug scopolamine—or my image of the volcanic islands as barren, rocky and covered with guano. But as it turned out, I absolutely loved the place, loved the odd birds and weird reptiles, loved the strange landscape, never minded the guano. The snorkeling was sensational. I absorbed a phenomenal amount of biological science.

It was, in the end, a journey that excelled on every level: the intellectual, the sensual, the physical, the emotional.

My tour was operated by Wilderness Travel of Berkeley, which offers a wide variety of excursions to the Galapagos throughout the year, on small vessels—and there were only seven people in our group. I chose an 18-day

one marine iguana, one yellow warbler, one ghost crab. The beach was pocked with craters where the green sea turtles had deposited their eggs; frigates soared overhead, waiting. We hiked across the lava to a pond where flamingos were feeding. All afternoon we drifted in the *panga* around the mangrove lagoons, observing the sea turtles and white-tipped sharks. A sea lion pup was thrashing about trying to swallow the spotted snake it had captured. In the evening the *garua*—mist that falls in the dry season when the cold Humboldt Current flows here—descended upon us, icy pinpricks on our bare legs and shoulders. We sped back to *Encantada*, her scarlet hull a beacon in the gray sea.

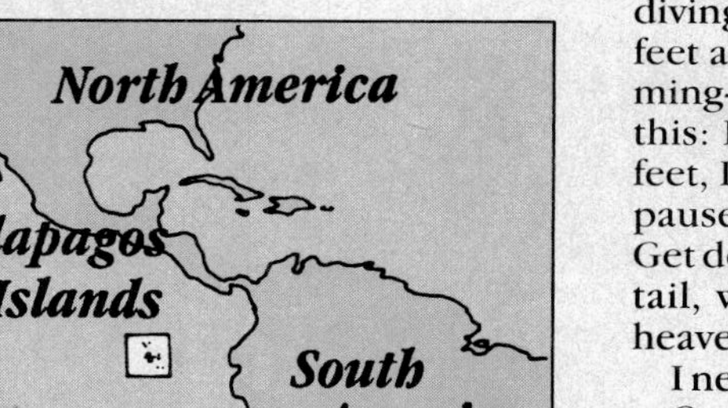

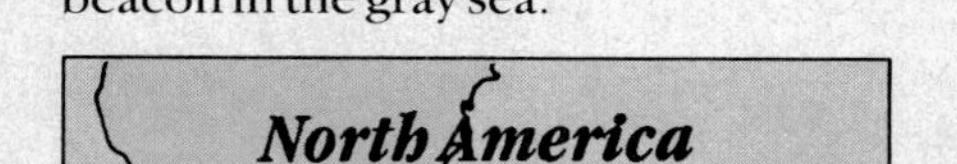

his chest, and with a great flapping of his stubby wings, answered her in kind. Afterwards, snorkeling in the castle of the king angels and moorish idols, I discovered one of the penguins "flying" underwater, at my side. Then, a shark, disappearing into the depths.

At almost every landfall, we encountered the endemic marine iguanas, the planet's only sea-going lizard. They graze in pastures of seaweed, then crawl ashore to warm their cold blood in the sun. Often they pile up by the hundreds. With their spiny backs, and snorting salt water from their nostrils, they seem like a convention of mini-dragons.

Most fun were the dance halls of the blue-footed boobies, those comical diving birds. I mean, their big webbed feet are the most brilliant blue, swimming-pool blue, and the whole idea is this: Hey, honey. You show me your feet, I'll show you mine. Lift one foot, pause. Nice, huh? Lift the other foot. Get down! Yeah! Then, sky pointing—tail, wings and beak pointed to the heavens—and whistling like crazy.

I never tired of watching.

One evening we stayed on Hood Island until dusk, spellbound, at the colony of waved albatross. This most marvelous of birds is large and regal, with

RACING THROUGH PARADISE

Story and photography by Sam Curtis

Sled dog racing, even

Galapagos/*from page 31*

have left their letters since the 1790s. The idea is that you pick up letters going your way; I came home with mail addressed to Berkeley and Livermore. Beyond the post office there is an opening to a lava tube; we carried ropes and rappelled about fifteen feet into the darkness, then followed the tunnel with flashlights as far as a sea-water pool.

Surprising for me was how much I enjoyed life on a sailboat. Often, after hiking or snorkeling, we would lie on the warm wooden decks, our daydreams lost in the billowing cloth above. Pink and black islands passed in the mist; columns of sunshine silvered the sea. Some nights the ocean was a still and glittering mirror, the stars at play among the riggings. Sometimes we pitched and rolled so fiercely that there was nothing to do but retire to our cabins and cling to our bunks.

About the climb of Volcan Alcedo: It was one of the most difficult and rewarding hikes of my life. We carried packs weighing 35 to 40 pounds, with all our food, water, tents and clothes, for three days. First by the light of the waning moon and then beneath the brutal equatorial sun, we climbed across a drab low forest of palo santo and clambered up through deep volcanic dust. We camped high on the rim, caldera floor and along the rim, we had found tortoises.

Now, months later, the images of that Galapagos voyage are still rich in my mind—the sails full of moonlight, the pale islands shrouded in mist, the joyful sea lions, the dancing birds. But mostly I think of the gentle tortoises, living up there on Volcan Alcedo. That there are only a few thousand of them, and more than four billion of us, and how much their race depends on our love and care to survive. I wish them well.

If you're going...

Galapagos tours are offered December through August by Wilderness Travel, 801 Allston Way, Berkeley, CA 94710; phone (415) 548-0420 or toll-free (800) 247-6700 (outside California). Prices start at $2620 per person, including airfare from Los Angeles.

Touring season in the Galapagos is usually December through August. Generally the weather is dry, cool and overcast May through December, and seas may be choppy. From January through April it is sunny and hot, with occasional heavy rains. Both seasons have their appeals.

Recommended books: *Galapagos: A Natural History Guide* by M.H. Jackson, and of course, two by Charles Darwin: *The Voyage of the Beagle* and *The Origin of Species*. A good quidebook is *Ecuador and the Galapagos Islands*, published by Lonely Planet. Best map

Photography by Dave Bartruff

MONTE CARLO'S INTERNATIONAL CIRCUS FESTIVAL

They come from north and south, east and west; from the four corners of the globe. They are clowns, high-wire artists, tumblers, mimes, and lion tamers—the cream of the circus world.

They come each year to Monte Carlo, the tiny Mediterranean community on the French Riviera. And they come at the royal invitation of His Serene Highness Prince Rainier III, Sovereign de Monaco.

A connoisseur of the circus art, Prince Rainier himself conceived the idea of an annual world competition. He and his wife, Princess Grace, the legendary Hollywood actress, welcomed the first performers in 1974, and personally awarded the top Gold and Silver Clown prizes to the winners.

The clowns are judged by an international jury of circus experts, and the grand prizes winners from places as diverse as Ecuador, North Korea, the U.S.S.R., Switzerland, The People's Republic of China, and Italy. The Gold Clown Award went to the Trapeze Troupe of Pyongyang, North Korea.

This year's festival will be held February 1-4. For further information and reservations, call 1-800-AF-PARIS.

of the giant tortoises live here, where there is ample food and moisture. An investment banker from New York kept track; by 10 a.m. we had counted more than 200 of them. (Each time we saw one, Macarena would cry, "Ah! Que lindo!")

One could never say tortoises are beautiful, but with their sweet manner, doleful E.T. faces and Darth Vader wheezing, I just loved them. It made us heartsick that mankind had been so cruel to them—early whalers and sailors carted away maybe 100,000 giant Galapagos tortoises to serve as fresh meat on their long voyages. Because they can live for months or a year with no food and water, they were stacked upside down in the moldy holds of ships, tossing on alien seas. Now they are threatened by the rats, goats, dogs, pigs and donkeys introduced by man.

We scrambled down to the caldera floor, walked across it to the sulfur fumaroles, climbed the far rim, and then continued around the north end—something we later heard no other tour group had ever done. After a dozen miles over faint donkey tracks, we stumbled exhausted into camp as night fell.

Everywhere we had gone, on the

capital cities in all of Latin America. At an elevation of 9300 feet, Quito has a cool, sunny climate. Snowy volcanoes tower over handsome Spanish colonial buildings, bustling markets and fascinating museums. Side trips can be taken to the famous Indian markets at Otavalo, Saquisili and Sangolqui, with overnight stays at charming centuries-old haciendas. My favorite Quito hotel, the Colon, has excellent service and good restaurants and charges about $100 for a double room. However, it is easy to find a nice place to stay for around $30. Meals are amazingly cheap. At the Colon, a gourmet dinner runs $8 to $10. One night a waiter prepared flaming crepes suzettes at my table; the tab was 75 cents.

It's been called the 500 miles of hell through paradise by people who have run it, but its official name is the Governor's Cup 500 Mile Sled Dog Race. For five days and nights, through southwestern Montana, dogs and drivers put in grueling hours to cover 500 miles of mountain terrain. That's the "hell" of it. But their route takes them over the Rocky Mountains, across frozen lakes, and through evergreen forests, and that, most mushers admit, is paradise.

Dragging a sled all day can be tiring.

"This is a beautiful race, beautiful country to run through," says Linwood Fiedler, winner of the 1988 Governor's Cup. "You know the backcountry of Montana—you can't beat it."

While spectators cannot follow the mushers and their teams through the backcountry, they can help get them off to a yapping start in Helena. They can also greet them at numerous check points along the way: Lincoln, Seeley Lake, Holland Lake, towns tucked in some of the most scenic spots in the West.

At these places and at the pre-race vet check, racers, handlers, and dogs are accessible to the public. These up-close opportunities go a long way in dispelling the myth that sled dogs are untouchable fighters that have to be chained up. In fact, before the race you can mingle with dogs that are clearly exuberant over the prospect of running. And at the checkpoints you can tiptoe past piles of very pooped puppies.

Although the Governor's Cup Race was just established in 1986, it carries on a long tradition of man and dog partnerships. With origins reaching back 4,000 years to the frigid Siberian landscape, dog sledding evolved as a way of life for many cultures. For centuries, in many snowbound communities it was essential for food gathering, transportation, communication, and exploration. It wasn't until the introduction of the snowmobile that dogs became less than necessary for many people's survival.

But certainly, somewhere back in the frozen history of Siberia, some playful indigenous people took time out from the serious business of hauling seal steaks home to the kids to see whose dog team could cross the ice flow first. However, sled dog racing didn't get going on an organized basis until the first All-Alaska Sweepstakes was held in Nome in 1908. From Alaska the sport caught on in Canada and finally reached Montana, Idaho, and California, where people from Sacramento and San Francisco went to Truckee to watch sled dogs run.

Although snowmobiles put a damper on the sport for a few decades, there were enough romantics around to start a resurgence of sled dog racing in recent years.

The Governor's Cup 500 attests to the re-growth in the popularity of dog sledding, and although the race is only five years old, it gets high marks in racing circles. According-

her hull was painted bright red, her sails were rust-colored. We had some surprising amenities: private (if tiny) cabins, clean sheets and blankets, even a hot fresh-water shower. Captain Rafael Gil ran a taut ship; he loved to fish, too, and his catch of grouper and tuna came to dinner. Once, with his bare hands, he caught a feral goat which became a tasty stew. He and the crew kept everything spotless and running on schedule. Benny, our smiling chef, worked in the tiny galley belowdecks day and night, cooking up hearty meals.

Our guide was Macarena Iturralde, an Ecuadorian naturalist with long years of experience in the Galapagos. She and Patsy had an abiding love for the islands; they knew the flora and fauna by both scientific and common name, and their habits and attributes. They were pretty good at bird calls and sea lion pup imitations, too.

We spent a couple of nights in the high mountain city of Quito, the splendid capital of Ecuador. From there we jumped a jet down to sultry Quayaquil, changed planes on the airstrip, and flew on to Baltra.

As our *panga*—wooden dinghy—pulled up to the first landfall, three locals stood on the beach to greet us:

For the next two weeks, we sailed a zigzag course, exploring various landfalls on twelve of these islands astride the equator.

Most of our visits were to the courtship and nesting places of birds, masked and red-footed boobies, waved albatross, flightless cormorants, magnificent frigatebirds. And we had the rare thrill of hiking to three areas where we found the famous giant tortoises in the wild: a beach on Isabela Island, a rainy upland farm on Santa Cruz, and the summit of Volcan Alcedo. We explored beaches of blinding white and hiked across glistening black lava that looked as fresh as if it had flowed yesterday—and in one place it was still steaming. We struggled into wetsuits to snorkel for hours in the clear, cold waters.

From the cinder cone of Bartolome we looked down into a small submerged crater where the white bellies of penguins flashed in the sun. Later, in the dinghy, we passed the penguins standing on a rock. Macarena called to them in penguin, a sort of high-pitched honk. The male stood high, puffed out

the East Pacific; almost all 24,000 of them come to this one island to court and nest. Its wingspan approaches seven feet; it can live fifty years, and it mates for life. Mating involves an elaborate and ecstatic ritual dance.

The "sighted" list of endemic species grew long: Lava gull, lava heron, lava lizard, lava snake, lava cactus. Four species of mockingbird. Galapagos hawk, penguin, dove and rail. Carpenter bee. And we learned to identify those thirteen little finches, whose adaptations so intrigued Darwin and influenced evolutionary theory. Vegetarian finch, mangrove finch, woodpecker finch, warbler finch, cactus finch, large cactus finch, sharp-billed ground finch. Small, medium and large ground finches and tree finches.

There was pathos, too—on South Plaza Island we found the big, colorful land iguanas starving; the prickly pears, their staple, had dried up in a drought.

On James Island we snorkeled in crystalline grottoes, swimming from pool to pool through dark submarine tunnels, while fur seals swirled about us in a fine interspecies ballet.

On Floreana Island there is a "post office" barrel where passing sailors

Continued on page 43

torque curve and provides good acceleration. It is also very efficient—we averaged 23.3 miles per gallon in our test, which includes equal amounts of city and freeway driving.

Interior appointments are top quality and include leather upholstery, excellent instrumentation, and convenient dome lights front and rear. Head and leg room are generous throughout. The sliding door on the right side of the van can be opened or closed with two fingers. Included as standard equipment are a roof luggage rack, cruise control, power door locks and windows.

Price as tested, $25,618.

Mazda 929 S

This is Mazda's biggest car, a full-size, luxury, four-door sedan which affords generous room for five, an excellent ride, and an attractive price. Over rough roads the 929's suspension soaks up the shock very well yet provides a high degree of stability in tight turns. The front suspension has MacPherson struts—roll bars are used front and rear. The steering is quite positive—a bit heavy in parking situations.

The 929 S model has Mazda's new, double overhead cam, 24-valve, V-6 engine. It provides excellent acceleration throughout all speed ranges and is coupled with a four-speed automatic transmission. Shift points are smooth and almost imperceptible. The driver can also manually select three lower gears in special driving situations.

The 929 S is an ideal car for long trips. The seats are comfortable and give good back support. The car is quiet at freeway speeds and controls are conveniently placed in logical positions, although the tiny buttons on the radio are a bit hard to find, especially at night. Included as standard on the 929 S are cruise control, power driver's seat, power moonroof, air conditioning, and a cassette player.

On our test loop we averaged 20.8 miles per gallon. Price as tested, $24,800.

Buick LeSabre Limited Sedan

The big, American car, perfectly suited to smooth, quiet, comfortable cruising on the big, American freeway is still with us—and the Buick LeSabre Limited Sedan is a fine example of today's updated version.

A 3.8-liter, 165-horsepower engine delivers power to the front wheels through a four-speed automatic transmission. Gear ratios are well chosen to make the car quickly responsive; there's always plenty of power. Both engine and transmission operate very smoothly. In fact, we found the Le-

Continued on page 53

SPECIFICATIONS OF CARS TESTED

	Displacement Liters	Horsepower	Axle ratio	Weight lbs.	Height In.	Length In.	Width In.	Wheel Base In.	Fuel Tank Gal.	Trunk Space
Pontiac Bonneville	3.8	165	3.33	3550	55.5	198.7	72.1	110.8	18.0	15.2
Chrysler Town & Country	3.3	150	3.02	3817	64.8	190.5	72.0	119.1	20.0	150*
Mazda 929	3.0	158	3.90	3581	54.5	193.9	67.9	106.7	18.5	15.1
Buick Le Sabre Limited Sedan	3.8	165	2.84	3297	54.9	196.5	72.4	110.8	18.0	16.4

*Rear seats removed

Galapagos tortoises, Alcedo, Isabela Island

After three days we came down from the summit of Volcan Alcedo, where the giant tortoises live, to Shipton Cove. We had seen the tortoises, wonderful hundreds of them, lumbering around the rim of the great caldera. Now we were sore, thirsty, and hungry. At the beach, this sweet scene: backpacks and dusty boots and clothes in a disheveled pile on the sand. Hikers lying back in the calm sea, gleefully soaking our blistered feet, washing away the dirt. Curious sea lions swimming among us, then teasing the pelicans like playful dogs. Offshore, *Encantada* lay at anchor, the crew readying for our departure. After a while they came to fetch us in the *panga*.

Dolphins riding our bow, we sailed away on freshening seas, bound for one last afternoon of snorkeling the waters around Sombrero Chino.

How it is: Every day the jets come screaming down to unload visitors on the island of Baltra, Galapagos Islands, Ecuador. Waiting in the harbor are the boats, large cruise ships and small sailing craft. These will carry the eco-tourists around the islands where, in 1835, young Charles Darwin took a hard look at the local animals and plants which weren't like any others, anywhere. He also saw that the same creatures varied a little bit from island to island. (He went home to England and mulled over his notes for a couple of decades and thought, hmmmm, this and this and this—aha! Then he published *The Origin of Species* and changed the intellectual history of the Western world.)

The Galapagos are now an Ecuadorian national park. Nature lovers are nuts about the place because the animals have almost no fear of man, and you can approach them so closely that you don't need binoculars or telephoto lenses.

These islands appear desolate, and there is almost no surface water, no permanent streams, only the seasonal rain puddles and a crater pond or two. For wildlife enthusiasts, this is a blessing—if these islands were as lush as Hawaii, there would be condominiums and high-rise hotels along every strand.

The Galapagos are purely oceanic in origin. They rose as volcanoes from the sea a few million years ago, so that every living thing (except the rapacious creatures introduced later by man) came on the wind, or vegetation rafts from the mainland, or in the bellies of birds. Over the millennia they evolved into species that can be seen nowhere else. It is the world's finest laboratory of natural selection.

Almost all the visitors explore the islands by ship; no camping is allowed on the beaches (although you can backpack up to a camp on the 3700-foot summit of Alcedo). The only hotels are in the rather dismal town of Puerto Ayora on Santa Cruz Island.

Each tour group must be accompanied by a licensed naturalist-guide trained by the local Charles Darwin Research Station. These guides lead their charges on marked trails at "official visitor sites" for intimate views of the wildlife. The guides are also there